PUBLIC ADMINISTRATION
Canadian Materials

Third Edition

edited by

Randy Hoffman

Diane Jurkowski

Victor MacKinnon

Janice Nicholson

James Simeon

Captus Press

PUBLIC ADMINISTRATION:
Canadian Materials, Third Edition

Copyright © 1998 by the editors and Captus Press Inc.

The publisher and the editors gratefully acknowledge the
authors, publishers and organizations for their permission to
reproduce their work in this book. Care has been taken to
trace ownership of copyright material contained in this book.
The publisher will gladly take any information that will
enable the rectification of any reference or credit in
subsequent editions and apologizes for any errors or
omissions.

Canadian Cataloguing in Publication Data

Main entry under title:

Public administration : Canadian materials

3rd ed.
Includes bibliographical references.
ISBN 1–896691–32–3

1. Canada — Politics and government. 2. Public law — Canada.
3. Civil service — Canada. 4. Comparative government.
I. Hoffman, Randy, 1944–   .

IL65 1991.P83 1998   320.471   C97–932628–1

Captus Press Inc.
Mail: York University Campus
        4700 Keele Street
        North York, Ontario
        M3J 1P3
Telephone: (416) 736–5537
Fax: (416) 736–5793
Email: Info@captus.com
Internet: http://www.captus.com

0 9 8 7 6 5 4 3 2 1
Printed in Canada

Table of Contents

Preface

The third edition of *Public Administration: Canadian Materials* has been substantially reworked. There are only four sections in this edition versus the six sections that were in the previous edition. The sections in the second edition dealing with the Canadian public policy process and cases studies in public administration have been removed. Section One includes a new chapter. Two chapters have been taken out of this section which appeared in the previous edition. Section Two has three fewer chapters and one updated chapter. Section Three remains substantially unaltered. Section Four has been entirely revamped with three new chapters. The Appendices for this edition have also been revised with two new contributions. While this edition is slimmer than the last, it still seeks to provide students and interested readers with timely and practical materials which thoroughly cover the field of Canadian public administration.

Again, we hope that those who use this current volume will find its content stimulating and thought provoking. One of its objectives is to allow the reader to quickly grasp the basic fundamentals of Canadian government and public administration.

We should like to thank all those who provide use with helpful suggestions and comments on our previous edition of this text. We have tried to incorporate many of these suggestions into the current edition. We continue to welcome your comments and suggestions for how this work can be improvement. *Canadian Public Administration: Cases and Materials* is an ongoing work in progress. Please send your comments and suggestions to Captus Press Inc., York University, North York, Ontario, M3J 1P3.

July, 1997
The Editors

Introduction

James C. Simeon

Most people are probably aware of the tremendous scope of government activity in their daily lives. To put this in some perspective, it is useful to keep in mind that the federal government, alone, spends more than the twenty largest Canadian corporations combined![1] According to the Organization for Economic Cooperation and Development (OECD), in 1988, government spending on all programs in Canada contributed to 35.2% of our Gross Domestic Product (GDP).[2] Government spending on social payments such as hospital and medical services, pensions, social assistance, public housing, and so on, came to 12.8% of Canada's GDP.[3]

Many of the public goods and services provided by governments are often taken for granted by people in Canada. For instance, such things as garbage collection, roads, water, electricity, mail delivery, drug testing, ferry services, food inspection, education, and so on, are provided by governments at all three levels, federal, provincial, and local, in Canada. For example, in September, 1991, three important public sector unions went out on strike at the same time: the Canadian Union of Postal Workers (CUPW), the Public Service Alliance of Canada (PSAC) and the transit workers union of the Toronto Transit Commission (TTC). The disruption caused to Canadian society, in general, and

1

to the residents of Metropolitan Toronto, in particular, as a result of these strikes, suggests just how important the public sector is in our daily lives. It is trite, but no less significant, to state that the government's impact on modern society is **all** pervasive. It follows, then, that given the significance of government in modern society that public administration would be an important field of study.

Not only are most Canadians inclined to take the public goods and services they consume for granted but they often also harbour misconceptions about how government and its administrative arm, the public service, function within the political process and the broader society. For instance, one common stereotype of public servants is that they lack incentives to work efficiently because they have job security. Another generalization that is frequently heard about government is that the public sector organizations are less efficient than the private sector. These negative stereotypes of public servants, in general, and public sector organizations, in particular, lead some people to believe the public service is highly unproductive and wasteful. These critics argue that the size and scope of government activity could be cut back substantially without adversely effecting society. In fact, it is further argued, if Canadians were to force their governments to make major spending cuts to programs, they could realize either tax savings or significant reductions in current governmental deficits and their accumulated debt.[4] This particular view of government and the public service in Canada reinforces their popular image as large, wasteful, unresponsive, monolithic organizations. In short, what is commonly understood to be a "bureaucracy." It also feeds the common bias and prejudice against public sector employees.

There is little doubt, of course, that modern governments are characterized by large bureaucracies. For instance, there are millions of people employed in the public sector in Canada at the federal, provincial, and municipal levels.[5] Further, the administration of vitally important policies and programs are entrusted to civil servants; for example, the provision of hospital and medical services, education, the management of the national and provincial economies, social assistance, and so on. Indeed, many services considered essential; for instance, such emergency services as police, fire, and ambulance, are provided by governments because the private sector is either unwilling or considered inappropriate for undertaking such tasks on behalf of society. This suggests that large bureaucracies will likely be an inevitable feature of technologically sophisticated, enormously large, and complex societies. Hence, it has been argued, that bureaucracies are an inescapable feature of modern mass societies.

Scholars continue to examine the implications of large bureaucratized governments and, by implication, the bureaucratized societies they operate in; for instance, modern society is characterized by large private international bureaucracies such as multinational corporations. A number of observers and researchers have been inclined to believe that the public sector has grown so large, and the scope of its activities have become so vast, that governments can no longer function effectively without the technical expertise and management skill provided by senior public servants. This implies, they argue, that it is the non-elected "permanent" public servants who wield incredible power in our society. Hence, under our parliamentary system of government it is not the elected politicians, who have become ever more dependent on their technical masters, the bureaucrats, for their policy advice and implementation of public programs, rather it is the public servants who rule. This view of the public service projects an image of an all-powerful, seemingly, non-accountable force in today's government and society.

Even though both of these popular images of the public service may have some element of truth, they do not capture the manner in which the public service actually functions and operates in Canada.

Indeed, one of the objectives of this volume is to give the reader a better understanding of the study and practice of public administration and the governmental process in Canada.

Naturally, given the size of the modern welfare state, one would expect that the field of public administration would be not only significant but a vast and diverse area of study. Accordingly, Kenneth Kernaghan and David Siegel have suggested dividing public administration into two components — as a "field of practice (or an occupation)" and as a "field of study (often referred to as a discipline)."[6] In other words, they remind us to keep in mind the old distinction between theory and practice. Public administration is both a field of study, for students and researchers, and an occupational field, as we have noted, for many people in Canada.

Government can be considered to undertake two major areas of action: (1) the enforcement of regulations; and (2) the provision of services. For instance, the enforcement of regulations can include such things as standards for foods and drugs, pay equity, and other standards for employment. The provision of services could include such things as maintenance of streets and highways, student grants and loans, mail delivery, and hospital and medical services. In both areas, it is obvious that the public service plays a central role.

Public administration, then, is concerned with the ways and means by which governments formulate and implement public policies and fulfil their onerous service and regulatory responsibilities.[7] This is not done, of course, by the government per se, that is, those elected to public office, but by the public bureaucracy.

As we have noted, public bureaucracies appear to be an inescapable fact of modern life. However, when the term bureaucracy is used in everyday conversation it is usually a pejorative term implying waste, delay, inflexibility. But when "bureaucracy" is employed as a term in social science it has a different meaning.[8]

In the etymological sense, bureaucracy means "**rule of offices**." It was first coined in France in 1745 by Vincent de Gourney who used bureaucracy to describe a form of government in which appointed officials play a central role.[9] Bureaucracy, in the social sciences, designates a particular kind of social structure for carrying out organized work.

1. Work is divided into impersonal roles or offices.
2. Positions tend to be specialized. There is, in other words, a high degree of division of labour.
3. Career commitment is demanded from employees. The complex roles within the organization can only be learned through long experience.
4. Careers are protected by some sort of job security or tenure.
5. Positions are filled by **merit recruitment** as opposed to patronage.
6. Bureaucracy is supposed to be a neutral instrument in the hands of those who command it. Authority flows from the top down within the organization.
7. The degree of discretion employees have to make decisions is minimized because policies and rules have been set by the authorities within the organization. As a

4

consequence, administration is regularized and made predictable.[10]

Bureaucratic forms of organization, of course, are not confined exclusively to government; for example, the Roman Catholic Church, non-profit volunteer organizations, and multinational enterprises are all examples of "private bureaucracies," as opposed to public bureaucracies.

The brilliant German sociologist Max Weber is considered one of the foremost students of bureaucracy. Weber devised what he called the "Ideal-Type" Bureaucracy. This was a hypothetical model or "intellectual construct" that could be used for studying and doing research on organizations to try and determine how closely an organization approximated the postulated "Ideal-Type." The way Weber viewed bureaucracy was as a system of authority relations that were defined by rules. And contrary to the popularly held view of bureaucracy as having a rigid and inflexible structure, Weber saw the "rule system," which is the fundamental basis of bureaucratic organizations, as constantly adapting and adjusting to changes in the broader environment.

Weber identified six key features in his "Ideal-Type" Bureaucracy:

1. **Rules** — tasks are organized;
2. **Division of Labour** — specialization;
3. **Hierarchy** — Superior–Subordinate relations;
4. **Decisions are made by technical and legal rules**;
5. **Administration based on files**;
6. **Administration as a vocation.**[11]

Given the importance of public bureaucracy in government and society it is not surprising that it would be the main focus in any study of public administration. Public administration then can be defined simply as the "study and practice of public bureaucracy."[12]

This book is divided into four sections covering various aspects of public administration in Canada. The first section covers the "Structure of the Canadian Government." This section overs the basic structural features of Canadian public administration. The second section, "The Constitutional Framework," outlines the major provisions of the Canadian Constitution and recent efforts at constitutional reform in Canada. The third section, "The Canadian Legal System," details the principal features of the legal environment in which public administration is practised in Canada. Section four, "Canadian Political Institutions," provides further detailed information on some of Canada's most important institutions and practices. The final section includes appendices that cover a number of supplementary materials that support the articles and case studies found in the previous sections of the book.

This book makes extensive use of comparative analysis. Canada does not exist in a global vacuum or as a self-contained political entity. The Canadian political system is affected by, while also simultaneously, affecting the wider world community of nation-states. Hence, we can neither artificially isolate our analysis and examination of Canadian government and public administration from external influences nor can we ignore the fact that the Canadian government and public administration also influence the outside world. Furthermore, comparative analysis is useful in its own right since it provides insights into the Canadian system that can be gleamed through no other mode of analysis. Accordingly, most of the sections of this book provide chapters that include comparative analysis or provide relevant examples of foreign nation-states that can serve as a basis of comparison for the Canadian case.

Each of the sections are largely self-contained and can be read on their own or arranged to follow an instructor's preferred teaching style and course requirements. Therefore, it is not essential to read each one of the sections or articles in sequence.

NOTES

1. Mark O. Dickerson & Thomas Flanagan, *An Introduction to Government and Politics: A Conceptual Approach*, 3rd Edition (Toronto: Nelson Canada, 1990), p. 331.
2. Linda McQuaig, "You get what you pay for in taxes," *The Toronto Star*, November 10, 1992, p. A19.
3. Linda McQuaig, "Social upheaval taught Europe value of stability," *The Toronto Star*, November 9, 1992, p. A13.
4. For instance, this is essentially the position of Preston Manning's Reform Party. Kirk Makin, "Reform urges massive cuts," *The Globe and Mail*, March 30, 1993, A1.
5. The total number of employees in the broader public sector was 2.1 million or 17.9 of the labour force in 1982. This figure includes hospital, educational, and Crown Corporation employees.

Sharon L. Sutherland & G. Bruce Doern, *Bureaucracy in Canada: Control and Reform* (Toronto: University of Toronto Press, 1985), p. 134.

6. Kenneth Kernaghan & David Siegel, *Public Administration in Canada: A Text*, 2nd Edition (Toronto: Nelson Canada, 1991), p. 5.

7. Ibid.

8. John McMenemy, *The Language of Canadian Politics* (Toronto: John Wiley & Sons Canada Ltd., 1980), p. 27. See also "Public Service (Administration)" on p. 217.

9. Fred A Kramer, "Organization Theories of Public Bureaucracy," in *Public Administration in Canada: Selected Readings*, 5th Edition, edited by Kenneth Kernaghan (Toronto: Methuen, 1985), p. 2.

10. Mark O. Dickerson & Thomas Flanagan, *An Introduction to Government and Politics: A Conceptual Approach*, 3rd Edition (Toronto: Nelson Canada, 1990), p. 337.

11. Fred A. Kramer, "Organization Theories of Public Bureaucracy," in *Public Administration in Canada: Selected Readings*, 5th Edition, edited by Kenneth Kernaghan (Toronto: Methuen, 1985), p. 3.

12. Ibid.

THE STRUCTURE OF
THE CANADIAN GOVERNMENT

Introduction to the Structure of the Canadian Government

James C. Simeon

Any study or examination that will ultimately lead or contribute to a fundamental understanding of public administration presupposes a familiarity and a comprehension of the operation and functions of the political process. This includes, of course, the basic principles, structural features, and processes of what constitutes the "government" within any particular jurisdiction. Accordingly, this section provides a broad overview of the Canadian system of government, its structural features, and Canadian public administration. To provide further insights and enhance one's appreciation for the Canadian system of government and public administration, comparative material is also included on two key institutions of Canadian government, the Parliament or legislature and federalism. Proposals for reforming the Canadian Senate have been made since the Canadian Parliament was established. The recent call for a "Triple E" Senate — equal, elected, and effective — are presented. Likewise, Anthony King outlines the weaknesses of the American system of government with its "never-ending campaign" which makes for overly vulnerable politicians and, in the end, results in public policies which do not serve the public interest.

Canadian Public Administration and Government

James C. Simeon

Government in Canada, as in other Western industrialized societies, is a complex organizational phenomenon. Government, which can be defined as the "process that makes and enforces rules and decisions for society,"[1] is enormous in modern societies. Spending by all governments in Canada (federal, provincial, and local) totals about 45 percent of the country's Gross National Product. The federal government's expenditures alone, exceeded $160 billion in fiscal year 1992–93, with close to $35 billion of this amount financed through borrowings; that is, through deficit financing. About 15 percent of the total labour force is employed by government in Canada. There are approximately 225,000 permanent civil servants who work for the federal government alone, not including Crown corporation employees or those in the military. Accordingly, given the enormous size of national governments and the scope of their activities, it is difficult to underestimate the significance of government in the lives of citizens in modern societies. In the Canadian government we have, perhaps, the foremost example of how governments can shape the quality of life as well as the very nature of the society in which it is found.

11

Two recent reports help to illustrate the significance of these points. Government Consultants International Inc. (GCI), one of Ottawa's largest lobbying firm, conducts an annual review of Canadian government contracts. For fiscal year 1991–92, it reported that the federal government had spent $9.4 billion on purchases for everything from computers to guided missiles. This prompted the lobbyists to state, "Government procurement continues to surpass all other business activity in Canada."[2] Clearly, this type of expenditure is an enormous stimulus to the Canadian economy. The C.D. Howe Institute, a private research organization, released a report that indicated that government debts in Canada were on the verge of threatening to put the country in a "debt crisis." The total government debt of the eleven major governments in Canada is about $665 billion, with roughly half this amount, $300 billion, in foreign hands.[3] The C.D. Howe Institute's report indicated that the total budgetary deficits of Canada's governments for 1992 was approximately $45 billion or about 6.4 percent of its Gross Domestic Product (GDP). The continuing escalation of Canada's public debts threatened to undermine Canada's financial standing among the international investment community. Over time, this could lower the value of the Canadian dollar and adversely affect the country's balance of payments which would, in turn, lower the standard of living in Canada. Government has acknowledged the seriousness of the problem but is not prepared to accept that it constituted a "debt crisis."[4] Evidently, the issue of growing government deficits and accumulated debt has the potential to drastically alter Canada's economic well-being.[5] Some analysts have referred to this as the "fiscal crisis of the state."[6] Not only do escalating government deficits and debts adversely effect the economy, they also limit the ability of governments to address the issues and problems of the day.

Both the GCI and the C.D. Howe Institute reports illustrate the power of governments in modern society as forces of good and ill. Again, this underscores the significance of government in modern society. Without a fundamental understanding of the structure and operations of government, one can not hope to understand or appreciate the way in which modern societies function. Nor can one hope to understand the broader forces that impinge on an individual's own life.

THE GROWTH AND DEVELOPMENT OF GOVERNMENT IN CANADA

The growth of the Canadian government has accelerated dramatically since the country was established in 1867. When the Dominion of Canada came into being on July 1, 1867, it consisted of a mere four provinces (Ontario, Quebec, Nova Scotia, and New Brunswick) and a small governmental apparatus largely inherited from the old United Province of Canada (formerly Canada East and Canada West) — the old provinces of Upper and Lower Canada, now Ontario and Quebec. By 1907, the Dominion of Canada stretched from "sea-to-sea" and consisted of the present ten provinces and two territories. Demographically, the country also grew from a population of 3.5 million in 1867 to 26 million by 1990.[7] Territorial and population expansion were two important factors which contributed to the growth of the Canadian government. Changing values, beliefs, and attitudes also account for the growth of the Canadian state over time. By the 1990s, Canada had developed into a mature "welfare state" which was providing a comprehensive set of social assistance and public assistance programs to those citizens in need.

The social security system consumes about 35 percent of the federal government's expenditures. Provincial and local governments make their own contributions to the social security system in Canada. Much of these social expenditures are coordinated in the form of "shared-cost" programs between the federal and provincial governments. Governments, since the end of the Second World War, also have been expected to be responsible for managing their nation's economy through the use of macroeconomic levers such as fiscal and monetary policies. This was unheard of prior to 1945. No public official, prior to the Second World War, would have dared advocate such a radical departure in the economic orthodoxy of non-governmental intervention in the economy or "laissez faire." However, the hardship of the Great Depression of the 1930s changed prevailing values away from laissez faire to the perceived legitimacy of government intervention in the economy to ensure high levels of stable employment, price stability, a sound balance of payments, rising productivity, and an equitable distribution of income.[8]

One catalyst for this change was the British economist, John Maynard Keynes, who argued in his famous book, *General Theory of Employment, Interest and Money* (1936), that high levels of unemployment could persist indefinitely in an economy without the intervention of government to increase aggregate demand. Keynes argued, in essence, that fiscal policy was necessary if a society hoped to achieve full employment. Keynes also demonstrated that an increase in public spending had a "multiplier" effect in terms of increasing income or the aggregate output of an economy.[9] Hence, the greater propensity to spend on the part of government, the greater the multiplier effect on the economy. After the Second World War, "Keynesianism" emerged as the prevailing consensus among Western industrialized countries with respect to macroeconomic management of national economies. Keynesianism, along with the professionalization of the discipline of economics, led governments to staff their Finance and Treasury Departments with appropriately trained economists who could advise and guide them on their overall management responsibilities for their national economies. Canada was no exception; and by the 1950s the federal Department of Finance, along with its officials, was one of the most important and influential departments in the Government of Canada.[10]

Governments in Canada are also noted for their use of public enterprises or Crown corporations. Indeed, Canada has a long history and tradition of using Crown corporations to serve public interest goals. Some of the most outstanding examples at the federal level in Canada are: Canadian National Railways (CNR) created in 1919; the Canadian Wheat Board set up in 1935; the Canadian Broadcasting Corporation (CBC) established in 1936; and more recently, the St. Lawrence Seaway Authority which was set up in 1954; Petro-Canada created in 1976; and the Canadian Development Investment Corporation (CDIC) established in 1982. Crown corporations tend to be concentrated in a few sectors of Canada's economy; for instance, energy, where we find the large public utilities such as Ontario Hydro, Quebec Hydro, B.C. Hydro and Power; communications, Canada Post Corporation and the Canadian Film Development Corporation (CFDC); transportation, such as VIA Rail and formerly Air Canada. In short, Crown corporations are concentrated in those areas that are considered part of the infrastructure of the economy. They help to facilitate the production, exchange, and distribution of goods and services within Canada's economy.

Through direct participation in the economy and through the vehicle of public enterprise, government makes a substantial contribution to the overall economy in Canada. The public

14

sector, then, is a significant contributor to the operation of the private market, free enterprise system. Hence, the apt description of Canada having a "mixed economy." It is "mixed" in the sense of having both public and private sector components which are essential to its effective operation. To varying degrees, all Western industrial societies have "mixed economies." Canada is outstanding, in this regard, to the extent that it relies more on public ownership than most other Western industrialized countries.

Herschel Hardin, in his book, *A Nation Unaware: The Canadian Economic Culture* (1974), has perhaps taken this point the furthest when he argues that public enterprise has been a fundamental feature of Canada's development. As a consequence, Canada has, he suggests, a "public enterprise culture."[11] Hardin argues that, without the high degree of public ownership and state intervention, Canada would not likely exist as a sovereign political entity. The small size of Canada's market and its geographical dispersion runs contrary to the north-south pull of continental economic forces. The disadvantages of Canada's relatively small economy and the fragile nature of our Canadian culture and identity necessitate state intervention. Thus, Canada is distinguished from the United States in its use of "public enterprise" and "state intervention." The Americans, in contrast, are firmly "laissez faire" and small "L" liberals in terms of their political culture. In the words of Graham Spry, Canadian nationalist and advocate of a public broadcasting system in the 1930s, the choice was between "the state or the United States."

What emerged by the end of the Second World War in Canada, which was typical of other Western industrialized countries, was a consensus on the mixed economy and the Keynesian welfare state.[12] This accounts, to a great extent, for the tremendous growth of government in Canada over the last 50 or 60 years. That consensus has helped to shape the current structure and operations of the Canadian government.

CANADA: A PARLIAMENTARY FEDERATION

The way in which forms of government tend to be classified is on their degree of centralization and decentralization and the relationship between the executive and legislative branches of government.[13] Canada is, therefore, classified as "parliamentary

15

federation." That is to say, it has a parliamentary system within a federal form of government. The parliamentary system of government is part of Canada's British inheritance, through its colonial origins of British imperialism. While Canada's federal form of government is attributable to the influence of the United States, "the world's first federal system."[14] Canada was, in fact, the first country in the world to combine a parliamentary system to a federal form of government. Australia, subsequently, followed the Canadian lead.

What is critical to a parliamentary system is the fusion of the executive and legislative branches of government. Only members of the House of Commons or the Senate are allowed to form the government in Canada's parliamentary system. This ensures that the government has the "confidence" of the House of Commons, the popularly elected lower chamber, before it can proceed with any important policy decision. This is also what is meant by "responsible government." If the Canadian government were to lose a "vote of non-confidence" in the House of Commons then, by convention, the government would be obligated to resign and, in most instances, the Governor General would dissolve Parliament and a writ would be issued for a national election to elect a new Parliament. This would not occur if the government lost a vote in the Senate, since the appointed upper house is not a "confidence" chamber. Following the national election, the Governor General would call upon the leader of the political party with the majority in the House of Commons (or, if no majority exists, the largest plurality) to serve as First Minister or Prime Minister and to form a government.

The government in a parliamentary system is therefore made up of the leader of the political party which enjoys a majority in the House of Commons, along with the other members of her or his political party that the leader may wish to call upon to serve in his or her administration. The Prime Minister and the other ministers who are appointed by the Prime Minister, are collectively known as the Cabinet. The Cabinet or government in a parliamentary system form the "political executive" while the Governor General, who represents the Crown and fulfils the ceremonial role of head of state, forms the formal executive. Both the formal and political executive are part and parcel of the legislative branch of government in a parliamentary system, since Parliament is comprised of three distinct elements: the Crown, represented by the Governor General; the

House of Commons, from which the Cabinet or government is formed; and the Senate, the upper house.[15] This is why the parliamentary system is called a "fusion of powers" system. The parliamentary system contrasts with the presidential system which is characterized by a "separation of powers" system.

In the United States, for example, the president and the members of his or her Cabinet are prohibited by the Constitution from holding seats in Congress. The sole exception is the U.S. Vice-President who serves as president of the Senate. It is a largely ceremonial role, and has the deciding vote in the upper house on the rare occasion of a tie.[16] The executive and legislative branches of government, therefore, are effectively separated from each other. The U.S. presidential system of government also embodies the "Mutual Theory of Checks and Balances" in which each of the three branches of government (executive, legislative, and judicial) can effectively check the other.[17] For instance, the President can veto legislation passed by Congress, while the Supreme Court of the United States can declare laws passed by Congress and signed by the President as unconstitutional. On the other hand, the President appoints members to the Supreme Court of the United States while the U.S. Senate has the power to ratify the appointees to office. The intention of the founders of the U.S. Constitution of 1789 for the "separation of powers" and the "mutual theory of checks and balances" was to avoid the concentration and abuse of power. It was, in the famous words of James Madison in *The Federalist*, to pit ambition against ambition. "In framing a government which is to be administered by men over men, the great difficulty lies in this: you must first enable the government to control the governed; and in the next place oblige it to control itself."[18] The "fusion of powers" found in the parliamentary system is premised, obviously, on a different philosophy of government: it is an approach to government which seeks to concentrate power within the executive branch of government, while at the same time entrusting the legislative branch with the responsibility for holding that power accountable for its actions.

Federalism is a decentralized form of government which divides sovereignty between a central or federal government and provincial, state, or regional governments. Canada has been described as one of the most decentralized federations in the world.[19] That is to say, that the provinces within the Canadian federation wield considerable clout in terms of deciding important issues of public policy. It does not necessarily imply that the provinces dominate the federal government in every field of public policy. This suggests that "federal-provincial relations" is an important aspect of the structure and process of Canada's system of governance.

Federalism is characterized by three principal features:

(a) A Constitution which serves as the supreme law of the land;
(b) A division of powers between a federal and provincial or state governments;
(c) Courts serve as the final arbiters or referees in disputes between and among governments.

Like so many aspects of Canadian government and politics, the Constitution is a hybrid of the British and American constitutional traditions. In other words, the Canadian Constitution is both written, like the U.S. Constitution, and unwritten, like the British Constitution. Its written portion is primarily encompassed by the Constitution Acts of 1867 (formerly the British North American Act) and 1982. (See Part VII, General, of the Constitution Act, 1982.) The unwritten portion of the Canadian Constitution consists of the conventions and traditions that were initially transplanted from Great Britain and that, subsequently, evolved in the Canadian parliamentary system. This is perhaps best exemplified by the Preamble to the Constitution Act of 1867 which states that "the Provinces of Canada, Nova Scotia and New Brunswick have expressed their Desire to be federally united into One Dominion under the Crown of the United Kingdom of Great Britain and Ireland, with a Constitution *similar in Principle to that of the United Kingdom.*" The single phrase, "similar in Principle to that of the United Kingdom," incorporated into the Canadian parliamentary system the customs and traditions of the British Westminster model of government. Responsible government is an example of the uncodified portions of the Canadian Constitution, as is the convention of Prime Minister and Cabinet government. It is important to remember that the uncodified sections of the Canadian Constitution are every bit as significant as the written text.

Section 52(1) of the Constitution Act 1982, clearly outlines the primacy of the Constitution of Canada by stating, "The

Constitution of Canada is the supreme law of Canada, and any law that is inconsistent with the provisions of the Constitution is, to the extent of the inconsistency, of no force or effect." However, it is in Sections 91 and 92 of the Constitution Act of 1867 where the division of powers between the two orders of government are found. Section 91 outlines a broad based set of federal powers to make "Laws for the Peace, Order, and good Government of Canada" and includes 29 Subsections "for greater Certainty, but not so as to restrict the Generality of the foregoing Terms of this Section." While Section 92 states explicitly, "In each Province the Legislature may exclusively make Laws in relation to Matters coming within the Classes of Subject next hereinafter enumerated." Section 92 then lists sixteen enumerated provincial powers. It is instructive to compare the most significant powers that are distributed to the federal and provincial governments in the Canadian Constitution.

Section 91: The Federal Powers*

(1) Public Debt & Property;
(2) Regulation of Trade & Commerce;
(3) Raising Money by any Mode or System of Taxation;
(7) Militia, Military & Naval Service, and Defence;
(14) Currency & Coinage
(15) Banking, Incorporation of Banks, and the issue of Paper Money;
(17) Weights & Measures;
(19) Interest;
(20) Legal Tender;
(21) Bankruptcy & Insolvency;
(22) Patents of Invention & Discovery;
(23) Copyrights;
(24) Indians, & Lands Reserved for Indians;
(27) Criminal Law, including the Procedure in Criminal Matters;

* Not all 29 Subsections are listed.

Section 92: The Provincial Powers*

(2) Direct Taxation within the Province;
(3) Borrowing Money on the Sole Credit of the Province;
(5) Management and Sale of the Public Lands belonging to the Province and of the Timber and Wood thereon;

19

(7)   Establishment, Maintenance, and Management of Hospitals, Asylums, Charities, and Eleemosynary Institutions in and for the Province, other than Marine Hospitals;

(8)   Municipal Institutions in the Province;

(10) Local Works and Undertakings other than:

(a) Lines of Steam or other Ships, Railways, Canals, Telegraphs, and other Works and Undertakings connecting the Province with any other, etc.

(b) Lines of Steam Ship between the Province and any British or Foreign Country;

(c) Such Works as, although wholly situated within the Province, are before or after their Execution declared by the Parliament of Canada to be for the general Advantage of Canada or for the Advantage of Two or more of the Provinces;

(11) Incorporation of Companies with Provincial objects;

(13) Property and Civil Rights in the Province;

(14) The Administration of Justice in the Province, including the Constitution, Maintenance, and Organization of Provincial Courts, both of Civil and of Criminal Jurisdiction, and including Procedure in Civil Matters in those Courts;

(16) Generally all Matters of a merely local or private Nature in the Province.

* Not all 16 Subsections are listed.

What is evident from this listing of some of the most significant federal and provincial powers in the Constitution Act of 1867 is that the federal government was granted most of the powers of finance and commerce. Whereas, the provinces were granted powers dealing with local matters and social policy. This is further corroborated by the fact that Section 93 grants the provinces exclusive powers to make laws in regard to education. Section 95 grants joint or concurrent powers over agriculture and immigration to the federal and provincial governments, with federal paramountcy in the event of conflict. Various students of the Canadian Constitution who have carefully studied the division of powers have made a number of relevant points regarding the intentions of the Victorian founders of Confederation and the nature of the Canadian federation.

Roger Gibbins, for instance, notes that the intentions of one of the leading founding Fathers of Confederation and Canada's first prime minister, John A. Macdonald, was to create a strong central government. The negative lesson from the American Constitutional experience, given the calamity of the U.S. Civil War which concluded in 1865, was the assignment of the "residual" powers (those not explicitly enumerated in the division of powers) to the States rather than the federal government.[20] Hence, the intention of the Constitution Act of 1867 was, undoubtedly, to make the provinces subordinate to the federal authority. The lessons of political history were not only relevant here, but, so too was the desire for commercial union and economic gain. The federal government would be endowed with those powers necessary for forging a national economy.

The repeal of the British Corn Laws in 1846, which led to the negotiation of the 1854 Reciprocity Treaty with the United States and its eventual abrogation in 1866, meant the British North American colonists had to provide their own means for economic prosperity. R.T. Naylor presents the persuasive argument that the mercantile capitalist class saw Confederation as a natural solution to their economic plight.[21] The federal government, accordingly, was vested with the powers necessary to ensure the commercial exploitation of the western hinterlands and the creation of a national economy.

The Canadian federation was also seen as the solution for the deadlock that plagued the United Province of Canada created by the Act of Union in 1840. For English Canadians the Act of Union ushered in responsible government. For French Canadians the Act of Union was an attempt to assimilate the French language and culture by making English the only official language of the legislative assembly and giving Canada East (formerly Lower Canada) and Canada West (formerly Upper Canada) equal representation in the legislative assembly, even though the population of Canada East exceeded that of Canada West by a wide margin.[22] Confederation, therefore, was intended to end the deadlock created by the Act of Union by, again, separating the two Canadas into Ontario and Quebec. Further, social policy would, henceforth, be a provincial matter under the terms of the new federal bargain.

This view was most forcefully presented in the Quebec Government's Report of the Royal Commission of Inquiry on Constitutional Problems (1956) or, better known as, the Tremblay Commission. It was the contention of the Tremblay Commission that Confederation was a "compact" between two founding nations which allows for the survival, and the peaceful co-existence, of the two dominant cultures. Thus, the Canadian federation was a compact between the English and the French and the division of powers in the Constitution reflected the principal concerns of both groups:

> The broad solution was to entrust the Dominion with the authority believed necessary to effective military defence and economic development, and in respect to which no cultural cleavages were anticipated, while the provinces would have jurisdiction over those classes of subjects where legislation would have a direct cultural incidence.[23]

Cultural dualism necessitated a federal form of government even though the preference of many of the founding Fathers of Confederation was a legislative union or a unitary form of government. Nonetheless, Canada began as a highly centralized federation or what some have even called a "quasi-federation." This would not last, however, as the courts, through their constitutional rulings on various cases, would eventually change the balance of the federation in favour of the provinces. This was begun by the Judicial Committee of the Privy Council (JCPC), the British law Lords at Westminster, who served as Canada's final court of appeal until the Supreme Court of Canada assumed this role in 1949. The impact of judicial rulings on the Canadian Constitution has been profound. Indeed, the relative power of the courts was enhanced when the Constitution Act of 1982, with its entrenched Charter of Rights and Freedoms, was proclaimed.[24]

The first 34 sections of the Constitution Act of 1982 constitute the Canadian Charter of Rights and Freedoms. It guarantees such basic rights as religion, thought and expression, the press, peaceful assembly and association as well as political rights such as the vote, to stand for public office, and the maximum duration of legislative bodies. Since the Charter has come into force, the courts have ruled on such pressing issues as abortion, mandatory retirement, Sunday shopping, pornography, the right to strike, random spot checks, and many others. In effect, the courts were making substantive public policy by deciding cases on these areas of vital public concerns. Consequently, the role of the courts in Canada was dramatically changed from one of "limited judicial review" to one of "full judicial review." The courts could, in other words, declare that neither the federal nor the provincial legislatures had the power to pass laws that infringed on the rights and freedoms of citizens. In addition, of course, the courts continued to play their traditional role of "final arbiter" within the Canadian federation by resolving jurisdictional disputes between the federal and provincial governments. New issues in federal-provincial relations along with the advent of the Charter are forcing the courts to rethink their approach to judicial decision making.[25]

CANADIAN PUBLIC BUREAUCRACY AND PUBLIC ADMINISTRATION

Kenneth Kernaghan and David Siegel define public bureaucracy as the "system of authority, people, offices and methods that government uses to achieve its objectives."[26] The Canadian public bureaucracy is, as previously mentioned, a highly complex organizational phenomenon which is comprised of some 27 federal departments and 400 agencies, boards, and commissions, including Crown corporations. The Canadian public bureaucracy, as in any liberal democracy, performs two fundamental roles in the governmental process. The first is to advise the political executive and the second is to execute or administer the laws and policies enacted by the legislative assembly.[27] The Cabinet or government is responsible for the public bureaucracy in a parliamentary system.

The Cabinet in a parliamentary system, with its "fusion of powers" system, is answerable to the House of Commons for its decisions and actions. This is affected in two ways. One is through "collective ministerial responsibility." The second is through "individual ministerial responsibility." The first requires that the government, as a whole, must assume responsibility for all major policy thrusts that are undertaken during the life of a Parliament. This is supported by the convention of Cabinet "solidarity" which requires that once a decision has been taken by Cabinet then all ministers are obligated to defend it publicly. Any minister that can not publicly defend the collective decisions of the government must resign. Ministers are also individually responsible for the decisions they take in directing their portfolio or departmental responsibilities. The most visible manifestation of this occurs in the daily Question Period which is held when the House of Commons is sitting. Ministers must defend their own departmental charges from the Opposition's questioning and attacks, while under close public scrutiny by the members of the press gallery and the public at large, through the daily coverage of parliamentary proceedings now available on the cable television channel. Therefore, the government is answerable on a continuous basis for its governance of the country.

Ministers are the political heads that direct the operations of each of the departments and other organizations in the Government of Canada. Collectively, the Cabinet or "Ministry" is responsible for directing the entire Canadian public bureaucracy. In the parliamentary system all legal authority is vested in the Crown. By convention, the Crown can only act on the advice of the Ministry or individual ministers. Thus, when ministers undertake particular actions, they do so on behalf of the Crown in Canada. Moreover, any action which is taken by a public servant is deemed to be taken under the authority of the minister who heads the department or organization that the public servant is attached. In this way, public servants and the public bureaucracy are held accountable through ministers to Parliament and, therefore, indirectly by the Canadian public who elects the Members of Parliament (MPs). Numerically, this means that 301 MPs, including the approximately 23 ministers, are responsible for holding some 500,000 public servants accountable in the public bureaucracy in Canada. Given the enormous size of the public bureaucracy, some would say that this is an impossible task. It has been argued that such a system may have been feasible in the 19th century when the Canadian public bureaucracy was relatively small but near impossible today with the tremendous size and scope of governmental activity. It is unreasonable, they argue, to expect Parliament, and more specifically the government, to be able to scrutinize the activities of half a million men and women employed in the Canadian public service. Nonetheless, this is in theory how the government in a parliamentary system holds the public bureaucracy accountable.

The Canadian government is centred on the Prime Minister to such a degree that some consider it more accurate to refer to the Canadian system of government as prime ministerial as opposed to parliamentary. There is no question that the person who occupies the Office of Prime Minister is one of the most powerful individuals in the Canadian political system. Despite the political clout wielded by the Prime Minister, she or he can not act alone. Indeed, the individual who holds the Office of

Prime Minister is dependent on the political support and advice of others to be effective in the position. The conventions and traditions of parliamentary government also constrain the power of the Prime Minister. For instance, one of the responsibilities of the Prime Minister is to lead the government in Parliament as well as the country. The success of a Prime Minister in this role will be judged, at least in part, to the degree that people are prepared to and willing to follow her or his lead. The influence of a Prime Minister will be directly dependent on his or her leadership skills.

Much of the First Minister's leadership skills will have to be displayed within government, leading the Cabinet and his or her party's caucus. Individuals are selected to Cabinet, in part, because they have emerged as the party's informal leaders in Parliament. The Cabinet decision-making system has developed into a highly sophisticated one, even though Prime Ministers have the prerogative to set up Cabinet operations in the way they feel most comfortable. The process of "institutionalization" which has taken place as Cabinet has evolved over time has been, essentially, built on the experience of previous Prime Ministers. It also has been necessitated by the changes which have taken place in Canadian society and government since Confederation as well.

Public administration can be defined as the "study and practice of public bureaucracy."[28] It is the Cabinet, as previously noted, that is responsible for the Canadian public bureaucracy as well as the major thrust of public policy in the parliamentary system. The Prime Minister and Cabinet, thus, are the apex of the power in the Canadian political system, and the locus of key decision making and control in the governmental process. An understanding of the Cabinet, as an "institution," and the process by which ministers reach decisions is, therefore, important to understanding the Canadian government.

J. Stefan Dupre has argued that the Canadian Cabinet has gone through three discernible stages of development. It has gone from the Traditional Cabinet to the Departmental Cabinet and then on to the Institutional Cabinet.[29] Canada's first Cabinet was appointed by Sir John A. Macdonald and had only 13 ministers. It had only one Cabinet Committee, Treasury Board, which remains the only statutory committee in the Canadian Cabinet. The first Cabinet was typical of the Traditional Cabinets in terms of its mode of operation, it was small in size and operated in an informal manner with no minutes kept of its proceedings. The Departmental Cabinet was larger in size, over 20 ministers, with minutes kept of its proceedings and a system of Cabinet Committees. With government departments increasing in size, senior civil servants were become more influential in government decision making. This period in Cabinet evolution saw the rise of the Ottawa "Mandarins."[30] The third stage in Cabinet evolution, the Institutional Cabinet, was marked by a large Ministry supported by a number of specialized Central Agencies to assist ministers in their policy-making responsibilities and sophisticated systems and procedures for managing governmental policy. The Institutional Cabinet presided over the mature Canadian Welfare State with its enormous public bureaucracy.

The work of the current Canadian Cabinet is divided into various standing and ad hoc committees. The two most important Cabinet Committees are the Priorities and Planning Committee (P&P) and the Operations Committee (OPS) of Cabinet. The Priorities and Planning Committee of Cabinet is often referred to as the "Inner Cabinet." It is chaired by the Prime Minister and consists of the most senior ministers in the government. P&P has the authority to ratify decisions on behalf of full Cabinet. In fact, full Cabinet meets infrequently and now serves mostly as a political forum on major issues; for the real work of Cabinet is being conducted in its committees. The Operations Committee of Cabinet is chaired by the Deputy Prime Minister and serves as a clearing centre or "traffic cop" for the flow of work within Cabinet. No policy or expenditure proposal can proceed without the approval of OPS. There are also a number of Policy Committees of Cabinet but their work has been limited due to the escalating debt problems of the federal government. It appears that ad hoc Cabinet Committees are a growing feature of the contemporary Cabinet system.[31] There are also a number of Coordinating Committees of Cabinet such as Legislation and Housing Planning, Communications, Special Committee of Council, and Security and Intelligence.[32]

Ministers are supported in their deliberations by an "elite core" of civil servants who are attached to a small number of high-powered governmental organizations referred to as Central Agencies. The most important Central Agencies include what is considered as the Prime Minister's department, the Privy Council Office (PCO). It also includes the Prime Minister's

Office (PMO) and the Federal-Provincial Relations Office (FPRO). A recent Canadian government publication explains the roles and relationships of these offices in the following way:

> The Prime Minister is supported directly on a day-to-day basis by personal staff working in three organizations within the Prime Minister's portfolio. The Privy Council Office provides public service support to the Prime Minister across the entire spectrum of policy questions and operational issues facing the Government. Public service support for matters relating to the provinces is provided by the Federal-Provincial Relations Office (FPRO). The personal political staff of the Prime Minister comprise the Prime Minister's Office.[33]

Two other important Central Agencies are the Treasury Board Secretariat (TBS) that supports the work of the Treasury Board which is a Cabinet Committee, and the Department of Finance. Both of these Central Agencies are responsible for the economic policies of the Government of Canada. Treasury Board manages and controls the expenditures of the government. The Treasury Board Secretariat assists the Treasury Board in this function but also has the important responsibility of compiling the annual budgetary Estimates of the Canadian government. With TBS responsible for the expenditure side of the budget, Finance has the responsibility for the revenue side of the budget. The Minister of Finance must deliver his or her annual budget statement to Parliament outlining the government's revenue requirements for the coming fiscal year, which starts April 1st and runs through to March 31st.

It is on this occasion that the Minister of Finance announces any tax changes or borrowing requirements that the government may need to meet its expenditures for the coming fiscal year. Since the government is also responsible for managing the economy to further its macroeconomic goals of high and stable employment, price stability, and sustained economic growth, etc., the Minister of Finance also presents an economic outlook statement on his or her economic projections for the coming fiscal year. The Minister of Finance's budget speech in the House of Commons is a significant annual occasion in the life of Parliament; since the Ways and Means Motions and the Appropriations Bills tabled by the Minister of Finance are considered to be a matter of "confidence." Should the Minister of Finance's bills be defeated in the House of Commons then the government would "fall" or be forced to resign.

Only the "best and the brightest" are selected to work in the Central Agencies from among the civil servants in the government. Civil servants who work in these Central Agencies are often called "Superbureaucrats" because of their access to ministers and the support and advice they give to the deliberations of Cabinet. These "high flyers" are recruited to work in the Central Agencies from line departments and serve in the Central Agencies for about two to three years before returning to their departments. When they return to their departments, "high flyers" usually get a promotion and are given more senior responsibilities. Needless to say, positions within Central Agencies are highly competitive, yet, highly sought after by ambitious civil servants within the Canadian government.

Below the Central Agencies, in the organizational hierarchy of the Canadian public bureaucracy, are the "Horizontal Coordinative Departments" and the "Vertical Constituency Departments." The Horizontal Coordinative Departments, whether they are "Policy Coordinative Departments," such as the Department of Justice and the Department of External Affairs, or whether they are "Administrative Coordinative Departments," such as the Department of Supply and Services, Department of National Revenue, and Department of Public Works, are responsible for matters that are of interest to the entire public bureaucracy. The Vertical Constituency Departments are the most numerous and include: the Departments of Agriculture, Labour, Veterans Affairs, Indian Affairs and Northern Development, Fisheries and Oceans, Transport, and so on. Vertical Constituency Departments service a particular group or sector of Canadian society while Horizontal Coordinative Departments service the entire government or cut across sectoral lines. The least influential departments on policy lines tend to be the Horizontal Administrative Coordinate Departments because they usually provide government-wide services for other organizations within the Canadian government. For instance, the Department of Public Works manages the Canadian government's real property assets and provides the office space for government departments, while the Department of Supply and Services issues the government's cheques and is the major procurement arm for the government.

One of the central tenets of a professional public service is the "doctrine of political neutrality." Civil servants are recruited *not* on the basis of "patronage", but on "merit." The "Merit Principle" demands that individuals appointed to the public bureaucracy are selected "exclusively on qualification or fitness for the job" and, furthermore, "all citizens should have a reasonable opportunity to be considered for employment in the public service."[34] The Public Service Commission (PSC) is the agency responsible for ensuring that the "Merit Principle" is enforced within the Canadian public bureaucracy. This implies that the public bureaucracy can well serve any political party that forms the government of the day, whether it is the Progressive Conservatives, Liberals, New Democrats, Reform, or Bloc Quebecois, etc. Therefore, selection to the civil service in Canada should not be based on one's partisan loyalty or affiliation. Indeed, for years civil servants were discouraged from any partisan activity even when it was outside their area of responsibility and it was on their own free time. This indicates the strength of the belief that politics and public administration are separate spheres and should not be mixed.

Despite the doctrine of political neutrality and the politics/administration dichotomy, few actually accept that the public bureaucracy is value free or little more than a servant of the state. For example, Ralph Miliband eloquently makes the point when he asserts:

> Formally, officialdom is at the service of the political executive, its obedient instrument, the tool of its will. In actual fact it is nothing of the kind. Everywhere and inevitably the administrative process is also part of the political process; administration is always political as well as executive, at least at the levels where policy-making is relevant, that is to say in the upper layers of administrative life.[35]

Perhaps those who are most noticeably at the cusp between the so-called political and administrative worlds in the Canadian public bureaucracy are the Deputy Ministers (DMs). Deputy Ministers are Order-in-Council appointments, which are made by the Prime Minister, and serve as the administrative heads of departments and work under the direction of the minister. The DM position is one of the most challenging and demanding roles within the Canadian civil service. One of the reasons for this is the overlapping and intersecting lines of responsibility and accountability that Deputy Ministers are subject to within the public bureaucracy. Although DMs are answerable to their ministers, they are conscious of the fact that they are also Order-in-Council appointments and serve at "the pleasure" of

29

the Prime Minister. On a DM's appointment, he or she will receive a "letter of instruction" from the PM. Since Canada has a
permanent civil service, appointments are made from within the
senior ranks of the public bureaucracy and on the advice of the
"Clerk of the Privy Council and Secretary" to the Cabinet, the
highest civil service post in the entire government. Accordingly,
the DM is also answerable to the Clerk of the Privy Council and
Secretary to the Cabinet who also has the responsibility for
evaluating the performance of DMs on an annual basis.

There are three pieces of legislation that directly impinge on
the responsibilities of DMs. Under the Departmental Act, ministers can delegate authority for departmental policy and management to a DM. The Financial Administration Act allows the
Treasury Board to delegate personnel and management responsibilities to the DMs. The Public Service Commission, under the
authority of the Public Service Employment Act, can delegate
specific responsibilities to the DM as well. As a consequence,
the DM not only answers to his or her Minister for certain matters but to the Treasury Board and the PSC for other matters.
Deputy Ministers are, therefore, held accountable by a number
of different superiors as well as agencies within the Canadian
government. DMs must face a complex working environment
with multiple authority centres. They are also the key links between the bureaucratic world of the department and the political world of the minister and the Cabinet.

MANAGEMENT IN THE PUBLIC
BUREAUCRACY IN CANADA

Public sector management is considerably different than management in the private sector. Grant Reuber who has served at the
senior levels in both the public and private sectors in Canada
offers these major differences between these "two cultures."[36]
Clearly, the objectives in the two sectors differ significantly
since one is profit oriented and the other is not, the exception
being certain Crown corporations. The private sector is largely
dependent on voluntary transactions while government can use
the force of law to ensure non-voluntary compliance to its direc-
tives. However, it is in the decisionmaking capacity of each
sector that we find the widest variation between the two sectors. Grant Reuber argues that public sector decision making is
characterized by overlapping jurisdiction and seemingly endless

consultations whereas private decision making has clear lines of authority and responsibility. The public sector is a complicated environment and as a result decision making takes much longer than in the less complicated environment of the private sector. Decision making within the public sector is defined by "support building." This is less of a consideration within the private sector given that objectives are more limited and more clearly defined. Furthermore, since there is greater uncertainty within the public sector environment, decision making tends to be more cautious. One of the major differences between the two sectors, Reuber suggests, is that public sector decision making takes place in a "goldfish bowl" where appearance counts as much as or more than reality.[37] The private sector has less interaction with the public and the media.

The public bureaucracy is, of course, many times larger than a large corporation. Unlike the private bureaucracy, the public bureaucracy is headed by a professional politician who may have little or no expertise in the area over which she or he is expected to preside. The planning horizon for the public bureaucracy tends to be limited to the term of office, the medium to short term from the perspective of business. Grant Reuber argues that selecting, developing, and rewarding talent is more difficult in the public bureaucracy than in the private bureaucracy.[38] The private sector does a much better job at harnessing talent for priority tasks. Part of the difficulty in the public sector is that DMs have limited control over staff and conditions of employment, as was pointed out in the last section. As a consequence, human resource management seems to be given a lower priority in the public bureaucracy than in the private sector. Senior officials seem to concentrate most of their time, energy, and talent on giving policy advice to ministers rather than on departmental administration.[39] In Grant Reuber's view, there is "excessive rigidity" in the public bureaucracy which prevent DMs from effectively managing their departments.[40]

There are, for instance, six pieces of legislation that govern and influence personnel practices in the federal civil service:

1. *Financial Administration Act (FAA), 1951.* This statute puts the Treasury Board in charge of personnel management in the civil service.

2. *Public Service Employment Act (PSEA), 1967.* This statute grants the Public Service Commission exclusive authority

to appoint to and within the civil service on the basis of merit, and to deal with appeals, layoffs, dismissals, and political partisanship.

3. *Public Service Staff Relations Act (PSSRA), 1967.* This statute creates the Public Service Staff Relations Board and provides the framework for the collective bargaining process in the civil service. It also deals with grievances and the resolution of disputes between unions and management.

4. *Public Service Superannuation Act (PSSA), 1975.* This statutes deals with pensions and death benefits for civil servants.

5. *Official Languages Act, 1969/1988.* This statute provides for the use of Canada's two official languages within the civil service.

6. *Canadian Human Rights Act, 1974.* This statute covers such matters as discrimination in hiring, promotion, and other employment practices and the privacy personal information. It also provides for pay equity within government and all organizations under federal jurisdiction.[41]

There are also three agencies that coordinate personnel management within the government:

1. *The Treasury Board Secretariat (TBS).* As outlined previously, the TBS is one of the key Central Agencies in the Government of Canada. With respect to personnel matters, it develops, interprets and monitors personnel policies, regulations and standards, and programs in the areas of: classification and pay; organization and establishment; terms and conditions of employment; and so on. It also represents the employer in the collective bargaining process.

2. *Public Service Commission (PSC).* As pointed out earlier, the PSC handles recruitment, selection, and appointments to and from within the civil service on the basis of the Merit Principle and also provides staff training and development programs as well as language testing and training. The PSC also hears and renders decisions on appeals against appointments, or recommendations for release or demotion for incompetence or incapacity. The PSC

investigates complaints under the Public Service Employment Act on alleged discrimination on the basis of sex,
race, national origin, colour, religion or age. It is responsible for administering regulations regarding political activity of public servants and reviews requests for "leaves of
absence" to participate in elections.

3. *Public Service Staff Relations Board (PSSRB)*. The PSSRB
    certifies bargaining units, deals with complaints of unfair
    practices, controls procedural aspects of collective bargain-
    ing, and has the responsibility for administering the Pub-
    lic Service Staff Relations Act. The PSSRB also has a Pay
    Research Bureau which studies salaries inside and outside
    the federal civil service.[42]

This complicated legislative and organizational environment in
the Canadian government supports Reuber's contention that public sector management is much more difficult than in the private sector.

Although many people incorrectly assume that once someone has been appointed to the civil service they are assured job
security for life, this simply is not the case. The recent budget
cutbacks in most jurisdictions in Canada, clearly demonstrates
this is no longer true, if it ever was in the public service in
Canada. Moreover, it is commonly perceived that this job tenure
undermines the desire of an individual to do their best work
and displaces the incentive to be as productive as possible.
What is less well known is that the Canadian government assesses the performance of all its civil servants on an annual basis and that these annual assessments have an important bearing
on employees' performance pay, opportunities for training, and
promotion.

The government-wide system of staff assessment — the Performance Review and Appraisal Report (PRAR) — is one of the
most important responsibilities of management. The PRAR is
seen as contributing to a "work force which is truly professional, responsive, and dedicated to the delivery of departmental
programs and the provision of services to the public."[43] The
PRAR was jointly developed by the TBS and the PSC. The
PRAR has four parts: Part A deals with Performance Review and
seeks to rank an employee's performance on a five-point scale,
from Outstanding to Unsatisfactory. Part B deals with the
Employee Appraisal and assesses an employee's abilities and

characteristics, again, using a five-point scale, and makes recommendations for promotion, probation, transfer, etc. Part C covers the Objectives for the Next Period, and, Part D includes the section for Signatures and Comments. For managers, the PRAR provides a structured method for assessing their employees and assisting them in realizing their full potential. In fact, managers are assessed on how well they do staff performance reviews and appraisals.

One of the most important, yet sensitive, areas of management is exercising disciplinary measures. Since disciplinary action is handled as an internal administrative matter, it rarely receives public exposure. This probably contributes to the public's general perception of the public sector as a lax work environment. Of course, disciplinary measures are used within the civil service but because they are internal departmental or agency matters and, indeed, in many instances are private matters between an employee and his or her supervisor, they are not publicly visible.

There are five disciplinary measures which can be used in the federal civil service:

1. Oral Reprimand;
2. Written Reprimand;
3. Suspension;
4. Financial Penalty;
5. Discharge.

Supervisors have the authority to issue oral or written reprimands. More serious penalties are dealt with by senior management. A supervisor can impose a provisional suspension in exceptional circumstances, if in the judgement of the supervisor the employee becomes a threat to persons or property in the workplace. Otherwise, the Deputy Minister has the discretion to determine what penalties should be applied for various kinds of misconduct within the guidelines of established precedent within their departments and across the Canadian civil service.

In the use of disciplinary measures, management must be sure that it does not violate the provisions of the collective agreement. Moreover, employees have the right to grieve against any disciplinary measures taken and to be represented by legal counsel in the hearing of such grievances. Furthermore, certain procedures must be followed prior to taking disciplinary action.

The employee must be given an opportunity to explain the circumstances surrounding the incident or incidents which may warrant disciplinary measures to be meted out by the supervisor. Such an interview should take place in private. The employee has a right to have a representative present at such an interview as does management. Determining an appropriate penalty for misconduct always requires good judgement. With respect to the federal government, its explicit policy is that the primary object of discipline is not punishment but to rehabilitate the employee, to make them a better and more productive worker. This is referred to as "corrective discipline."[44]

The control and direction of financial resources is also a key aspect of public sector management. As already discussed, this is primarily the responsibility of two key Central Agencies within the government, Finance and the TBS. The Minister of Finance is responsible for the "revenue budget" while the president of the Treasury Board is responsible for the "expenditure budget." Both of these ministers perform essential functions in the same "budgetary process" in the Canadian government.[45] The two ministers and their respective Central Agencies must work together not only to ensure there is coordination but to maintain coherence and consistency in the budgetary process.

Much of the work of Parliament is centred on the documents presented by the Minister of Finance and the president of the Treasury Board. The Budget Resolution and accompanying bills and the Estimates embody two fundamental parliamentary principles: "no taxation without representation;" that is, no monies can be raised by the executive without the approval of the representative assembly; and, no monies can be spent by the executive unless duly authorized by the representative assembly. These are two of the most fundamental constitutional principles in the parliamentary system.

The Minister of Supply and Services, who is also designated the Receiver General for Canada, also plays an important role in the budgetary process. The Minister of Supply and Services is responsible for the disbursement of public funds and for the preparation of the "Public Accounts." These are the records of the actual expenditures of the Canadian government during the fiscal year.

The Estimates, tabled by the president of the Treasury Board, and the Ways and Means Motions, which are presented by the Minister of Finance as part of the government's budget, are collectively known as the Appropriation Acts after they have been approved by Parliament. The Appropriations Acts provide the authorization for the Minister of Supply & Services to dispense public funds, which is done under the direction of the Treasury Board. After the end of the fiscal year and usually in the fall, the Minister of Supply and Services tables the Public Accounts in the House of Commons. The Public Accounts are then reviewed in detail by one of the most important Standing Committees in Parliament, the Public Accounts Committee. This is the only committee in Parliament which is chaired by a member of the Opposition. When specific departmental expenditures are being reviewed, the Public Accounts Committee will request the presence of the minister and his senior officials to explain and defend their expenditures to the committee members. This is one of the ways in which the House of Commons can hold the government accountable for its financial management of public funds.

INTERGOVERNMENTAL RELATIONS AND CANADIAN PUBLIC ADMINISTRATION

As a parliamentary federation, Canada has two orders of government which are constantly interacting on a wide range of issues and concerns. This is to be expected given these governments have jurisdiction over the same people and territory. As noted before, Canada's governments also have overlapping responsibilities and concurrent powers under the Constitution in such fields as, agriculture and immigration, the administration of justice, and the environment. Federalism has been, in fact, defined as a "political system in which the powers of the state are formally divided between central and regional government by a written constitution but in which these governments are *linked in an interdependent political relationship.*"[46] (Emphasis added.) This definition suggests that intergovernmental relations are a typical feature of federal forms of government.

Canada has, perhaps, one of the most refined processes of intergovernmental relations of any federation in the world. It has evolved a complex network of intergovernmental structures which are intended to facilitate the smooth and harmonious interaction between and among governments in Canada. The most well known and visible structures facilitating intergovernmental

36

relations in Canada is the "First Ministers Conference," (FMC). This is the pinnacle of the federal-provincial interaction process and involves the Prime Minister and the premiers supported by their most senior ministers and officials. The FMC is the institution in which some of the most important and contentious issues are addressed within the country.

The FMC is the forum for the resolution of outstanding constitutional issues in Canada. In the last several decades, such constitutional amendments as the Victoria Charter, 1971, the 1982 Constitution Act, the Meech Lake Accord, 1987, and the Charlottetown Accord, 1992, were all forged at First Ministers Conferences. Both of the most recent failed attempts at constitutional reform, the Meech Lake Accord and the Charlottetown Accord, sought to constitutionalize the First Ministers Conference. At present there is no basis for FMCs in the Canadian Constitution, therefore, it has been put forward that the role of the FMC, in the Canadian political system, needs to be better defined and based in law rather than custom and tradition.

In addition to FMCs, there is also a plethora of ministerial meetings that take place to coordinate policy between and among the governments in Canada. There are at least annual meetings of ministers of Finance and Treasurers, Attorneys-General and the ministers of Justice, Health ministers, Environmental ministers, and so on. Meetings also take place at the official level to deal with these various substantive policy fields. There are regular meetings of DMs, Assistant Deputy Ministers, Director Generals, Executive Directors, and the like. Meetings at the official level are intended to deal with the technical issues before they can be resolved by the politicians, to facilitate the exchange of information and to do the "leg work" in advance of ministerial meetings. There are literally thousands of intergovernmental meetings which take place each year in Canada.

All of this intense activity, as one would expect, has engendered an elaborate infrastructure to facilitate the process of ongoing consultation and negotiation between and among governments. Quebec was the first province to establish a Department of Intergovernmental Affairs in 1961. Other provinces quickly followed the Quebec lead. In 1968, the federal government decided to establish a Federal-Provincial Relations Secretariat within the PCO. By 1975, it was decided that the Secretariat should be upgraded to an office and separated from the PCO. So in that year, the Federal-Provincial Relations Office was established as a separate Central Agency within the Government of Canada. In 1973, the federal and provincial governments decided to establish the Canadian Intergovernmental Conference Secretariat to help organize federal-provincial meetings. Ottawa's old railway station, across the road from the Chateau Laurier and down the street from Parliament Hill, was converted into a meeting facility and serves as the National Conference Centre; that is, the site for FMCs and other federal-provincial meetings in Ottawa. The Canadian Intergovernmental Conference Secretariat is jointly funded by the provinces and the federal government.

Intergovernmental relations is developing into a highly specialized area within Canadian public administration. Civil servants, whether federal or provincial, who work in this field are considered to be "process experts." They are involved on a full-time basis in the ongoing processes of consultation and negotiations. Their principal goal, of course, is to protect and advance their government's interests in a particular policy field. Moreover, with the process of federal-provincial relations growing in complexity, these officials are considered to be growing in influence as well. These developments are considered to have a number of consequences for Canadian government and politics.

Some have argued the growing number of specialists within the civil service in the area of intergovernmental relations is leading to greater conflict between governments. Unlike substantive experts, say in the field of accounting, engineering, law, teaching, etc., who operate from common assumptions and values and use the same technical language, process experts have no common assumptions or values. Where substantive experts may seek technical solutions and the refinement of public policy, the process experts sincerely seek to advance their government's interests in negotiations. Without common assumptions, values, and goals among the main participants in the process of federal-provincial relations, the degree of conflict will likely increase.

This process of intergovernmental relations which involves ongoing interactions among governments has been coined "Executive Federalism" by Donald Smiley.[47] Smiley draws a number of conclusions from the recent Canadian experience with Executive Federalism. First, agreements are more likely to be reached when Ottawa negotiates with individual provinces or when officials are concerned with specific programs as opposed to the broader aspects of public policy. Second, agreements are more likely when governments are in continuous communications. Enhanced communications among participants will lead to a better understanding of the interests and motivations of all parties involved. As a consequence, agreement is more likely to result.[48] Although most of the literature on Executive Federalism tends to decry conflict, not everyone is of the opinion that collaboration or cooperation would necessarily advance the public interest. Indeed, given the size of the country, the diversity of its population, and the ideological and class divisions, conflict may be inevitable in intergovernmental relations in Canada.

CANADIAN PUBLIC ADMINISTRATION AND THE STRUCTURE OF GOVERNMENT

The structure of government in Canada, as we have seen, conditions public administration in Canada. The modern Canadian governmental system is an incredible mix of structural components and procedures which impact on the daily lives of Canadians. The size and complexity of the Canadian government is partially due to Canada being an advanced welfare state, with all that this entails in terms of the role of the state in Canada's "mixed economy." This implies that the public sector makes a significant contribution to the Canadian economy both in terms of employment and in the creation of wealth. Public administration, therefore, is essential to the overall operation of Canadian government and to the general well-being of Canadian society.

Canada's parliamentary system of government is directed by the executive branch of government. At the apex of the governmental structure, then, we have the Prime Minister and Cabinet supported by the Central Agencies and departments. Under responsible government it is the Cabinet, through "collective" and "ministerial" responsibility, that reports to the House of Commons in the daily Question Period when Parliament is sitting. Government, thus, is held accountable on an ongoing basis by Parliament and periodically in national elections by the Canadian electorate. Since the government is accountable for directing the public bureaucracy, the public bureaucracy is only indirectly accountable to the legislature. Nevertheless, civil servants are still held accountable in a myriad of other ways for their actions or inactions within government. For instance, the

Deputy Minister who is appointment at the "pleasure" of the Prime Minister is the senior administrative official who has the responsibility for deciding the more serious matters dealing with disciplinary measures within her or his department. Despite common misperceptions among the public, civil servants are terminated for a number of reasons, including incompetence. The parliamentary system imposes its own system of accountability and control on public administration through a government which is "fused" to the legislature.

Clearly, public administration in Canada, at least at the senior levels, is perhaps one of the most challenging vocations that anyone can pursue. The material rewards may not be as great as for comparable positions at the senior levels in the private sector, but the intangible rewards of serving the public interest and one's country can not be found within any private sector position or, in fact, in most other occupations. The implications of the decisions taken within the public sector usually impact on all Canadian citizens, unlike the limited impact of decisions taken within firms, regardless of their size. In the end, it is the extent and range of power and influence exercised within the governmental process that marks the difference between the public and private sectors in Canada.

NOTES

1. Mark O. Dickerson & Thomas Flanagan, *An Introduction to Government and Politics: A Conceptual Approach*, 3rd Edition (Toronto: Nelson Canada, 1990), p. 21.
2. "Ottawa shops until it drops $9.4 billion," *The Toronto Star*, February 17, 1993, A11.
3. Bruce Little, "Debt crisis looms, study warns," *The Globe & Mail*, February 16, 1993, A1–A2.
4. "Mazankowski rejects tax rise to cut deficit," *The Toronto Star*, February 17, 1993, D6.
5. Terence Corcoran, "What a debt crisis might look like," *The Globe & Mail*, February 17, 1993, B2.
6. See James O'Connor, *The Fiscal Crisis of the State*. (New York: St. Martin's Press, 1973)
7. Robert J. Jackson & Doreen Jackson, *Politics in Canada*, 2nd Edition (Scarborough: Prentice-Hall Canada Inc., 1990), p. 41.
8. Stephen Brooks, *Public Policy in Canada: An Introduction* (Toronto: McClelland & Stewart, 1989), p. 180.

9. "The Search for Keynes," *The Economist*, December 26, 1992–January 8, 1993, pp. 108–10; and Don Patinkin, "Keynes, lost and found," *The Economist*, January 23, 1993, p. 65.
10. See Richard D. Phidd & G. Bruce Doern, *The Politics and Management of Canadian Economic Policy* (Toronto: MacMillan of Canada, 1978).
11. Herschel Hardin, *A Nation Unaware: The Canadian Economic Culture* (Vancouver: J.J. Douglas, 1974).
12. Ramesh Mishra, *The Welfare State in Capitalist Society: Policies of Retrenchment and Maintenance in Europe, North America and Australia* (Toronto: University of Toronto Press, 1990), p. 1.
13. Mark O. Dickerson & Thomas Flanagan, *An Introduction to Government and Politics*, Chapter 15, "Classifications of Political Systems."
14. Ibid., p. 251.
15. For a further explanation on the operation of the Parliamentary system, see David Siegel, "The Public Sector in Canada: Sector and Processes," in *The Canadian Profile: People, Institutions, Infrastructure*, edited by Jerry Dermer (Toronto: Captus Press, 1992).
16. Ronald G. Landes, *The Canadian Polity: A Comparative Introduction*, 2nd Edition (Scarborough: Prentice-Hall Canada Inc., 1987), p. 117.
17. Andrew Hacker, *The Study of Politics: The Western Tradition and American Origins* (Toronto: McGraw-Hill Book Company Inc., 1963), p. 65.
18. James Madison, *The Federalist*, No. 51, as quoted in Mark O. Dickerson & Thomas Flanagan, *An Introduction to Government and Politics*, pp. 245–6.
19. Robert Jackson & Doreen Jackson, *Politics in Canada*, 2nd Edition (Scarborough: Prentice-Hall Canada, Inc., 1990), p. 252.
20. Roger Gibbins, *Conflict and Unity: An Introduction to Canadian Political Life*, 2nd Edition (Toronto: Nelson Canada, 1990), p. 36.
21. See R.T. Naylor, "The rise and fall of the third commercial empire of the St. Lawrence," in *Capitalism and the National Question in Canada*, edited by Gary Teeple (Toronto: University of Toronto Press, 1972), pp. 1–41.
22. Roger Gibbins, *Conflict and Unity*, p. 13.
23. Donald V. Smiley, "The Two Themes of Canadian Federalism," in *The Canadian Political Tradition*, edited by R.S. Blair & J.T. McLeod (Toronto: Methuen, 1987), p. 65.
24. David Vienneau, "The Charter's Quiet Revolution," *The Toronto Star*, Saturday, April 11, 1992, A1 & A12.
25. Richard Van Loon & Michael Whittington, *The Canadian Political System*, 4th Edition, (Toronto: McGraw-Hill Ryerson Limited, 1987), p. 267.

26. Kenneth Kernaghan & David Siegel, *Public Administration in Canada: A Text*, 2nd Edition (Toronto: Nelson Canada, 1991), p. 5.

27. Mark O. Dickerson & Thomas Flanagan, *An Introduction to Government and Politics*, p. 338.

28. Nicholas Henry, "The Intellectual Development of Public Administration," in *Public Administration in Canada: Selected Readings*, 5th Edition, edited by Kenneth Kernaghan (Toronto: Methuen, 1985), p. 64.

29. J. Stefan Dupre, "Reflections on the Workability of Executive Federalism," in *Perspectives on Canadian Federalism*, edited by R.D. Olling & M.W. Westmacott (Scarborough: Prentice-Hall Canada Inc., 1988), pp. 233–6.

30. J.L. Granatstein, *The Ottawa Men: The Civil Service Mandarins, 1935–1957* (Toronto: Oxford University Press, 1982).

31. James C. Simeon, "The British and Canadian Cabinet Systems: Cabinet Decision-Making Under Prime Ministers Margaret Thatcher and Brian Mulroney," in *Public Administration: Canadian Materials*, 2nd Edition, edited Hoffman et al. (Toronto: Captus Press, 1993), pp. 54–67.

32. For a further description of the Canadian Cabinet system, see Robert Jackson & Doreen Jackson, *Politics in Canada*, Chapter 7, "The Inner Circle."

33. *The Privy Council Office*, September, 1991, pp. 3–4.

34. Kenneth Kernaghan & David Siegel, *Canadian Public Administration: A Text*, p. 640.

35. Ralph Miliband, *The State in Capitalist Society* (London: Quartet Books, 1973), p. 47.

36. Grant Reuber, "Better Bureaucracies: Public versus Private Sector Administration," in *Public Administration in Canada: Selected Readings*, 5th Edition, edited by Kenneth Kernaghan (Toronto: Methuen, 1985), p. 101.

37. Ibid., p. 102.

38. Ibid., p. 104.

39. Ibid., p. 105.

40. Ibid., pp. 105–6.

41. Kenneth Kernaghan & David Siegel, *Public Administration in Canada: A Text*, 2nd Edition, pp. 511–2; and Treasury Board of Canada Secretariat and Public Service Commission, *Personnel: A Manager's Handbook* (Ottawa: Supply & Services Canada, 1982), pp. 4–5.

42. Treasury Board of Canada Secretariat & Public Service Commission, *Personnel: A Manager's Handbook* (Ottawa: Supply & Services Canada, 1982), pp. 5–8.

43. Ibid., p. 3.

44. Ibid., p. 57.

45. Evert A. Lindquist, "The Budgetary Process," in *Politics: Canada.* 7th Edition, Edited by Paul Fox & Graham White (Toronto: McGraw-Hill Ryerson, 1991), pp. 475–83.
46. Kenneth Kernaghan & David Siegel, *Public Administration in Canada: A Text*, p. 417.
47. Donald Smiley, *The Federal Condition in Canada* (Toronto: McGraw-Hill Ryerson Limited, 1987), p. 83.
48. Ibid., p. 98.

Understanding Canadian Parliamentary Government

George E. Eaton

This paper is intended to be of assistance to students being introduced to the study of public administration. There are two usages to the term public administration. In the broadest sense it encompasses the entire machinery of government including:

(a) the legislative decision-making bodies (Parliament) through which national or provincial goals and priorities are articulated, debated and translated into specific public policies, programmes, or measures;

(b) Executive Organs — including the Crown and Cabinet and the public services especially the Civil Service, through which the policies are not just interpreted and implemented but are often initiated, and given practical effect to the population at large; and

(c) the Judicial and Legal Services, through which disputes over constitutional questions and rights, as well as other forms of civil litigation and redress are adjudicated, and justice meted out to those accused of violations of laws governing social conduct and order in society.

In its other and more restricted usage, the term public administration is often used to refer to the executive organs of government, mainly the Cabinet and civil or public service.

The focus in this paper will be on the term in its broadest usage — looking then, at how society deals with the ordering and running of its affairs in short — with public affairs.

The public administration or the machinery of government, involves a complex of institutions and activities, and its purposes are correspondingly varied. They range all the way from establishing and maintaining representative decision-making bodies or institutions, to the allocation of the tasks of government so that they can be performed in a manner considered acceptable by the citizenry, (which usually involves considerations of efficiency and economy) to defining areas of authority and responsibility of administrative units, so that they can be made properly subject to constitutional and political controls.

In Canada, the machinery or structure of government has been greatly shaped and influenced by the British (UK) Constitution or arrangements of government. Let it be noted right away, that there are differing views and perceptions of what a constitution is or is not depending on one's professional or academic orientation. Thus we can discern at least 5 concepts of constitution — philosophical, structural, legal, documentation, and procedural.

From the purely structural point of view, the constitution defines and provides for the establishment of the main organs of government. If, however, the constitution is viewed as a political process embodying certain ideals of government, then the focus will be on the methods or techniques used to establish and maintain effective restraints upon political and governmental action.

The British model of parliamentary government is widely referred to as the Westminster model and/or the Whitehall model and we should be clear as to what these terms connote. The "Westminster" model derives its name from the physical location of the Houses of Parliament at Westminster, London, England and is used to identify the classic (British) model of parliamentary government as well as the countries, typically former British colonies, which have inherited or retained the same functional organization or system of government. There is, however, only one authentic Westminster model and that is to be found at Westminster itself, and there is a lot to be said

45

for reserving the label for the original. To illustrate; a fundamental tenet of British constitutionalism, is the doctrine of the
Supremacy of Parliament. This doctrine asserts that in the
making of laws, Parliament's control over conduct is direct and
absolute and not subject to the regularized restraints of fundamental law.

Accordingly, there is no single document or British Constitution which sets out overriding principles of constitutional government or basic rights of citizens which can be enforced
against Parliament through and by, the courts. The result is that
some of the most fundamental aspects of the political and government system are regulated not by law but by "conventions of
the constitution." Conventions, it may be noted, are variously
customs, usages, rules, or principles which are adhered to although they may not be legally enforceable. A breach of a convention may be unconstitutional but not unlawful or illegal. It
is often this gap between formal theory and practice, between
the stated and the unstated, which leaves student's confused,
and makes the workings of the system of government so difficult to comprehend.

If the Westminster model more appropriately identifies the
unique experience and system of government of the United
Kingdom, the "Whitehall" model is used to denote the colonial
or overseas adaption of the Westminster model. The adjective
"Whitehall" gives recognition to the fact that civil servants in
Whitehall (The Colonial Office) have been intimately involved in
the process of drafting "independence" constitutions, certainly
for the newly emergent nations such as all found for example,
in the Commonwealth Caribbean.

Some of the features or basic tenets of the Whitehall model
which serve to distinguish it from the Westminster model are —
a Bill of Rights or Charter of Rights and Freedoms (A Charter
was incorporated into Canada's Constitution in 1982) which
diminishes the legislative supremacy of Parliament; the entrenchment of certain constitutional articles or provisions which require
special and more difficult amending procedures, which likewise
diminish the legislative supremacy of Parliament; and the incorporation of previously unwritten conventions into the Constitution. For example, where the dissolution of Parliament remains a
convention in the Westminster model, the Constitutions of Trini-
dad and Tobago and St. Lucia in the Commonwealth Caribbean

deal explicitly and differently with the power of dissolution of Parliament.

Let us now turn to the workings of, and interactions between the three main organs or functional branches of the public administration (or government), Legislature Executive and Judiciary.

The Legislature or Parliament

One of the suppositions of liberal democracy is that the power to set up forms and institutions of government, i.e., constituent power, as well as sovereignty, the notion of an ultimate source of authority and power which may be exercised within a country, and brought to bear against citizens, are both deemed to be vested or inhere in the people. Of course, for many subject (colonial) peoples, constituent power or the right to self-determination were or are qualified rights, as more often than not they have had, sometimes on the basis of armed struggle, to negotiate the terms and constitutional instruments of political independence with an imperial power and to submit draft constitutions for approval. The distinction made earlier between the Westminster and Whitehall models of parliamentary government underscores this point. That sovereignty inheres in the people is all well and good, but how do the people give expression to, and implement their wishes and will, when societies and nations number in millions of people? Even in mini-states such as in the Commonwealth Caribbean where populations number over 100,000 it is considered either impractical or inconvenient for citizens to come together in the arena or market place as they did in the ancient Greek city states, to discuss and vote directly on matters of public concern. Nor should we forget that this ancient Greek ideal of direct participation in government rested on a foundation of slavery which gave citizens of the city state the time and leisure to congregate in the marketplace.

The only practical alternative where vast numbers are involved is indirect representation, where representatives are chosen through the electoral process, to give expression to the desires and will of citizens individually and collectively.

In democratic theory, the Legislature (in our case the elected House of Commons or Lower House as distinct from the Senate, or Upper House, whose members are appointed) represents the people or community. Parliament (the House of Commons) is supposed to exercise general surveillance over the

Executive to ensure that governmental power is exercised for the benefit of the people and not against them.

Two hundred ninety-five members of Parliament (MPs) currently sit in the House of Commons, each having been chosen in electoral districts or ridings or geographical constituencies to represent that constituency and collectively the nation of over 25 million persons. Because Canada also operates a federal system of government about which more will be said later — the principle of representation according to population in the Constitution applies only to provinces as such.

How have we been able to decide who can best represent our interests and communal welfare in Parliament? The major instrument or mechanism which evolved as a worldwide phenomenon between 1850 and 1950 to facilitate the process of representation and to enforce electoral accountability has been the political party, or party system of politics.

Party Politics and Electoral Representation

It is not our purpose to trace the development of the national parties or the Canadian party system. Generally speaking, at the national (and provincial) level, Canada has followed the tradition of the Westminster model of a two-party system of government of "ins" and "outs" despite having three major parties — Liberals, Progressive Conservatives, and New Democrats.

As with the concept of constitution — so too the functions of political parties are variously categorized, depending on the predilections of the scholars/practitioners involved. A listing of functions is likely to include some if not all of the following:

(a) Articulation and aggregation of interests — this they do through the brokerage of ideas and interests and presentation of an election "platform or manifesto" designed to attract the widest possible community or regional electoral support. Parties bridge the gap geographically between voters, who at the furthest ends of the country, north or south, east or west, can be united behind a particular party. On an ongoing basis also, parties help to organize public opinion and to communicate demands to the centre of governmental power and decision making.

(b) Political recruitment — that is to say — the selection of political office holders and political leadership.

(c) Articulation of the concept and meaning of the broader community (national consensus) even if the aim of the party is to modify or destroy the community and replace it with something else.

If we accept the essentiality of the functions and role attributed above to political parties, then quite apart from any consideration of how well they perform their functions, we must conclude that political parties lie at the heart of the democratic process. In spite of this, political parties are not mentioned in the Canadian Constitution.[1] Following the Westminster model, they are private and voluntary bodies which control their own internal processes and are formally outside the Constitution. In effect, the most dynamic element of the political process and system of government remains part of the convention of the Constitution. Since the general election of 1993, there has been an interesting turn in the configuration of the three well established and enduring national parties.

The Progressive Conservative or "Tory" Party (PC), which had won a landslide victory in 1984, taking 211 of 282 seats, and a historic follow-up victory in 1988 was devastated in 1993, and reduced from 169 to 2 seats, one in Quebec, the other in New Brunswick. The New Democratic Party (NDP) fell from 43 seats in 1988 to 9 seats in 1993, with representation being confined to the western provinces of British Columbia (BC), Manitoba and Saskatchewan. Both the PCs and the NDP forfeited official party status in the House of Commons, which requires a minimum of 12 seats.

Also making their first appearances as official parties in 1993 were the Bloc Quebecois (BQ) and the Reform Party. The BQ emerged as a single-issue party, its purpose being to work for the separation of the Province of Quebec from Canada. By winning 54 of the 75 federal seats and 49% of the popular vote in Quebec, BQ created a situation, the ultimate in irony, of becoming "Her Majesty's Loyal Opposition," while being dedicated to achieving the break-up of Canada as a nation state.

The Reform Party, a right-wing populist coalition and anti-Eastern Canada protest movement growing out of, and reflecting, Western Canada alienation, also won 52 seats, concentrated in the provinces of Alberta (22 seats) and British Columbia (24 seats).

Finally, the Liberal Party, the predominant ruling party since Confederation, survived as such and took 177 seats to form a majority government.

In the June 1997 general election, the Liberal Party again won another majority term in office with 155 seats but, while it gained modest or respectable representation in the Atlantic provinces, Quebec and the western provinces, its ability to form a majority was made possible by winning 100 of the 103 seats in the Province of Ontario.

The PC party regained official party status by winning 20 seats but realized support primarily in the Atlantic provinces (13 seats) and in Quebec (5 seats).

The NDP won 21 seats, likewise regaining official party status but with support concentrated in the Atlantic provinces (8 seats) and in the western provinces (12 seats).

In turn the Reform Party won 60 seats, all in Western Canada, thereby displacing the BQ as the official Opposition in Parliament.

In effect, therefore, the traditional two-party system of government of "ins" and "outs" at the national level has been replaced by a collection of region dependent political parties. Whether this is a transitory phenomenon or the harbinger of the new Canadian political reality remains to be seen.

The fragmentation of parliamentary representation does, however, compound the unresolved dilemma of representative and responsible liberal democratic government, namely, meaningful (as distinct from formal) electoral accountability. One of the suppositions of the Westminster model is that "the political party forms the government but does not govern." The rationale underlying this rather subtle distinction appears to be the desire to differentiate between liberal democratic government constrained by checks and balances and totalitarian forms of government in which the political party stands above the government and dictates to it. Be that as it may, the fact remains that in Canada, political parties solicit the support of the electors to give them a mandate to implement their respective electoral platforms or "manifestos." Quite often, however, when party leaders in their capacities as leaders of government or the public administration are quizzed by followers or the electorate at large about failure to adhere to, or implement, their mandated manifestos, the usual rejoinder is that the political administration represents and acts on behalf of all the citizenry and in the national or country's interests and not just on behalf of the factions who voted on behalf of the party candidates. Of course, the converse situation may apply where a ruling party commits itself single-mindedly to carrying through its campaign manifesto even when the electorate may become alarmed and disenchanted with the social consequences. In both situations, whatever may be the avenues available to influence a government during its term in office, in the final analysis, the electorate may be obliged to await the next general election for a reckoning. However, this periodic exercise in electoral accountability may be dominated by the desire to vote against the incumbent party in office rather than to vote positively for an acceptable alternative regime. In other words, the ruling party is punished while its successor wins by default.

An often touted solution which was ardently espoused by the Reform Party as part of its electoral platform and campaign in 1997 is the device of "recall." It allows constituents by way of petition to express a vote of non-confidence in a sitting member. If the petition succeeds, a by-election must be held in consistency. The recall mechanism is intended to achieve two objectives concurrently — to encourage the parliamentarian to keep in touch with constituents and to give citizens the assurance that they are, indeed, the ultimate sovereign; that the elected representative is a servant and not master of, the people. In Canada, the Province of Alberta flirted with the recall mechanism as early as the 1920s, but the enabling legislation was repealed when the premier became the subject of a recall petition. The courts also were of the view that recalls violated the principle of the supremacy of the legislature.

It may be noted, by way of comparison, that in the United States about nine states have recall provisions in their constitutions. However, while recall is permitted at the state and local levels, it is not, at the federal level of government. Local recall is allowed in at least 37 states with various signature percentage requirements ranging from 5% to 50%.

The Legislature — The Gap between Formal Theory and Practice

As was the case when specifying the functions of political parties, so too, the functions of Parliament have been variously enumerated to include: law-making, surveillance or control of the Executive, representation and electoral conversion, recruitment, socialization and training (of political leadership) and conflict management or integration, and legitimization.

This writer's preference is to see Parliament as having three functional roles — (1) As Legislature (2) As Representative Assembly and (3) As Deliberative Assembly.

In formal theory, the primary function of Parliament as Legislature is to enact legislation. The primacy of the law-making function is consistent with the notion of the supremacy and sovereignty of Parliament. It grew out of the long struggle in Great Britain between monarch or Sovereign and Parliament over control of the purse string. Buttressing the principle of no taxation without representation was the conviction that freedom and liberty of citizens might best be assured by a separation and balance of powers and function — between legislation (the Legislature), execution (the Executive) and the enforcement of laws and administration of justice (the Judiciary). To the extent also that Parliament came increasingly to embody the principle of representation, and of public deliberation, it seemed best placed and suited to serve as the counterpoise to the powerful Executive — the Sovereign.

The notion of supremacy of Parliament rests on a number of propositions:

i) that there is no higher legislative authority than Parliament

ii) that there is no limit to Parliament's sphere of legislation

iii) that no Parliament can legally bind its successor or be bound by its predecessor and,

iv) that no court can declare Acts of Parliament to be invalid.

Parliamentary supremacy is also reinforced by the principle of Parliamentary Privilege, that is, a series of rights given uniquely to the legislature to ensure that Parliament as an institution and its members are collectively and individually protected against outside control. Thus, while the House of Commons is sitting, members are exempt from the laws of libel while within its chambers and also need not respond to subpoenas requiring attendance at court trials. Parliamentary Privilege also allows the legislature to determine remuneration of members, set its own rules of procedure and conduct and to discipline members. Indeed, it may determine its own membership and expel members temporarily or even permanently as was done at the provincial level by the Saskatchewan legislature in relation to a member who was convicted for the murder of his wife.

The Westminster notion of supremacy of Parliament has, however, been qualified in Canada, firstly by the operation of a federal system, under which exclusive areas of jurisdiction have been allocated to two levels of government — central or federal and regional or provincial. Secondly, and more recently, the Charter of Rights and Freedoms incorporated into the Constitution in 1982, gives formal recognition to, and enshrines the rights of individuals. These rights are now protected by the Constitution and their enforcement falls within the jurisdiction of the courts. Parliament therefore performs its functions subject to these additional constitutional restraints.

The one area over which Parliament historically has been most concerned to assert its supremacy as Legislature has been in the area of public finance, to which we have already alluded. The formal supremacy of Parliament, and I stress formal, has been reflected in the application of special rules to so-called money bills. Bills for the appropriation of public funds or for the raising of any tax or duty must originate in the House of Commons. *But*, special rules applied to money bills also *confine initiation of financial measures to responsible Ministers*, which in effect means the Cabinet. Furthermore, the House of Commons may not adopt any financial measure unless recommended to the Commons by the Governor General (the Formal Executive) which as we shall see also means the Cabinet or political executive. Thus, while Parliament has formal primacy in the sense that it gives effect to policy by legislating, *it is the Cabinet* — the political executive, which decides what Parliament may legislate.

The fact is that Parliament is no longer the prime initiator of legislation, having been superseded by Cabinet dominance of the machinery of government. Realistically, therefore, it is the two other functions of Parliament, as Representative and Deliberative Assembly, which have become the main function of Parliament today. As a representative Assembly, Parliament gives legitimacy and authority to government and facilitates stable government by reassertion of confidence in political administrations. As a Deliberative Assembly, Parliament engages in public/popular education by bringing public policy issues into focus, examining the pros and cons; engages in propagandizing i.e., the selling by the government and belittling by the Opposition of government programmes with a view to influencing the electorate. In the process of parliamentary give-and-take, a measure of integration of conflicting interests and views is achieved.

Freedom of speech (and immunity against laws of slander and libel within Parliament) is considered essential to the representative and deliberative functions of Parliament. But freedom of speech cannot be absolute, as democratic expression has to be tempered by considerations of efficient performance — or getting things done. Hence, the need for rules of procedure and rules of debate and in particular rules of closure of debate, and in this the office — and role of the Speaker — as presiding officer, is crucial. One of the reforms recently carried out to enhance the independent and impartial status of the Speaker, is that the holder is now chosen in secret ballot by MPs rather than by the Prime Minister as a sinecure to be bestowed.

THE SENATE OR UPPER HOUSE

The Senate has a normal complement of 104 members (Ontario 24, Quebec 24, Maritime provinces, 6 each totalling 24, western provinces, 6 each totalling 24, Newfoundland 6, the Northwest Territories, and the Yukon, 1 each). However in 1988, the Conservative Prime Minister Brian Mulroney invoked, for the very first time, a provision thought by the conventional wisdom to be inoperative by virtue of disuse, to increase the membership to the maximum allowable at any time, namely, 112. Sections 26–28 of the Constitution Act of 1867 provide for the addition of from 4 to 8 senators representing equally the Four Divisions (Regions) of Canada. The procedure was invoked to prevent the Liberal-dominated Senate from blocking passage of the very unpopular Goods and Services Tax legislation. The appointment of the additional 8 senators withstood legal challenges and raises speculation as to whether other provisions of the Constitution deemed to have been made inoperative by the convention of disuse could, likewise, successfully be invoked in appropriate circumstances. Of particular interest are the powers of the federal government, unrestricted at law, to disallow provincial legislation and to direct the withholding of assent to provincial bills by the Lieutenant Governor, the representative at the provincial level, of the Queen (Head of State) of Canada. The Lieutenant Governor also has the constitutional power to reserve a bill for the signification of the Governor General, the representative of the Head of State in Canada.

Canadian senators used to be appointed for life, but since 1965 must retire at age 75.

The Senate of Canada was intended to play an important role at the time of Confederation and to be a social balancing mechanism between Upper (English) Canada and Lower (French) Canada, hence the equal representation and appointment rather than election to office; it was also designed to serve as a restraint on "hasty or ill-conceived legislation" (which might compromise the interests of private property) emanating from the popularly elected House of Commons.

Criticism of the Senate has been the favourite past-time of students and practitioners of Canadian politics and public administration, but more recently of the premiers of the western provinces. Now, virtually entrapped in a posture of western alienation — based on alleged bias of the Canadian government towards the dominant concerns of Quebec as a distinct society and Ontario as the industrial heartland of Canada — western political leaders have been arguing for a Triple E Senate (Elected, Equal, Effective).[2] In 1989, the Government of Alberta under the leadership of Premier Don Getty of the ruling Progressive Conservative Party instituted a province-wide election to choose a senator-designate to fill a Senate vacancy. A political complication arose when a maverick candidate put forward by a fringe (separatist) party gained the majority vote — and thus became the Senator designate. Premier Getty has, however, forwarded his name to the Prime Minister of Canada for appointment, raising a number of interesting constitutional and political issues which cannot be pursued here.

Both friends and foes of the Senate have conceded that the Senate has made a useful and often significant contribution in discharging its functions as a revising chamber for general legislation originating in the House of Commons. The Senate retains a critical role in the process of constitutional amendment as its approval is needed for any amendments to the "safeguarded" or "entrenched" clauses and that would extend to the status of the Senate itself. Actually, the Senate can delay certain motions (constitutional amendments) passed by the House of Commons for a maximum of 180 days, after which it can be approved by the Commons unilaterally. What this means is that senators cannot indefinitely block amendments that would reform or abolish the Senate itself.

PARLIAMENTARY GOVERNMENT AS CABINET AND/OR PRIME MINISTERIAL GOVERNMENT

The Formal Executive — Queen and Crown

The Queen of the UK is also the Queen of Canada and the government of Canada is conducted in her name. However, she herself does not — by constitutional convention — govern, either in the UK or in Canada. The monarchy is institutionalized in the Crown, the legal entity or institution which embodies all the powers of executive government, whether exercised by ministers or public officials. Put another way, the Crown as a legal abstraction represents the government but is not accountable for the actions of the government. The Queen of Canada can do no wrong and cannot be sued, but the Crown (by virtue of the Crown Liability Act of 1952) can be.

The powers of the Crown derive from two sources — statute and common law.[3] The statutory powers both to administer laws (executive power) and to make laws (legislative power) are conferred upon the Crown by Parliament and is thus a delegated power subject to the discretion of Parliament. (e.g., to summon senators, to summon or call the House of Commons, appoint the Speaker of the Senate, assent to or refuse to assent to bills which have been passed by both houses of Parliament and so on).

The fact is, however, that the exercise of these statutory powers is subject to *convention*, or long established constitutional doctrine, that the Governor General, the Queen's personal representative acts on the advice of the Privy Council (The Cabinet).

The common law or residual powers may be considered part of the prerogative powers. The Sovereign (Queen) also possesses certain "personal prerogative powers" which are still important constitutional reserve powers. as for example, the right to act independent of ministerial advice in certain circumstances.

The most important prerogative power of the Crown exercised in Canada by the Governor General is the finding of the

Prime Minister, in the choice of which the Governor General acts on his own authority (prerogative). The Governor General likewise has a prerogative right to be consulted in the appointment of ministers of the Crown, and the much more controversial right to refuse the Prime Minister's request for the dissolution of Parliament.

The exercise of prerogative power again shows how formal theory and requirements may, and have been, circumscribed by *convention*. In normal circumstances, convention requires that in the choosing of the Prime Minister, the Governor General call upon the leader of the political party which has gained a majority of seats in the House of Commons to accept the Prime Ministership and form the government. The Governor General, may however, enjoy much greater scope for discretionary prerogative where no party has a clear majority or where a Prime Minister becomes incapacitated or dies in office, and his party has not yet chosen a successor.

DOMINANCE OF THE CABINET OR POLITICAL EXECUTIVE

The Cabinet has become, and is, the unchallenged centre of political power in the Government of Canada. Technically the Cabinet is comprised of the Crowns' confidential advisers and is a Committee of the Privy Council.[4]

The Cabinet, however, is not mentioned in the Canadian Constitution. While also there are other statutory references to the position of Prime Minister, there is no legal definition of the Office of Prime Minister. The earlier title — First Minister would imply that the Prime Minister was supposed to be the first among equals (primus inter pares) but has achieved a degree of pre-eminence that it is now plausible to speak of Prime Ministerial government rather than Cabinet government. Indeed, it is fair to say that the life of the Cabinet is linked to the will and life of the Prime Minister.

The power of the Prime Minister stems in part from the exclusivity of certain functions which he performs and in part from the nature of electoral politics and the role of the media in mass society.

The Prime Minister advises the Sovereign (Queen) on the appointment of the Governor General, her personal representative in Canada. He alone recommends to the Governor General the appointment, dismissal or acceptance of resignations of ministers. He has the right to determine what ministerial offices are entitled to Cabinet rank and who may attend Cabinet. His own resignation may bring not only his own ministry but his government to an end. The Prime Minister has the right to advise on the dissolution of Parliament, a threat which he can hold over the heads of fractious or rebellious colleagues.

The Prime Minister presides over the Cabinet and Cabinet Secretariat, so that he, in effect, controls the agenda and recording of decisions. He can easily dominate Cabinet proceedings, more so when he is a highly popular or charismatic leader on whose coattail many party candidates may have been carried into political office.

In this writer's experience based on three and a half years of participation in Cabinet and Cabinet Sub-Committee meetings in a comparable Whitehall model situation, that genuine free for all discussion takes place in Cabinet only when the Prime Minister does not have a very direct personal interest in a matter and plays the role of elder statesman. If there is a strong opposing consensus, the Prime Minister is likely to remind that it is he who will have to pull the political chestnuts out of the fire and repair the electoral damage. When there is dissatisfaction with the Prime Minister's performance, it is the other ministers who bear the brunt of Cabinet shuffles designed to give the administration a new look or a new lease on political life.

Again, and most surprisingly, the mystique of the Cabinet appears to be at its strongest in the privacy of closed meetings, where ministerial colleagues and close political associates who would otherwise address the Prime Minister by first name (and this applies to close relatives also) feel constrained to use formal address of Prime Minister or Sir.

The Prime Minister has the right to issue orders in any department or ministry with or without consulting the incumbent minister and may indeed place any ministry under his direct control or trusteeship, so to speak.

It is also the Prime Minister who exercises the prerogative of advising the Governor General whether Cabinet secrecy may be relaxed, so that a disaffected, dismissed, or resigning minister may find himself effectively gagged from publicly telling his side of the story because of the constraint of the Official Secrets Act and the Privy Council oath of secrecy.

The nature of electoral politics in mass society and the influence of the media, especially television, also serve to enhance the dominant role of the Prime Minister. The ruling political regime is identified by the name of the Prime Minister. He can, at short notice, pre-empt prime time of the electronic media, commandeer the print media to press conferences, photo opportunities, and so on.

Paradoxically also, high levels of popular education in the modern administrative or bureaucratic state with its emphasis on rational/legal procedures and administration have not diminished the tendency towards veneration of political leadership. As social existence and interaction and the world of work become more complex and the rapid rate of socio-economic change becomes more bewildering, it appears that even an educationally more sophisticated electorate seems inclined to suspend its critical faculties and to seek a leader or saviour who will provide the solutions or lead into the promised land.

The challenge to enhance citizenship participation in the democratic processes and the politics of participation, or to make Parliament a more effective instrument of representation may lie not in making political parties or Parliament more effective instruments of democratic will, but in curbing the power of the Prime Minister and making the holder of the office a first among equals, and nothing more.

The dominance of the Executive generally — over the Legislature — from which ministers are overwhelmingly drawn (Senators may be appointed to ministerial portfolios but cannot sit in and report to the House of Commons) has also been made possible by the invoking of party discipline and voting on strict party lines in the House of Commons. Full and frank exchange of views on the part of MPs especially back-benchers who do not hold ministerial or junior ministerial appointments, tend to take place within the confines of private party meetings (caucus) held before the sitting of Parliament. Once the caucus has agreed on a government or opposition position MPs are expected to toe the line in the Commons and vote along strict party lines. Only on issues of conscience (e.g., death penalty or abortion) are MPs especially on the government side, free to vote in accordance with personal and/or constituency inclinations.

A device often used to allow MPs to avoid embarrassing voting dilemmas is "pairing" where an MP of one party may join an opposite colleague to both absent themselves from the Commons and thus not jeopardize the outcome of a vote.

Failure to observe party line and party discipline in the House of Commons is likely to impact unfavourably on the career prospects of a recalcitrant or rebellious back-bencher or even parliamentary secretary (minister in training). A powerful Prime Minister, also can as party leader, but obstacles in the way of re-election of the troublesome MP as a candidate for the general election the next time around.

Other factors which have served to promote the dominance of the political executive are the sheer volume of governmental activity arising from the expanded role of government in the Modern Welfare State — even parliamentary committees tend to be overburdened — and the complexity of the issues in the modern state, which require expertise which is found concentrated in the Civil Service — the permanent arm and mainstay of the Executive.

THE CIVIL SERVICE

The basic unit of organization in the Civil or Public Service is the ministry or department. A ministry is a grouping of governmental functions or departments headed by a minister. A measure of confusion has been created by the fact that in the British tradition the term ministry is used interchangeably with department, thus the Ministry of Finance is referred to as the Department of Finance.

Strictly speaking, a department is an agency or major unit of government, usually discharging a single substantive function (e.g., Department of Labour or of Public Works). In some countries the department is known as Bureau, Service, Office, or Administration.

A department may be headed by a political officer or a technical officer or a career official. A department usually is structured into Divisions, Branches, or Sections.

The underlying principle of organization is functional homogeneity — that is to say usually there is an attempt to group functions into units as nearly related or as homogeneous as possible.

However the grouping of ministries or departments to constitute the portfolio of a minister is in the final analysis a political function. The Prime Minister may realign ministries/departments because of particular skills (or lack of skills) of a MP earmarked for Cabinet appointment or for other purely political considerations.

THE FUNCTIONS AND ROLE OF THE CIVIL SERVICE OR BUREAUCRACY

The main thrust of this paper has been to try and make the Canadian parliamentary system (Westminster/Whitehall model) more comprehensible by distinguishing between formal theory and actual practice, between legally enforceable constitutional provisions and informal provisions or conventions which are accepted as part of the political culture.

It is in examining the functions and role of the Civil Service that we can best get an overview of the conventions which link the machinery of government together and appreciate the extent to which certain of these conventions have persisted as rationalizations or folklore of "responsible" government, long after they have ceased to describe or correspond to political and administrative realities.

In the Westminster/Whitehall tradition, the constitutional convention which defines the responsibilities and role of the public service especially in relation to the Legislature and political executive is known as the doctrine or model of neutrality. Strict adherence to this conventional doctrine would require that the following conditions be met.[5]

1. The separation of politics and policy-making from administration with politicians making the policy decisions and public servants executing them.

2. Public servants are independently appointed and promoted on the basis of qualifications and merit rather than on the basis of political patronage, that is to say, on the basis of party affiliation or contributions.

3. Public servants do not engage in partisan political activities.

4. Public servants do not express publicly personal views (in praise or criticism) on government policies or administration.

5. Public servants provide the best and honest advice they can to political executives who in turn accord them "anonymity" (no-name-calling) by accepting ministerial responsibility for departmental decisions and actions.

6. Public servants, regardless of their personal opinions or social philosophy zealously carry out the decisions of the party in power irrespective of the latter's ideological commitment and programme emphases.

POLITICS AND ADMINISTRATION

According to the doctrine and model of political neutrality, politics is concerned, in all spheres of government, with the whole business of deciding what to do and getting it done. Deciding what to do properly belongs within the realm of policy formation which is equated with politics and is thus the prerogative and responsibility of legislators and political executives. Getting things done, on the other hand, falls with the realm of administration and is thus the concern of administrators or public servants. Given this dichotomy, policy decisions are political, administrative decisions are non-political.

However, this distinction between policy formulation or politics, and policy execution or administration, cannot be sustained in today's administrative state. The fact of the matter is that while the legislators may give legal effect and governmental force to certain directions in policy or priorities in terms of programmes and activities, it is in the process of implementation by way of delegated powers and authority, that policies become meaningful and make their impact on particular groups or the society as a whole. It is no secret that much of the legislation which is enacted by Parliament or the legislative authority (as much as 80–90%) originates within the Civil Service and certainly the regulations made to give practical effect to enabling legislation are almost always subject to the decisive influence of civil servants.

Public servants also have been forced increasingly by the logic of the development of the administrative or Welfare State to assume the role of social change agents. Not only do ministers of government expect and seek advice from senior civil servants on policy, but they encourage them to promote new and innovative solutions to social problems. These expectations are

62

derived from the status and role of senior civil servants. If their academic and professional training as well as long experience in public affairs guaranteed by security of tenure of employment mean anything, it should mean the ability to anticipate social and economic problems and to help find solutions to them. Hence, the job of a senior civic servant or public servant must involve to a greater or lesser extent, ongoing evaluation and scrutiny of the ideas and proposals that emerge from the political process. It is difficult to see how it could be otherwise. The administrative and advisory role of the senior civil servant places him or her in a special relationship to the minister, the limits of which are set by mutual confidence and respect rather than formal constitutional theory or supportive rationalizations.

Another of the realities faced by the senior civil servant in the parliamentary system of government is that of growing exposure to pressure groups or interest groups seeking to influence policy formation and policy execution. Given the dominance of the Cabinet as the principal instrument of policy formation and execution, and the strict adherence to party discipline which requires voting along party lines in the Legislature, the individual member of Parliament usually has relatively limited sway or ability to influence policy measures and/or subsidiary regulations. Interest groups have recognized this by shifting their representations and lobbying to the ministries of government and to the senior public servants who advise and influence ministers.

In the Westminster/Whitehall tradition the permanent civil service head of a ministry typically is known as the "Permanent Secretary." The very designation itself carries a certain number of connotations. For one thing, it suggests that the civil servant is the permanent and immovable expert while the political executive is essentially a transient amateur or "bird of passage" to be tolerated until another comes home to roost temporarily. For another, it could reinforce the impression that the Permanent Secretary is the sole repository of executive authority and the only person constitutionally responsible for the proper administration of a ministry or department whereas it would be far more helpful to view the office as that of Chief Executive or General Manager, coordinating the efforts and activities of the senior management team.

In some Caribbean (though not Commonwealth Caribbean) jurisdictions, the designation used is Vice-Minister while in many Western European and Afro-Asian jurisdictions with much the same British civil service traditions, the title used is Director General. Whatever, the title used, the fact remains that the permanent chief administrator is a co-policy maker and joint executive with the political administrator (minister).

The Canadian public administration has given recognition to the unique role played by the chief administrator by an innovative adaptation of the Westminster model. The Permanent Secretary has been redesignated "Deputy Minister" and is an appointment which is the prerogative of the Prime Minister who is supported in the selection process by other senior officials. Deputy Ministers are legally appointed by, and serve at, the pleasure of the Governor General, acting on the recommendation of the Prime Minister. The performance of Deputy Ministers is appraised annually by a Committee of Senior Officials (COSO) or Executive Personnel with inputs from the appropriate Ministers and central agencies. The committee reports its findings to the Cabinet and it is on the basis of these recommendations, that the Cabinet makes its determination of performance and compensation awards. Appointments below the grade of Deputy Minister are made by the Public Service Commission after consultation with the Deputy Minister.

The convention has developed that, provided the Deputy Minister does not become too publicly identified with the political regime in office, or becomes too overtly partisan in his support of the policies and programmes of the government in office, he or she enjoys much the same security of tenure enjoyed by other officials below the grade of Deputy Minister. This arrangement thus leaves open the possibility of a new government being able to appoint a Deputy Minister from outside the ranks of the civil service, although here again the convention is that the outsider should have professional qualifications or experience and attainments at least equal to, if not more impressive than, candidates with the public service who may be considered logical contenders.

POLITICAL PATRONAGE

The appointment of persons to the government service on the grounds of contributions to the governing party or political or ideological affiliation is regarded as a blatant violation of the traditional doctrine of political neutrality. The main objection is that such a course of action is at odds with the merit principle, the premise of which is that public servants are appointed on the basis of merit or fitness for the job rather than on the basis of political affiliation or contribution.

It may be noted that this problem usually becomes particularly acute when a political party comes to office espousing significant shifts in programmes or governmental policies, or alternatively a more radical ideology which envisages profound reconstruction of the socio-economic and political systems. The argument most often heard is that the natural tendency of the bureaucracy towards administrative inertia will be compounded by resistance to, and sabotage of, change. It is further contended that the resistance to change may be expected because career officials will most likely have been recruited from the dominant social (and wealthier) groups within the state and will be loyal only to the political leadership which evidences the same political attitudes as those held by the permanent officials.

To prevent political patronage and other considerations from impinging on the establishment of a career responsibility for recruitment, appointment, transfers, discipline, promotions — in sum — career advancement and development is vested in a relatively autonomous Public Service Commission. There appears to be a great deal of misunderstanding, however, about what political neutrality means. If it means non-direct involvement in partisan political activities, it is a reasonable proposition. If it means a lack of political awareness and acumen, it is not.

Politically, the administrator must not only be responsive to external direction and control but have a "political sense" which leads to an appreciation of major political shifts of opinion and the pressures to which members of the political directorate are subject. They must have faith then, in popular values and popular institutions.

Satisfactory public service is best guaranteed by public service employees with professional competence. If not, inability to perform new tasks or meet new challenges is likely to be mistaken for disloyalty and sabotage.

POLITICAL ACTIVITY

The tradition of political neutrality requires that public servants do not engage in partisan political activities. Historically there has been a close link between the patronage and spoils system

65

and political activity on the part of public service officials. Political sterilization of public servants was deemed to be a reasonable quid-pro-quo for the elimination of spoils and patronage in the public services.

It still appears to be a reasonable expectation and a practical consideration that public servants do not become actively engaged in partisan political activity in the course of performing their duties and responsibilities. It may be noted that the Public Service Employment Act of 1967 provided that public servants, with the exception of Deputy Heads, may, with the approval of the Public Service Commission, take leave of absence to stand for election to public office, but must resign if they are elected. There is a continuing embargo however against public servants actively campaigning for or against a candidate or political party.

PUBLIC COMMENT

The prohibition against publicly expressing personal views on government policies or administration is another integral component of the doctrine and model of political neutrality. Increasingly, it is a prohibition largely observed in the breach, because public servants unavoidably become involved in public comment in the regular performance of their duties.

The prohibition is also at odds with the growing demand for, and trend towards, openness in government and greater participatory democracy. Citizen participation in the political and governmental processes can have no meaning unless politicians and officials are prepared to, and are capable of, discussing basic policy issues in the public arena.

ANONYMITY AND MINISTERIAL RESPONSIBILITY

The concept of anonymity on the part of public servants depends upon and reinforces, the doctrine of ministerial responsibility, which however, has been suffering erosion for some time. Ministers of government are no longer expected to resign in response to revelations or disclosures of maladministration in ministries and departments.

Government and the public administration have become so large and complex that ministers can hardly be expected to have knowledge and control of all the activities and actions of officials. As the Head of the British Cabinet Office observed to the Expenditure Committee of the British House of Commons which undertook an extensive review of the structure and role of the Civil Service between 1974–1977 "The concept that because somebody whom the Minister has never heard of, has made a mistake, means that the Minister should resign, is out of date, and rightly so. I think equally, that a Minister has got a responsibility which he cannot devolve to his Permanent Secretary, for the efficiency and drive of his Department."

TENURE AND PERMANENCY IN OFFICE

The changing role of public servants and the increasingly high profile of so-called "mandarins" have led to the questioning of the principle of security of tenure or permanency in office on the part of public servants.

Increasingly, also the right to security of tenure (not just for public servants but for university academics for whom it is an equally hallowed tenet), has been made subject to budgetary considerations. The fact of the matter is that security of tenure is no longer the unique or characteristic feature of public service employment that it once was. The quest for job security is no less a preoccupation of the private sector, and grievance procedures in collective agreements and employment contracts for managers and professionals are being used to offer a measure of job security. What may really be at issue is not the principle of security of tenure but revision of extremely cumbersome and time-consuming procedures by which public servants can be separated for valid causes.

THE STATUS OF THE DOCTRINE OF NEUTRALITY

The doctrine of neutrality, based as it is on a presumed dichotomy between politics and administration is difficult to sustain. It is also based on a definition of politics which is narrow, misleading, and dangerous. Politics is concerned with the exercise of power and not just with the manoeuvrings of politicians, political parties, and interest groups.

The distinction between policy or politics and administration, undoubtedly has served some purpose, otherwise it would not have so long survived as one of the canons of parliamentary government. Analytically, the dichotomy makes it possible to distinguish between the constitutional and legal functions of political executives and permanent administrators. Practically, it has served the interest of both civil servants and politicians. Civil Servants have been shielded from attacks by politicians and the public while politicians have invoked it to maintain appearances before the public giving the impression that they may be acting more objectively than is in fact the case.

The greatest limitation and danger of the doctrine of neutrality is that it exposes the society at large to fraud and the Civil Service to moral corruption. To fraud, because political and administrative decisions can be taken without fear of awkward enquiry or demands for public scrutiny either by Parliament or other legislative body, the press, and the citizenry at large. To moral corruption, because if *all* governments are to be served with equal impartiality and legality there can be little grounds for criticizing the officials who serve regimes which commit heinous crimes and infamy against a society or even humanity.

A recurrent theme appearing in the now fashionable genre of political biographies of former or retired political leaders is the feeling of frustration and inadequacy engendered by the inertia and/or resistance to change, especially ideologically inspired change, on the part of the administrative bureaucracy. But apart from recourse to special advisers who are political appointees and may play a facilitative but not executive role, no attempt has been made to provide a more appropriate constitutional framework or set of principles to reconcile the concept of responsible and responsive bureaucracy with the more positive role of public servants as agents of social change. The starting point would have to be explicit recognition that the public administration is managed jointly by a political and administrative directorate rather than by presumed political masters and self-effacing and neutral public servants. The traditional concept of neutrality can only serve to make even less meaningful, the already difficult task of enforcing governmental and administrative accountability.

THE JUDICIARY

The Judiciary and courts in Canada have drawn their decisive legal and judicial traditions from Great Britain. In the Westminster model, because of the assertion and acceptance of the supremacy of Parliament, the Judiciary cannot declare legislation unconstitutional, and are limited to interpreting the meaning of legislation when disputes turning on its meaning and application arise.

Unlike Britain, which is a unitary state, the British North America Act of 1867 created a federal union, with legislative power and functions being assigned, explicit and otherwise to the federal Parliament and provincial legislatures. The Canadian courts since then have emerged as the arbiters of the balance of the Constitution, with the authority to declare laws ultra vires or null and void when a litigant whether individual or corporate citizen or one level of government or the other, alleges that there has been an encroachment upon or usurpation of jurisdiction. Since 1949, final interpretation of the Canadian Constitution has fallen mainly to the Supreme Court of Canada. Before that the Judicial Committee of the Privy Council of the UK had constituted the ultimate court of constitutional appeal.

Outside of its role as arbiter of the constitutional balance of powers, however, there was little scope for judicial activism, as the Judiciary felt constrained by the notion of the supremacy of Parliament.

The inclusion and proclamation of the Charter of Rights and Freedoms has enlarged the role of the Canadian courts, giving them a more central role in deciding public policy and social values. A case, in point, was the decision of the Supreme Court of Canada in 1989, that the provisions of the Criminal Code governing accessibility to abortion infringed upon certain rights of women under the Charter of Rights and was therefore null and void. To the extent therefore, that the courts may now entertain litigation contending that a contested law is not only beyond the jurisdiction of the enacting legislature, but may also be in contravention of the Charter, the Canadian courts will now be closer to the American system of courts, where the Supreme Court has served as the "living voice" of the Constitution. In the US Constitution, the application of the doctrine of separation of powers between Legislature, Executive, and Judiciary, has resulted in a system of constitutional checks and balances designed to achieve limited government.

In Canada, the independence of the Judiciary has become a matter of fundamental constitutional principle, rather than of fundamental law. It is reflected in the guarantee of security of tenure, both general and specific to judges and autonomy in the operation of the courts. The general right of tenure ensures that judges of all but the lowest level of courts, once appointed, may serve without fear of being removed from the bench until age 75. The specific right of tenure is reflected in the requirement of specific procedures for the removal from the office of the judges in question.

It may be noted that while the judicial branch is treated as distinct and independent, there is in fact a near fusion of the Legislature and Executive. Legislature and Executive are inextricably intertwined in that the political executive is drawn from the Legislature and the government will not survive a vote of no-confidence unless it can command a majority vote in the House of Commons. We also saw that while Parliament gives effect to policy by legislating, it is the Cabinet or Executive which decides what Parliament is to legislate. At the same time, under the concept of ministerial responsibility, the political directorate are accountable to Parliament for the direction of their respective ministries or portfolios.

CONCLUDING OBSERVATIONS

While Canada has a written constitution based on the British North America Act of 1867, and other related legislation, the functioning of the system and the machinery of government depends a great deal on conventions or unwritten rules. As we saw, while the Cabinet (as distinct from the (Queen's) Privy Council of Canada) is not mentioned in the Constitution — there are the Cabinet conventions — of Cabinet Solidarity (ministers collectively accepting responsibility for Cabinet decisions), of ministerial responsibility to Parliament, which also entails according anonymity to civil servants.

Likewise the Governor General in his choice of a Prime Minister is bound by the convention that he should first call upon the leader of the majority party to form the government. In the exercise of statutory and prerogative powers, the

Governor General is likewise bound by convention to accept the advice of the ministers of the Crown — or the Cabinet. The very appointment of the Governor General is done by the Queen, as Queen of Canada, on the advice of the Prime Minister of Canada. There is the firm, unwritten rule, that the government must hold the support of a majority of the House of Commons or resign.

Political parties are not mentioned in the Constitution, but constitute the lynch-pin of responsible representative government and political debate and voting in the House of Commons takes place normally on the basis of party affiliation and party discipline. The convention of the doctrine of neutrality governs the role and relationships of the Public Service to the Political Executive and Legislature although certain of its tenets no longer appear to be congruent with objective reality constitutional change may also be brought about by the disuse of a convention. For instance under the BNA Act, the federal government has the power, unrestricted in law, to disallow provincial legislation. The power has not, however been used since 1943, and its usage is now highly improbable, given the coming of age of the provinces.

The federal government also has the power, again unrestricted in law, to instruct the Lieutenant Governor, the Queen's representative at the provincial level, to withhold assent to provincial legislation, but this power must now be considered incongruous and a constitutional anomaly as it use would put the provinces in a position of inferior (colonial) status.

It is by recognizing the gaps between formal theory and practice and action, and by linking constitutional and legal requirements with constitutional conventions, that we can make sense of the Canadian parliamentary system of government.

NOTES

1. The British North America Act of 1867 which created the Federal Union of Canada and its subsequent amendments, stood as the basic Constitution of Canada until the passage of the Constitution Act of 1982, which modernized the Canadian Constitution. It did so by patriation of the Constitution which had been domiciled in the UK because of the lack of an amending procedure. The Constitution Act of 1982, not only remedied this defect but incorporated the Canadian Charter of Rights and Freedoms.

2. It is a development arising out of the Meech Lake Constitutional Accord which is dealt with in the next article.

    The idea behind the Triple E Senate, is that with election and each province having equal representation — the Senate could more effectively balance provincial interests.

3. See J.R. Mallory, *The Structure of Canada on Government*, Rev. Edition (Gage, 1984), for extended discussion.

4. In the 12th century, the King of England was advised by a Great Council of the principal men of the Kingdom. The King developed his own Inner Circle of that Council. It in turn evolved into sections based on functional separation and the general purposes section became the permanent council or privy council.

5. For extended discussion see K. Kernahan and D. Siegel, *Public Administration in Canada: A Text* (Toronto: Methuen, 1987), Chapter II.

Federalism in Canada and Australia

Helen Nelson

The enduring concern in all federations is where to draw the line between those matters that can be most effectively dealt with at the national level and those that are more appropriately left to be decided by the individual constituent units. Although the division of powers that characterises federal systems would seem, in theory, to determine the allocation of functions between the federal (national) government and the regional (or provincial or state) governments, the limitations of constitution-making and the practicalities arising from a system in which two governments rule over the same territory and the same population ensure that, in practice, neither government can operate totally independent of the other. The need for some form of interaction, and the interplay of the strengths and weaknesses that each government brings to the relationship, means that the balance of power between the two levels of government will be in constant flux. The written words of the constitution might not change but other factors, such as, for instance, judicial interpretation of the constitution, control of financial resources and, even, the personalities of political leaders, will have an impact on the location of decision-making in the federation. It is the constantly changing balance between the forces pulling the federation towards a more centralised structure and those pulling in the direction of decentralisation, allowing more power to the constituent units, that is the source of much of the fascination of federal systems of government.

The dynamic interplay of centripetal (centralising) and centrifugal (decentralising) forces is particularly evident in the histories of the Canadian and Australian federal systems. The Canadian federation, founded on a centralist vision, has evolved into one in which the provincial governments have become ever more vocal in the protection and extension of their rights. Conversely, the Australian federation, built on a concept of federalism that favoured a weak central government, with a limited range of powers, has developed so that the central government has become the dominant partner in the federal-state relationship. In each case, different factors have worked to advance or limit the position of one or other level of government.

Four areas that have been critical in the evolution of the Canadian and Australian federations are: the constitutional division of powers; the method of constitutional change; the role of judicial review; and the management of financial resources.

DIVISION OF POWERS

In both federal systems, the original constitutional division of powers has remained largely unaltered since the time of federation (see sections 91–95 and sections 51–52 of the Canadian and Australian constitutions respectively). The powers allocated to the national government in each country are fairly similar and include: international relations, defence, trade and commerce, customs and excise taxes, postal services, currency, banking, naturalization and aliens, marriage and divorce, and weights and measures.

Both constitutions also nominate areas of concurrent power. The Canadian constitution lists agriculture and immigration, with the proviso that in cases of incompatibility federal law should take precedence over provincial legislation (section 95). The Australian application of concurrent powers is more extensive, although again, when legislation conflicts, section 109 provides that federal law will prevail.

The differences between the two constitutions are more evident in the treatment of the role of the provincial/state governments. The Canadian constitution-makers' intention to promote a centralist concept[1] is seen in sections 92–95. They provide for a set of provincial powers that includes direct taxation, hospitals, education, local government, mineral resources development and export, prisons, and "property and civil rights." Although the range of provincial powers is extensive, their listing in the constitution denotes an intention that provincial lawmaking should be confined. The Australian constitution provides for no such limitation. Federal government powers alone are stipulated and the residual powers — those not specifically mentioned in the constitution — are left to the states. Such an arrangement is a source of constitutional strength for the states, not least because it means that in all areas not mentioned in the constitution, including all "new" areas of public policy, they can act immediately, whereas the federal government must find a less direct means of entering any field not specifically designated in the constitution as a federal power.

The allocation of the residual powers in the Canadian constitution is a matter of dispute, although the original intention appears to have favoured their allocation to the central government.[2] Other factors, however, have worked to encourage expansion of the role of the provincial governments. The modern "big-spenders" in public policy — in particular, education, health and welfare — are primarily provincial responsibilities and, even when they rely on federal financial assistance in order to carry out policy, the provinces' constitutional position has boosted their ability to exercise policy control. Similarly, the ownership of natural resources has been both an economic and a political strength in sustaining and advancing the position of the provincial governments in the federation.

Although the formal division of powers is a significant source of provincial/state strength in the balance of federal-regional forces, the practice of public policy has blurred the distinction. Were it ever feasible to discuss a federal system in which all levels of government could operate with total independence, it is no longer the case. The growth in the range and scope of government activities has brought also a growing interdependence between the federal and constituent governments, and a need to share responsibilities and resources. There are now few areas of public policy that do not entail some form of participation by both levels of governments.[3] A comparison of cabinet portfolio titles at federal and provincial/state levels illustrates the involvement of both in a similar range of policy areas. In both Canada and Australia, policy areas once thought to be the responsibility of provincial/state governments, such as health, natural resources and development, have acquired portfolio equivalents at the federal level. Similarly, "new" areas of government activity, not mentioned in the respective constitutions, such as, the environment, arts and sports, and consumer affairs, are now among the portfolio titles at both levels.[4]

The interdependence of governments in public policymaking is promoted further by what Kenneth Wittshire refers to as "linkages" between the functions of government, that is, the overlap between policy areas so that "alterations to any aspect of the conduct of one function induce immediate and direct reaction to others."[5] Policies regarding public health, for instance, have a direct link with policies in areas such as sanitation, pollution, sewerage and irrigation. Wittshire lists also the direct links between: trade and commerce, and industrial relations; navigation, irrigation and conservation; immigration and employment, schools, hospitals, welfare and other functions related to social infrastructure.[6] In each instance, intergovernmental cooperation is necessary in order to overcome the constitutional distribution of responsibilities.

When governments are involved in the same, or linked, policy areas, the constitutional division of powers will still influence of *nature* of their involvement. As Peter Leslie notes, the constitution "underpins" the federal-provincial/state relationship: "The constitution does not effectively separate the policy areas in which federal and provincial governments, respectively, are active, but it does impose limits on the range of powers — often defined in instrumental rather than substantive terms — that each may legally exercise."[7] For instance, as mentioned above, agriculture is a concurrent power in the Canadian constitution and the Canadian federal government therefore has a direct influence on policy. In the Australian case, agriculture is a state responsibility. The federal government has extensive involvement in the area, but it depends upon its powers over exports and its financial dominance in order to exert a policy influence. In both federations, the federal government's financial superiority tends to give a fiscal emphasis to its involvement, especially in policy areas formally designated as the function of the provincial/state governments. In such cases, the nature and extent of federal participation will depend upon its willingness to use its financial leverage to enforce its own policy preferences. Observation suggests that the Australian federal government has been more willing, and more ruthless, in flexing its financial muscle in order to impose national priorities than has the government in Ottawa.

FORMAL CONSTITUTIONAL CHANGE

When federal governments use their financial powers to dictate policy directions in an area formally the responsibility of the regional governments, or when federal and provincial/state governments pool their resources to cooperate in the formulation and implementation of a new policy program, their actions can often be seen as bringing about a type of *"informal"* constitutional change. Such arrangements can introduce flexibility into an otherwise rigid division of powers. *"Formal"* constitutional change refers to changes in the actual wording of the constitution. In both federations, the "informal" variety has been much easier to achieve, and has occurred more frequently, than "formal" change.

The story of constitutional change in the Canadian federation is one of the search for an appropriate method of constitutional amendment. It is a story that illustrates well the evolution of a federal system that recognises the separate, special interests of the provinces. The Australian amendment formula was written into the Constitution Act of 1900. The formula has rarely been challenged, despite that it has proved to be a serious obstacle for proposed alterations to the constitution. Its effect has been to preserve the original "federal bargain" and the curtailment of central government powers.

The continuing Canadian debate regarding an amendment formula is well documented.[8] The British North America Act, 1867, which established the Canadian federation, did not include provision for its own amendment. It was an Act of the British parliament and amendments to the Act were carried out by that same parliament, albeit only upon formal request from Canada. By convention, requests to the British parliament required the approval of both houses of the Canadian parliament. The provinces were brought into the process in 1906, as part of a consultation process, although the practice was never formalised. Of the twenty amendments to the constitution during the period 1907–82, seven had a direct impact on provincial powers: federal subsidies to the provinces (passed in 1907); jurisdiction over natural resources for the four western provinces, thereby placing them on equal footing with the other provinces (1930); endorsement of the Statute of Westminster (1931); federal government acquisition of powers in the area of unemployment insurance (1940); federal government concurrent jurisdiction over pensions, subject to provincial paramountcy (1951); extension of federal powers to include certain supplementary and disability benefits (1964); and patriation of the Canadian constitution, and other changes including a Charter of Rights and Freedoms (1982).[9]

The British parliament's involvement in the amendment process continued until "patriation" of the constitution in 1982. The amendment formula adopted in the 1982 revision[10] was the outcome of half a century of sporadic debate, during which the main source of contention was the place of the provinces in the amendment process. Indicative of the protracted search for agreement, there are six different procedures for amending the constitution, the appropriate procedure depending on the issue under consideration:

- the general procedure, requiring that a proposed amendment be approved by both federal houses of parliament and the legislative assemblies of at least two-thirds of the provinces (i.e., seven out of ten) representing at least 50 per cent of the population. Provision is made for any province to "opt out" of any amendment that affects its existing responsibilities. In addition, when the matter concerns the transfer from provincial to federal level of provincial powers relating to "education or other cultural matters," the dissenting province will receive "reasonable compensation" from the federal parliament;

- unanimous consent, to apply to proposals affecting the monarchy, the minimum number of representatives in the House of Commons from any one province, bilingualism at the federal level, the composition of the Supreme Court, and the amending formula itself;

- the approval of some but not all provinces, for matters such as individual provincial boundaries and bilingualism within provinces;

- the Canadian parliament alone, for executive government matters;
- individual provincial legislatures alone, on changes to the respective provincial constitutions;
- without Senate approval, that is, Senate objections can be overridden by the House of Commons after a period of 180 days.

The above provisions, set out in sections 38–49 of the Constitution Act, 1982, reflect both the elitist style of Canadian constitutional politics and the determination of the provinces to gain control in those areas important to them. The new procedures extend constitutional change beyond the exclusive realm of the first ministers, but they still restrict participation to the federal and provincial legislatures. Only the federal houses of parliament or the provincial legislative assemblies can initiate constitutional amendment proposals and only they can vote on such proposals. An earlier suggestion for amendment by popular referendum was rejected. D.V. Smiley explains the choice in political culture terms:[11]

> what Canadians mean by democracy is representative democracy unmixed with popular elements and according to which those whose credentials derive from popular elections have the unfettered power, as conferred and regulated by the Constitution, to make any and all choices for the popular community.

The "opting out" clause is extraordinary. It is described by Peter Meekison, however, as the "cornerstone" of the new formula. Under its protection, no province is obliged to bend to the will of the others. The alternative, in the context of the Canadian debate, was that the unanimity requirement be applied to all amendment proposals — a requirement that would effectively block all other constitutional change.[12]

At the time of writing (1989), only one amendment has been made under the new formula. Under the general procedure, an amendment was proclaimed in 1983 extending the constitutional rights of aboriginal peoples to include rights acquired through land claims agreements and a guarantee of equal rights for aboriginal men and women.[13]

The new amending formula was part of a larger package of constitutional changes that included also a constitutional bill of rights. The package enacted in 1982 was accepted by the federal and provincial governments, with the exception of Quebec. The debate therefore continues. The Meech Lake Accord, announced in 1987, represents a new attempt to reach an agreement with Quebec. At the time of writing, it has still to gain ratification by all provincial legislatures. The on-going process, with its emphasis on the respective roles of the federal and provincial governments, reflects a continuing concern about the very nature of Canadian federation. In the process, Canadian constitutionalism has become, according to Peter Russell, more "covenantal": "The very fact that the leaders of all three of Canada's major political parties have been committed to negotiating an agreement with Quebec — even though Quebec's rejection of the 1982 settlement has no legal significance — demonstrates the wide political consensus which exists in Canada on the fundamental nature of the social compact."[14]

The constitutional concerns that have been such a large part of Canadian political debate during the last two decades have no parallel in Australia. The constitution is not high on the Australian political agenda. The "constitutional crisis" in 1975, when the Governor-General exercised his constitutional powers to dismiss the government of the day,[15] gave rise to considerable discussion about the need to review the constitution, but the debate was not sustained and, fifteen years later, there has been only one, relatively minor, constitutional change to the provisions that were so critical at that time.[16] The federal government has from time to time established various Royal Commissions and inquiries to make recommendations, but their reports have yielded little response.

The history of constitutional change in Australia might be seen to reflect popular endorsement of the constitutional *status quo*. The amending formula, established at the commencement of federation in 1901, has remained intact[17] and few, mostly minor, amendments to the constitution have been enacted. Under section 128, proposals for constitutional change are initiated by the federal parliament and then submitted to popular referendum. In order to be passed, proposals must receive not only a majority overall, but also, a majority in a majority of the states (that is, four out of six). Of the 42 constitutional questions put to referendum since 1901, only eight have cleared the hurdle. Most have had small impact and have concerned mainly machinery-type matters or the validation of existing arrangements. The most significant have been the validation of a financial agreement on state debts and the establishment of the Loan Council to coordinate federal and state government borrowing (1928), the extension of federal powers in the social services field (1946) and the granting of concurrent power to the federal government to legislate with respect to aborigines.

Opposition from state governments has been a factor in the poor record. More often, party politics, with the two major parties taking opposing sides on the issue, has been crucial. L.F. Crisp mentions also the possible impact of the Australian compulsory voting requirement: "...it coerces to the polls many uninterested and ignorant electors who would not otherwise have bothered to come but, having come, frequently vote "No" from natural caution, to "cock a snook" at the politicians, or out of sheer resentment at the compulsion."[18] The possibility that electors might actually be exercising a vote for or against the federal *status quo* arises from a study of referendum voting patterns by Sharman and Stuart. Their work shows a suggestive parallel between state voting returns and changes in the status of the states within the federation.[19]

There are marked differences between the two federations in the saliency of constitutional issues. Yet the record of actual constitutional change, in qualitative terms, is testimony to the durability of their respective constitutions. Alan Cairns' observations about Canadian constitutional politics apply also — perhaps even more so — to the Australian experience:[20]

> The bias of established systems is to favour continuity. The existing system thus illustrates the reach of the past into the present. In the same way, the new amending formula, the Charter, and other components of our recent constitutional change will be our gift to our successors and will confront future generations as givens, incapable of easy modification.

Judicial Review

When courts adjudicate on questions concerning the division of powers and other constitutional matters, they take on the role of an umpire, poised to "blow the whistle" when players step over the boundary lines. The process of judicial review in Federal systems can be seen then as setting the bounds for government action. Judicial decisions, as Peter Russell points out, "shape the constitutional capacity of government." But the courts are constitution "shapers," not makers. The degree to which the "constitutional capacity" is taken up and exploited is a matter for political decision, constrained by political criteria. "Constitutional capacity" is an important resource for governments, but the use of that resource will be influenced by political factors such as public opinion and electoral considerations.[21]

The British North America Act of 1867 did not make specific provision for a system of judicial review. Until 1949, the Judicial Committee of the Privy Council in the United Kingdom was the final court of appeal for Canadian constitutional cases. The Judicial Committee's record is seen generally as one that favoured the forces of decentralisation. Its impact was to contain expansive use of federal powers in favour of upholding the place of provincial governments in the federation. Although the Privy Council's record in judicial review has drawn a great deal of criticism, it is seen also as corresponding well with contemporary public opinion.[22] Any sharp trend towards centralisation world have been contrary to the external developments that stressed the diversities inherent in the federation.

The Supreme Court of Canada took over the Privy Council's role in 1949. Appointments to the Court are made by the federal government and, at least until the 1970s, the Court kept a low-key profile.[23] Russell's analysis of its record shows "an uncanny balance" in decisions favouring federal and provincial powers respectively. He goes on to argue, however, that the *political* impact of Court decisions has been "more useful" to federal politicians, in the sense that the "constitutional capacity" resource has been applied more extensively at the federal level.[24]

Since the mid-1970s, the role of the Supreme Court and the political potential of judicial review has become more visible. A sharp increase in the amount of constitutional litigation and the introduction of the Charter of Rights and Freedoms has expanded the range of matters now subject to judicial review. As the Court has moved more into the limelight, it has attracted more political attention. D.V. Smiley identifies three likely consequences:[25] increased demands from the provinces for a say in the jurisdiction and composition of, and appointments to, the Court; increased public attention on appointees; and increased awareness of, and questioning of, the Court's role in shaping the political framework, thereby raising questions of judicial accountability.

The High court has been the main actor in the Australian system of judicial review. Until 1975 (and until 1986 in the case of the state courts), the Privy Council was the final court of appeal on constitutional matters, with the important exception that no question concerning the limits *inter se* of Commonwealth and state powers could go forward unless granted a certificate by the High Court. Although the "constitutional credentials" of the High Court are written into constitution, the Court and the role of judicial review were still subjects of heated political debate in the early years of the federation. the early appointments to the Court were of judges who had participated in the federation debates. Their view of the constitution reflected the intentions of the constitution-makers and their record was one of maintaining the position of the states. After 1920, however, the Court practised a strictly legalistic approach to judicial review, focusing on the actual words of the constitution and omitting reference to the intent. Brian Galligan has argued that the strategy of adopting "techniques and public rhetoric of a 'strict and complete legalism'" for constitutional cases and the government's appointment of "apolitical" legal specialists as judges were critical factors in establishing and consolidating the prestige of the Court as the official interpreter of the constitution and umpire in federal disputes.[26] The outcome of the long period of application of the positivist approach, from the 1920s to the 1970s, was that the Court came to be seen as a neutral player in federal-state relations. Geoffrey Sawer concluded in 1976 that Australia was "constitutionally speaking, a pretty frozen continent." A more recent analysis by Galligan argues that the period produced a "persistent, if irregular, incremental centralization."[27]

During the last decade, both the position and the direction of the High Court have changed so that, like its Canadian counterpart, it has become more politicised. The appointment of a former Labor government Attorney-General to the Court, made by the Whitlam Labor government during its term of office, 1972–75, and that government's attempts to make more expansive use of federal powers, roused awareness of the political relevance of judicial review. This has been reinforced by recent Court decisions that are clearly centralising in their potential impact. In particular, the *Franklin Dam Case* (1983) gave a broad interpretation to the federal government's external affairs power, so that the government might give effect to its obligations under and international treaty even when the matter concerned is traditionally an area of state jurisdiction.[28]

Australia has no equivalent of the Canadian Charter and its federal government has, to date, exercised caution in exploiting its new-found constitutional capacity to the full. In both federations, however, the impact of constitutional litigation has become acknowledged increasingly as an important source of informal constitutional change. The words of a constitution might not change much, but clearly, interpretations of the words can and do vary.

FEDERAL FINANCIAL RELATIONS

Control of the purse-strings is not the only source of power in intergovernmental relations, but it is arguably the most influential. Nowhere is the changing balance of federal-provincial/state powers in Canada and Australia better mirrored than in the respective changing patterns of federal financial arrangements. In both federations, the terms of the original bargain allocated the chief source of revenue — at that time, customs duties — to the federal government. In the Canadian case, it was anticipated that the federal government would use its financial superiority to subsidise the activities of provincial governments. And yet, by the 1980s, the provinces' independent revenue resources represented a larger proportion of total revenue than did the federal government's. In the Australian case, the customs tariff was regarded a providing far in excess of the needs of the new central government, with its narrowly defined set of constitutional responsibilities, and provision was made that, for the first ten years of federation and then by further agreement, three-quarters of the total federal revenue from customs and excises would be returned to the states for their independent use. And yet, by the 1980s, the states were almost totally reliant upon the federal government for their financial needs. This turn-about in federal financial relations, in opposite directions in the two federations, has occurred without any formal change to constitutional provisions.[29] It has been more influential than any other single factor in shaping the relationship between federal and provincial/state governments.

A major source of contention in federal finances arises from problems in achieving vertical balance, that is, of ensuring a balance between the revenue and expenditure needs of the various governments. The ideal that the government that raises the revenue should be responsible also for its expenditure is difficult to achieve in federal systems. The division of powers make its almost inevitable that there will be some form of financial adjustment between governments in order that each level of government might meet its expenditure demands. In the Canadian and Australian federations, for instance, the national level of government was allocated superior revenue raising resources, but the responsibility for providing services in large, revenue-intensive areas such as education, health and social welfare, was given to the provinces/states. In order to achieve vertical balance, either the provinces/states must yield some of their "big-spender" constitutional responsibilities to the federal government, or, the federal government must yield revenue raising resources to the provinces/states. Both Canada and Australia have taken the latter course, although their paths have differed. Prior to World War II, the federal and provincial/state levels of government each exercised taxation powers. For the period of the war, financial control was in the hands of the respective federal governments. Since then, whereas Canadian fiscal arrangements have worked to establish provincial financial independence, the Australian states have remained in a subservient position.

Post-war, the Canadian federal and provincial governments, with the exception initially of Ontario and Quebec, and later only Quebec, returned to a system of tax rental agreements, whereby the provinces forewent their right to collect income and succession duties and instead, "rented" their taxation bases to the federal government in return for a system of uniform per capita grants. The tax rental agreements were renegotiated at five-yearly intervals. By the 1970s, income taxes were the chief revenue source for provincial governments, which began to enact their own provincial tax measures, albeit within the framework of a scheme administered federally and subject to contain conditions regarding the definition of the tax base, the allocation rules and the rate structure.[30] In 1986, the taxation agreement was modified so that provinces could levy their own income taxes, independent of the federal framework.

In the Australian federation, financial arrangements have become the primary source of federal government domination. In 1942, the federal government decided to take over the income and corporate taxation field to itself. It imposed a level of taxation that prohibited the states from imposing additional taxes of their own. There is, after all, a limit to the amount of blood that can be drawn from the tax-paying stone. In return for its monopoly, the federal government offered to "reimburse" the states for the monies collected. When the Commonwealth's action was challenged before the High Court, it was supported on constitutional grounds: section 51 (ii), which granted the Commonwealth concurrent taxation powers; section 109, which provided that when federal and state enactments in areas of concurrent power were in conflict, federal will would prevail; and section 96, under which the federal government could pay such monies as it saw fit to individual state governments. Developments since then have created a system of federal finance in which the vertical imbalance is greater than in any other federation. The method of revenue transfer has changed from the original "taxation reimbursement grants" to, in 1959, a system of "financial assistance grants" to, in 1976, a slightly more formalised system of "tax-sharing grants."[31] The common thread was a system that rested on annual bargaining between the federal and state governments, with the federal government holding the upper hand in a process that has been characterised a "bloodsport." In 1985, the revenue-sharing concept, based on taxation collections, was replaced with a new form of "financial assistance grants," incorporation an initial increase in annual grants in line with CPI movements and a guarantee for future years of a set percentage increase in real terms. The new system introduces some predictability into federal-state financial relations, in a system in which the federal government retains its control of the purse.

Other components of federal financial arrangements, such as conditional grants and equalisation payments,[32] have histories that repeat the pattern outlined above. The different financial histories point to the differences between the two federations in the conceptualisation of the federal relationship. As Kenneth Wittshire has pointed out, the Canadian federal government has taken on the role of "the collection agency for the provincial share of income taxes"; the Australian federal government "assumed that sovereignty accompanied tax collection and saw itself as the arbiter of both the vertical and horizontal distribution of the state governments' share of this money."[33] It is perhaps no accident that whereas the Canadian federal and provincial governments entered into tax "rental" agreements, the Australian federal government merely "reimbursed" the states for taxation revenues that had once been theirs by right.

CONCLUSION

There are striking similarities between Canada and Australia. They share British colonial backgrounds, Westminster-based parliamentary systems and federal systems of government. As federations, each comprises a relatively small number of component units, with two dominant provinces/states. In both federations, the original division of powers has evolved into a complex system of intergovernmental interdependence across a broad spectrum of policy areas. There are also some similarities in their respective records of formal constitutional change and judicial review. Where differences arise, most markedly in the area of federal financial arrangements, they bring into focus the underlying differences in the two federal cultures. Gordon Robertson's summary of differences in fiscal arrangements applies to other areas of federal-provincial/state interaction: "In brief, where differences exist in the fiscal relations between federal and regional governments in Canada and Australia, they seem to be both the reflection and the sources of greater provincial strength and greater inter-provincial differences in Canada than exist among the Australian states."[34]

Were this brief overview to be extended to include consideration of current Canadian debate regarding, for instance, accommodation with Quebec through the Meech Lake Accord, changes in the Senate's composition and role, and the impact of the Charter of Rights and Freedoms, the common theme world be again the demands of the provinces in protection of their independence. Although the Australian federation has seen a revitalisation at state level in recent years, there is no federal-state debate that challenges the fundamental federal principles that are currently under reconsideration in Canada.

As indicated by Robertson, above, much of the difference relates to the greater inter-provincial differences within the Canadian federation, not only in relation to Quebec, but between the provinces generally. The cleavages in the Australian population — for instance, class differences and urban/rural differences — might be as strong, but they are not territorially based and they do not manifest themselves in federal-state terms. Similarly, although the Australian political party system is state-based, the same two (or, more accurately, two-and-a-half) parties compete at both the state and federal level and can therefore take consensus-building role at the federal level, as well as at the constituency level. The Canadian party system is more fragmented, with some parties that operate at provincial level only and others that operate with separate provincial and federal organisations. Such an arrangement might be seen to reinforce territorial divisions.

Finally, in seeking an explanation for the differences between the two "federations," it is worth noting that the Australian federation comprises six states, all of which were parties to the original federal agreement, which was then ratified by popular referendum. For Australians, the rules were set in 1901. Although the federal system and set of relationships has evolved in unexpected ways, it has done so within that "settled" framework. The Canadian Confederation was, and has remained, a bargain worked out and then implemented by political elites.[35] The new amending formula extends the process to include the legislative forums. It may be that a "settled" framework awaits yet further extension of the endorsement process to include involvement by the electorate at large.

NOTES

1. See, e.g., D.V. Smiley, *The Federal Condition in Canada* (Toronto: McGraw-Hill Ryerson, 1987), pp. 36–38.
2. Garth Stevenson, "The Division of Powers" in Richard Simeon (ed.), *Division of Powers and Public Policy*, vol. 61, Research Studies for the Royal Commission on the Economic Union and Development Prospects for Canada (Toronto: University of Toronto Press, 1985), pp. 80–81.
3. On the "entanglement" of federal and provincial policy responsibilities, see Peter M. Leslie, *Federal State National Economy* (Toronto: University of Toronto Press, 1987), pp. 48–63.
4. Stevenson, pp. 88–91.
5. Kenneth Wiltshire, *Planning and Federalism* (St. Lucia, Queensland: University of Queensland Press, 1986), p. 128.
6. *Ibid.*, pp. 127–33.
7. Leslie, p. 63.
8. Garth Stevenson, *Unfulfilled Union*, 3rd Edition (Gage Educational, 1989), pp. 235–66; Alan C. Cairns, "The Politics of Constitutional

Conservatism" (1983) and "The Canadian Constitutional Experiment" (1984), both reprinted in Douglas E. Williams, *Constitution, Government, and Society in Canada. Selected Essays by Alan C. Cairns* (Toronto: McClelland and Stewart, 1988), pp. 195–256; Peter MeeKison, "The Amending Formula," *Queen's Law Journal,* 8:1–2, 1982–83, 99–122. For a Canadian/Australian comparison, see, Peter H. Russell, "The Politics of Frustration: The Pursuit of Formal Constitutional Change in Australia and Canada" in Bruce W. Hodgins, John J. Eddy et al., *Federalism in Canada and Australia: Historical Perspectives, 1920–1988* (Peterborough: First Centre for Canadian Heritage and Development Studies, Trent University, 1989), pp. 59–85.

9. Russell, "The Politics of Frustration," pp. 61–62.
10. See, Meekison, "The Amending Formula," pp. 99–122.
11. Smiley, *The Federal Condition*, p. 47.
12. Meekison, "The Amending Formula," p. 112.
13. Russell, "The Politics of Frustration," p. 76.
14. *Ibid.*
15. See, e.g., C. Howard and C. Saunders, "The Blocking of the Budget and Dismissal of the Government" in Gareth Evans (ed.), *Labor and the Constitution: 1972–1975* (Melbourne: Heinemann, 1977).
16. Amendment to the Constitution in 1977 provided that a casual vacancy in the Senate should be filled by a person from the same party as the Senator who occupied the position previously.
17. *Final Report of the Constitutional Commission*, vol. 2 (Canbera: Australian Government Publishing Service, 1988), pp. 851–93.
18. L.F. Crisp, *Australian National Government*, 5th Edition (Melbourne: Longman Cheshire, 1983), p. 51.
19. Campbell Sharman and Janette Stuart, "Patterns of State Voting in National Referendums," *Politics*, XVI(2), November 1981, 261–70.
20. Cairns, "The Politics of Constitutional Conservatism," pp. 227–8.
21. Peter H. Russell, "The Supreme Court and Federal-Provincial Relations: The Political Use of Legal Resources," *Canadian Public Policy*, II(2), 1985, 161.
22. See, e.g., Allan C. Cairns, "The Judicial Committee and Its Critics" reprinted in Williams (ed.), *Constitution, government, and Society in Canada*, pp. 43–85.
23. Stevenson, *Unfulfilled Union*, pp. 59–69.
24. Russell, "The Supreme Court," pp. 161–70.
25. Smiley, *The Federal Condition*, pp. 55–7.
26. Brian Galligan, *Politics of the High Court* (St. Lucia, Queensland: University of Queensland Press, 1987), pp. 71–2.
27. *Ibid.*, p. 250.
28. Leslie Zines, "Judicial Review in Australia and Canada" in Hodgins et al. (eds.), *Federalism in Canada and Australia*, pp. 122–3.

29. A chronological table of the "major events" in federal finances in Canada and Australia, from the time of federation to the 1980s, is set out in Kenneth Wittshire, "Federal State/Provincial Financial Relations" in Hodgins et al. (eds.), *Federalism in Canada and Australia*, pp. 189–92.

30. For more detail, see Economic Council of Canada, "Tax Collection Agreements and Tax and Fiscal Harmonization" in R.D. Olling and M.W. Westmacott (eds.), *Perspectives on Canadian Federalism* (Scarborough, Ont.: Prentice-Hall, 1988), pp. 167–81.

31. See Richard M. Bird, *Federal Finance in Comparative Perspective* (Toronto: Canadian Tax Foundation, 1986), pp. 106–45.

32. See, e.g., Bird, *Federal Finance*, pp. 106–45; Wittshire, "Federal State/Provincial Financial Relations"; Olling and Westmamott (eds.), *Perspectives on Canadian Federalism*, section 4.

33. Wiltshire, "Federal State/Provincial Financial Relations," p. 193.

34. Gordon Robertson, "Intergovernmental Financial Relationships in Canada and Australia" in R.C. Mathews (ed.), *Public Policies in Two Federal Countries: Canada and Australia* (Canberra: Centre for Research on Federal Financial Relations, 1982), cited in Bird, *Federal Finance*, p. 108.

35. Cf., Stevenson, *Unfulfilled Union*, pp. 20–42, esp. pp. 38–41.

The Case for a "Triple E" Senate

Howard McConnell

Canada is demographically, sociologically, and in the unevenness of distribution of its natural resources, one of the most disparate federations on the globe. It is a country riven at times with regional conflicts. No matter what political party is in power federally, there are regional issues on which a strong central Canadian majority in the lower house can dictate policy to the peripheries. The regions, whether they be in the east, west, or north, can be overridden with relative impunity because their comparatively sparse population gives them scant weight in a House of Commons dominated by Ontario and Quebec. This has engendered much frustration, and could lead to disunity, since the outlying provinces and territories lack a countervailing voice, such as exists in the American and Australian senates, in our central parliamentary institution. It will be argued here that the present moribund Senate should be replaced by an elected Senate, with effective powers, in which, as in the US and Australia, the constituent units would possess equal representation. While such a revised body would have a special responsibility to

From *Queen's Quarterly* (1988), 95(3): 683–98. Reprinted by permission of the author.

articulate provincial and regional concerns there are constitutional safeguards which would still maintain much of the House of Common's present dominance in Parliament.

A "Triple E" senate refers to a reformed upper house which is "equal, elected, and effective," having the same number of senators from each province, elected by the provincial electorates, and possessing effective legislative powers to offset, at least temporarily, initiatives by the House of Commons deemed harmful to the provinces or regions. It seeks to provide a countervailing regional voice in a lower house having 282 members, 180 of which (or just under 2/3 of the total) represent the two large central provinces.

If the upper houses in the federal systems bearing the closest resemblance to Canada are examined, it will be seen that they play a far more vigorous role in representing local interests than does the Canadian Senate.

In the US there was extensive debate between the large and the smaller states at the Philadelphia convention in 1787 on the rival principles for apportioning seats in the Senate.[1] It was agreed there that seats should be allocated proportionally on the basis of population in the House of Representatives, and there were some who favoured the same method of distribution of seats in the upper house. An unsuccessful motion by Charles Pinckney of South Carolina and James Wilson of Pennsylvania would have provided for a variable number of senators for the states, the number depending on approximate population density, with Rhode Island having one, New York three, and Virginia five, and the other states being ranged in population groupings with from one to five senators. Population having been used as the distributive principle in the lower house, however, the smaller states were adamant that equality should be the rule in the Senate. "The smaller states can never give up their equality," said Jonathan Dayton of New Jersey. "For myself, I would in no event yield that security for our rights"; a colleague, Roger Sherman of Connecticut, stressed that it was not solely the interest of the small states that was at stake; all states should be represented on an equal basis in the upper chamber. That chamber should reflect the interests of all state governments. (Peters 126).

James Madison, one of the erudite expositors of the ideas underlying the American Constitution, describes the outcome in *Federalist* No. 39:

> The House of Representatives will derive its powers from the
> people of America; and the people will be represented in the
> same proportion and on the same principle as they are in the
> legislature of a particular state, so far the government is *na-
> tional* not *federal*. The Senate, on the other hand, will derive
> its powers from the states as political and co-equal societies;
> and these will be represented on the principle of equality
> in the Senate.... So far the government is *Federal* not na-
> tional. (244)

The resulting legislative system, accordingly, united the national
and the federal governmental principles. The lower house represented the people and the upper house the states. Either principle without the other would result in a perversion of federalism,
since in a legislative body organized according to population
alone there would be no assurance that imperilled regional or
state interests — which might not much preoccupy that lower
house since it represents the "people" — would be adequately
taken into account. The loose coalition or "league" of states represented by the Articles of Confederation (1781–89), on the
other hand, with its excessive dependence by Congress on the
states both for funds and the execution of its decrees, had little
real contact with the citizenry. It erred too much in the other
direction. For true federalism, on the Madisonian model, the
people should be represented according to population in the
lower house and the states, or local units, on the basis of equality in the Senate. Although the two chambers would respond to
the same issues, they would take different constituencies into
account in making laws and policies, and the interests that they
respectively represent, as will be argued later, must both find
effective expression if the central legislative organ of the federation is to respond both to popular and to regional concerns.

The same contention between states' rights and centralized
authority helped to shape the Australian Senate, with Sir John
Cockburn of South Australia declaiming at the 1891 Convention:

> We know that the tendency is always to the centre, that the
> central authority constitutes a vortex which draws power to
> itself. Therefore, all the buttresses and all the ties should be
> the other way, to enable the States to withstand the destruc-
> tion of their powers by such absorption.... Government at
> a central and distant point can never be government by
> the people, and may be just as crushing a tyranny under re-
> publican or commonwealth forms as under the most absolute
> monarchy. (Cockburn 155, 157)

The balancing of central and regional concerns, again, was an influential factor in the design of the Australian upper house. As L.F. Crisp states in his work, *The Parliamentary Government of the Commonwealth of Australia*, "Central to the position of the 'States' Rights' spokesmen was their idea of the constitution of the Senate. It must, they urged, be founded alike in equal representation of the States and in equality of status with the Lower House in respect of powers over all classes of legislation"(26). Although the Australian Senate has sometimes been criticized for not being sufficiently energetic, when required to do so it has played a significant role as a guardian of local interests. To give just two examples, in 1939 Western Australian senators helped to defeat a gold-tax bill which in their judgment would have retarded the expansion of the gold-mining industry in their state. A later, more acceptable bill, at a reduced tax rate, was subsequently passed. In 1958 Southern Australian senators ensured over strong opposition that their state would get an equitable share of River Murray water for a hydroelectric project which drew largely from their local resources (*Australian Senate* 5).

A common problem mentioned by Crisp is that an overzealous and encroaching executive power will sometimes virtually pre-empt policy formulation or effective debate by taking initiatives that present Parliament with a *fait accompli*. For example, the Australian Commonwealth government made decisions at the 1931 Ottawa Economic Conference intimately affecting the economic interests and industries of Australian states without consulting them. Neither was there effective debate by the Senate at Canberra of the issues raised at the Conference (Crisp 189). While the Senate cannot really be a substitute for inter-governmental consultation, in areas of central-regional conflict it could perform a more effective role in putting forward provincial or regional points of view.

From its inception in 1867, the Canadian Senate possessed only very modest powers; it did not, as did its American and Australian parallels, represent the constituent federal units equally, nor was it effective, having no popular constituency to appeal to; in any confrontation with the elected lower house it could do little more than delay unwanted initiatives for a limited time. Its weakness arose not through inadvertence but by design. A noted Canadian historian has summed up well the purpose of the Senate as envisaged by the Fathers of Confederation:

> Though the designers at Quebec turned naturally to the United States to study federalism in North America, they did so largely to see what to modify or avoid. The Canadian Senate, for example, had only the same name as the powerful American chamber. As an upper house on the British parliamentary model it was not meant to be more than a revising body, or a brake on the House of Commons. Therefore it was deliberately made an appointed house, since an elected Senate might prove too popular and too powerful, and be able to block the will of the House of Commons. The Canadian Senate was really the old British colonial legislative council under a new name. Besides, it did not represent separate provinces or states, as in the American system, but sections; Ontario and Quebec each had twenty-four members, and Nova Scotia and New Brunswick twenty-four together. This 'section' principle was continued as new provinces were added to the Dominion. (Careless 256–57)

The present complement of 104 senators was made up by adding a new "western section" of 24 senators to the other three in 1915, composed by six senators from each of the four western provinces (Constitution Act, 1915), six more for Newfoundland on its admission to Canada in 1949 (Constitution Act, 1949), and one each for the Northwest Territories and the Yukon in 1975 (Constitution Act, 1975).

As with the case of the colonial legislative councils to which Careless rightly compares the Canadian Senate, appointments to the upper house are the virtually unfettered gift of the incumbent prime minister. Those to whom political debts are owed have a greater claim on the appointing authority's beneficence than those who have achieved distinction in various areas of national life. In Canada where, historically, there have been long periods of one-party dominance, of the Conservatives in the nineteenth century and the Liberals in the twentieth, this can lead at times to disconcerting political imbalances. One of the most glaring examples of this trend occurred in 1955 when, after 20 uninterrupted years of Liberal federal power, a minuscule Conservative opposition of seven senators faced 75 Liberals in the then 102-seat Senate. Even so, Prime Minister Louis St Laurent refused either to relinquish such an important source of patronage or to make new appointments as vacancies arose, leaving a large number of seats to be filled in 1957 when the Conservatives, after 22 years in the wilderness, unexpectedly achieved power under John Diefenbaker (McConnell 68).

It was episodes like the above, along with the moribund nature of the institution, which led to various reform proposals for what most observers saw as a very imperfectly constituted legislative chamber with little real power.

One of the most recent reform proposals emerged in the twilight days of the second Trudeau administration in 1984, when a joint Senate and House of Commons committee recommended the future election of senators, representing major "regions" of the country as well as minority groups (Canada Special Joint Committee). The present chamber would be expanded to 144 seats to provide additional representation for the smaller Atlantic and western provinces. One-third of the reconstituted House would be elected at two-year intervals. Under the proposal, Ontario and Quebec would each retain its present complement of 24 senators, while the four western provinces would be enlarged from 6 to 12 each, with Newfoundland, Nova Scotia, and New Brunswick also being increased to 12 and Prince Edward Island advancing from four to six. Instead of their single senator, as at present, the Yukon would receive two and the Northwest Territories four.

Any such uneven allocation of seats to the various provinces and territories raises important issues. If relative population density is the criterion, why should British Columbia, with three times, or Alberta with twice Saskatchewan and Manitoba's population, receive the same number of seats? Or why should British Columbia, with more than 20 times Prince Edward Island's population, receive only twice the number of the island province's contingent? Some areas of the country are growing relatively more rapidly than the others, and there are indications that others are stagnant or could even be in decline. Substantial population shifts are bound to take place in future. If we assign such uneven numbers, it is inevitable that further reallocations will be needed at indefinite intervals in the future. If, a hundred years hence, the four western provinces acquired a greater population than central Canada, would the latter region agree to giving a preponderance of senators to the West? Would not the better course be to assign all the provinces an equal quotient of seats, since population density is *already* taken into account in the lower house, and the upper house should give the provinces equal representation so that valid provincial concerns will not simply be overwhelmed by numbers. By definition, the Territories have a subordinate constitutional status, and some numerical discrimination against them is justified until they become provinces.

Relative population disparities among the varied constituent units have not been an impediment to equal representation in the American or Australian senates. In fact, as mentioned above, the reason for equal representation is to forestall undue domination of the lesser-populated peripheries by the centre. If the examples of Wyoming or Alaska are taken in the US, for example, the populous state of California has more than 50 times the population of either, yet each of these three states has the same entitlement to two members in the US Senate. While population disparities in Australia are not so great, the small state of Tasmania, with about one-tenth the population of New South Wales, has the identical representation, ten senators, as the other five states of the Australian Commonwealth.

Another contentious feature of the 1984 reform proposal is the limitation of senators to a single nine-year term, with incumbents not being eligible for a second term. The purpose of creating a single relatively longer term was evidently to make the elected Senate a genuinely independent body by relieving its members of some of the political pressures and anxieties contingent on the necessity of presenting themselves for periodic re-election, pressures that would be felt particularly towards the end of their terms. The undesirable concomitant of such a proposal, however, would be that the valuable fund of accumulated experience of long-serving members in other upper houses (one thinks of Senators Fulbright or Goldwater in the US or Lords Beaverbrook or Shinwell in Britain) would be lost in the Canadian upper house. Independence could be better achieved by reconstituting the upper house on different lines, with a distinct mandate, which would create a dynamic interaction between the two chambers: former Prime Minister Pierre Trudeau's concept of the "counterweight" comes to mind here. There would arise a creative interplay between two legislative bodies each considering the same laws and policies, but with the needs of different constituencies in view. Because of party discipline, lack of political legitimacy and effective power, the present Senate cannot perform such a role. It is as moribund and stagnant as a "federal" chamber as it is in other respects.

Another reform plan with some of the same undesirable features was Trudeau's proposal, in Bill C–60 (Constitutional Amendment Bill), advanced in the spring of 1978, to establish a new upper house along lines radically different from the present Senate. Rather than the existing 104-member Senate appointed by the governor-general on the recommendation of the prime minister, a 118-member House of Federation was to be elected indirectly, with half of its membership being contingent, respectively, on the relative proportion of votes received by the various parties in the last preceding elections for the provincial legislatures and the House of Commons. With each successive such election, consequently, the composition of the new upper house would undergo a shift. While there would be some increase in seats for the Atlantic Provinces and the West in the new body, with Ontario and Quebec retaining their present numbers, representation would still be unequal. The new chamber would accede to such novel functions as confirming federally-appointed judges and senior federal executive appointees. It would also act as a watch-dog of French-English linguistic rights, with a double majority of English- and French-speaking senators (federators?), constituted for this purpose as separate "colleges," so to speak, being required to approve basic changes in language laws.

Some critics, and notably William Lederman of Queen's University law school, strongly contested Trudeau's contention that Parliament acting by itself possessed constitutional jurisdiction to reform the upper chamber. The prime minister's assumption appeared to be that Parliament as a whole was a *national* legislature: if the provinces could unilaterally reform provincial legislatures (e.g., Premier Jean-Jacques Bertrand's abolition of the Quebec legislative council on 31 December 1968), then Parliament, by a simple bill, could reconstitute the Senate into a House of the Federation. There was no need, indeed, for prior provincial consent to a constitutional amendment for that purpose. The doubts of experts like Lederman, however, prompted Trudeau to initiate a constitutional reference to the Supreme Court to determine whether Parliament possessed the challenged jurisdiction. The tribunal held unanimously against the prime minister's proposal (Authority of Parliament). One of the main factors persuading the Court against the initiative was the compelling argument that the Senate, as originally conceived, was designed expressly to protect sectional or provincial interests[2] and Bill C–60 was attempting fundamentally to alter the character of the upper house without seeking provincial consent.

The federal government did not dispute that the historical intention was to create an upper chamber representing local interests, but it contended that the present Senate no longer performed such a task. It had been superseded long ago as a guardian of provincial or regional interests by a "federalized" cabinet, the members of which were drawn from every province in the country. The fact, nevertheless, that the Supreme Court had so emphatically rejected the logic underlying the government's argument (which, it might be added, was still valid in an empirical if not in a strictly constitutional sense) dramatically emphasized the need for genuine reform of the upper house so that the reconstituted body could more effectively discharge its original constitutional mandate.

But what are the types of controversies which so imperatively demand such an alteration of the upper house? There are significant provincial and regional issues with respect to which the lack of an appropriate forum places the smaller provinces, particularly, but all provinces potentially, at a decided disadvantage. For example, take the controversy in October 1986 between Manitoba and the federal government about the awarding of the CF–18 maintenance contract to Canadair of Montreal rather than to Bristol Aerospace of Winnipeg. According to documentation later obtained by the *Globe and Mail* under the Access to Information Act ("Taken for a Ride"; York)[3] the awarding of the contract to the Quebec firm, as determined by the federal government's own experts, "would cost 13 per cent more in the first four years of the contract and 1.8 per cent more each year after that. While the Canadair bid was technically acceptable, the advisers preferred the Bristol bid 'based on a significantly higher technical assessment'" ("Taken for a Ride"). Although not everything was revealed about the award of the contract to Canadair, enough was known at the time for the matter to be debated vigorously in a chamber more aptly designed to ventilate regional grievances. In the lower house, with its substantial central Canadian majority, the issue did not provoke the intense debate it should have. In all frankness, the leaders of opposition parties were just as much aware as was the prime minister that Quebec had 75 seats in the House of Commons as compared to Manitoba's 14, and did not want considerations of equity to interfere inordinately with partisan electoral prospects in the coming general election. From a realistic standpoint, as practical politicians, they could hardly be censured for such an assessment, especially when Quebec voters were in a volatile mood in the wake of the September 1984 federal election.

Had there been an independent, elected senate, where each province had equal representation, and minority viewpoints would not have been inundated by sheer force of numbers, such regional issues could have been more rationally dissected and debated. Senators who owed their seats not to one or another prime minister, but to the electorate in their respective provinces, could have debated such matters with greater vigour and independence, and without the inhibitions imposed in the lower house by party discipline. Such a body could act as a real brake on possible excesses by the dominant lower chamber, balancing provincial and regional requirements against the unconstrained "popular will" to which the more *jacobin* House of Commons is designed to give expression. In such a reconstituted Parliament, whenever the regions or provinces lost out, as they not infrequently would, they would at least be cognizant that their viewpoints had been articulated and duly weighed before being rejected.

It is not merely the smaller provinces, however, which would benefit from such a reconstituted senate. Sometimes, a province such as Ontario finds itself in disagreement with the other provinces on matters of high provincial interest. In 1980–81 during the acerbic national debate over the patriation of the Constitution and the adoption of the Charter, Ontario and New Brunswick found themselves isolated from the rest of the provinces in their support of Trudeau's unilateral constitutional initiative. Much of the rancour and bitterness that surrounded that incendiary debate might have been avoided were it not for the strong perception, at least until the Supreme Court's cautionary decision in September 1981 (Reference re Amendment), that the ultimate fate of patriation would be determined by a centralist-dominated House of Commons in which there was no authentic provincial presence. Everybody expected, under current constitutional arrangements, that the Senate would more or less uncritically follow the lead of the lower chamber, as indeed it did. This would not have happened, of course, in a truly "federal" senate with eight provinces opposing, and only two supporting, Trudeau's original project. Some might say that in such a new institutional framework we still might not have patriation or the Charter. More likely, we would probably have achieved both, but perhaps in an altered form, and arguably with greater political legitimacy. It is also likely that Quebec, the shunned partner, would not have been subject to a midnight deal consummated in a kitchen behind her back. It would have been, rather, a continuing party to the negotiations and the outcome, and we would, mercifully, never have heard of the Meech Lake Accord. Instead of this, the perception that parliament was a monolithic entity with a single corporate will produced a mood of exasperation in those who questioned either the process or the substance of what our prime minister was doing.

More recently, Premier David Peterson of Ontario has diverged from a large number of his fellow premiers in opposing the US-Canada free trade pact. As Canada's richest and most industrialized province, Ontario assuredly has a high stake in the economic consequences of the deal, and could be severely hurt by a bad result. But where is the parliamentary forum where the distinctive Ontario point of view, rather than that of national party leaders, can be put forward? There is, of course, no such forum. What is needed is a new upper house where issues dividing the regions and the centre can be resolved. When it comes to matters of detail, for example, Peterson challenges the mandate of Ottawa, under the free trade agreement, to dictate the prices of imported wines on the shelves of his province's liquor stores. Citing the Privy Council's 1881 ruling on trade and commerce (Citizens Insurance), and its 1937 decision in the International Labour Organization (ILO) case on the treaty-implementing power (Labour Conventions), Donald S. Macdonald, a strong proponent of free trade, puts the federal argument in its most uncompromising form: "A federal statute, therefore, assuring the nationals of a foreign state freedom from discriminatory trade barriers would take precedence over provincial trade restrictions, and so it should" (Letter). Would Ontario's present discretionary legal competence to set prices for wine in its liquor stores constitute a "discriminatory trade barrier?" How far would the trade pact go, without a further constitutional amendment, to empower Ottawa to regulate matters formerly considered as falling under provincial jurisdiction? Surely, local jurisdiction over wine pricing, local marketing, and consumer protection, falling as they do under the provincial head of "property and civil rights in the province" (Constitution Act, 1867), would not be transferred to federal jurisdiction by the trade pact alone? Does the 1937 ILO case (Labour Conventions) *really* support Macdonald's (or the federal government's) position? Should not such issues profitably be debated in a reformed upper house? It is of some interest that a closely related issue was raised in the US Senate by Senate Bricker in 1954, when he proposed a constitutional amendment which would have allowed treaties to become effective only through legislation valid in the absence of the treaty (Corwin 133) (which is, *pace* Macdonald, the present Canadian position). The fact that Bricker's proposal ultimately failed to attain the required two-thirds majority by only one vote is not the point; the point is that it was possible to debate fully in the American Senate this issue of primary importance to the federal system and to bring it to a resolution after canvassing both the national and the local implications of the contested constitutional jurisdictions. With members of the Canadian Senate (disregarding some untypical recent exceptions) (Lynch) deferring excessively to their national leaders in the lower chamber, either through political impotence or the strong tradition of party discipline, the Senate too often is simply a weak echo of what happens in the other place. What is needed, again, is a reconstituted second chamber reflecting provincial concerns with greater authenticity, with a mandate from provincial electors which would give its members greater independence.

Other specific contemporary issues which have occasioned sharp federal-provincial discord have been numerous and often protracted. Among such disputes was the recent disagreement between Alberta and Ottawa over the taxation and regulation of energy; the controversies between British Columbia and Ottawa, and between Newfoundland (and some other Atlantic provinces) and Ottawa, over the ownership and control of mineral rights in the sub-soil under territorial waters and in the adjacent continental shelf; the dispute between Saskatchewan and the federal government over the rescinding of the "Crow rate" for hauling grain, a dispute, indeed, with large ramifications for all of western Canada; the disputes between provinces on both coasts and Ottawa over the fisheries; the disputes between New Brunswick and, incipiently, Manitoba, with the federal government and other provinces over the ratification of the Meech Lake Accord; and the ongoing dispute between Quebec and Ottawa over educational language rights (as well as related disputes on the rights of linguistic minorities both inside and outside Quebec);

and other contentious political conflicts, all of which might more effectively be debated in a revised upper house.

In addition to such specific disagreements, there are more general, over-arching issues which impinge on both orders of federal government, which could be canvassed in a reformed senate. Among such issues would be the respective federal-provincial responsibilities for the establishment of aboriginal self-government, and for environmental controls, and oversight of the constitutional division-of-powers generally. It has been suggested at times that the upper house could also oversee Canadian compliance with treaties, especially in the human rights area, and that a subcommittee of the reconstituted senate could confirm prospective federally-appointed judges and senior government officials.

Another general issue that could be debated more effectively in the upper house of a federation constitutionally committed to reducing regional disparities (Constitution Act, 1982) would be the overall equity with which Ottawa treats the different provinces and regions. This is a matter best not left to prime ministers with huge majorities in the lower house, or to opposition leaders who must soon confront the regional electorates they might otherwise accuse of enriching themselves extravagantly from federal coffers. Party leaders may be more frank on the hustings than within parliament, of course. At a nomination meeting in western Canada, for example, NDP leader Ed Broadbent (who was very muted in his criticism in Parliament of the CF–18 deal) charged that "Pierre Trudeau's Liberals spent 13.9 per cent of the federal procurement budget in the west where 29 per cent of Canada's population live, while in the past four years the Mulroney government has used just 11.5 per cent of the budget beyond the Manitoba-Ontario border..." (qtd. in *Star-Phoenix*). Even if Broadbent's numbers are right the federal government may have a good explanation for them: the problem is that the bald statistics are troubling, and are not likely to be effectively discussed in a legislative chamber with a weighty majority from central Canada. In a senate with equal representation from all provinces there would be a more propitious climate for dealing with such figures adequately. But how could such a "Triple E" senate be set up, and what might some of its powers be?

As a senate of about the present size seems practical, an elected upper chamber with 10 senators for each of the provinces, with perhaps two for the Yukon, and four for the somewhat large and more diverse Northwest Territories, would be workable. When the Territories became provinces they too would be entitled to equal provincial representation. This would establish an upper house with 106 members as compared to the present 104. A smaller senate would probably not have enough numbers adequately to perform committee work and other legislative responsibilities.

There is a certain arbitrariness about any internal boundaries, but the continuance of the practice of maintaining "sectional" rather than provincial equality in the Canadian Senate is simply not justifiable. It is "provinces" not "sections" whose constitutional and political rights may be jeopardized by action in the House of Commons. It is typically provinces which are in confrontation with Ottawa, rather than sections, although there may be moments where there is a considerable degree of "sectional" agreement on certain issues. There can also be, and often are, disagreements between provinces in a section of the country on important issues. The possible continuation of "sectional" representation raises the question of just how many shared interests there are between adjacent provinces. How much sectional or regional homogeneity is there? Alberta and Saskatchewan disagreed on the Crow rate, for example, and Saskatchewan and Manitoba for many months had major differences on constitutional patriation. Nova Scotia and Newfoundland had distinctly different perspectives on the ownership of offshore resources, and if central Canada is considered as a region, Quebec and Ontario have strong differences on free trade. The differences in industrial development between Prince Edward Island and Nova Scotia, or between Saskatchewan and Alberta make it difficult to classify either pair, on rational criteria, as members of a common section with uniform interests. In most ways, with some exceptions, our typical perspective is provincial rather than regional or sectional. It would seem to underlie the postulate of equal sectional representation that there is a community of economic or other interests binding together members of a section, but there isn't. Even if Ontario is taken as a "section" (which apparently it was) the northern Ontario hinterland has more affinities with the adjacent prairies than it does with the industrialized south of the province, and "sectionalism" might be questioned even here.

Taking the 10 provinces, then, as the more typical federal units, for representative purposes, the units in which constitutional rights, duties, and interests inhere, *these* are the entities which must be accorded representation in the upper house, and that representation must be equal. The provinces must have equal status in the upper house because the more populous areas of the country already have greater weight in the lower chamber. In a properly balanced federal system the weight of population should not be felt in *both* houses, since that would tend towards an overcentralized *national* rather than a balanced federal polity.

As in other federations, continuity in the upper house could be ensured by providing for a six-year term for senators, with one-third of the body being elected at two-year intervals.

Like the other provinces, Quebec would be represented by 10 senators. If the criticism were made that the proposed new upper house did not adequately take Quebec's specific interests into account, it could be met by providing that no legislative action could be taken derogating from the province's linguistic, cultural, or other rights without the assent of a majority of Quebec senators, present and voting, which would be considered as a unit for that purpose. This would not, in any event, seem to be a major obstacle, since some of Quebec's most important existing rights are already entrenched and beyond alteration by a simple parliamentary bill: a constitutional amendment would be needed for that purpose. The protection envisaged here, however, contemplates that cultural or linguistic rights in ordinary legislation specifically protecting Quebec's interests would not be abrogated without the "collegial" consent of the province's senators.

As argued above, the primary aim of the reconstituted Senate would be more effectively to advance provincial points of view, so that there would be an authentic central legislative organ in Ottawa to articulate local interests there that are not now adequately put forward. Far from exacerbating regional tensions, such a revitalized body would inject needed harmony into federal-provincial relations. Much of the fractiousness between Ottawa and the provinces in recent years has arisen because there was no "presence" in the national capital to effectively represent the provinces. The new Senate would in no manner replace the intermittent meetings of federal and provincial First Ministers, or so-called "executive-federalism," which is an extra-parliamentary, extra-constitutional forum without specific legislative powers. The First Ministers do valuable work, but their task is essentially that of inter-governmental consultation and compromise, and is more specific in character, being largely confined to constitutional and economic matters. These areas are, assuredly, of great importance, but the work of the Senate would be more continuous and of even greater breadth, embracing virtually all jurisdictions, and it would have its appropriate legislative dimension which the First Ministers, as an executive body, lacks.

And to be truly effective, the new Senate should have not merely a delaying power, or "suspensive veto," but a real veto on virtually all laws emanating from the lower house, except for constitutional amendments,[4] and for the not always clear restrictions circumscribing the action of the upper house where the "spending power" is concerned. If a mere delaying power were involved, in any federal controversy the lower house would need only to wait through the moratorium period and then unilaterally do whatever it pleased. Disagreements, even so, would not be very frequent; they are not endemic in other federations. Where such disagreements did arise, a "conference committee" of both houses could decide on joint action. A possible device to break any unusually intractable disagreement could be similar to that contained in section 57 of the Australian Constitution. That provision provides that in such a contingency the governor-general can convoke a joint sitting of both federal houses, with an absolute vote of both senators and members of the lower house, sitting together, being necessary to break the log-jam.

But in collaborating in the establishment of such a potentially powerful new legislative body, would the House of Commons be crating a powerful rival? In some respects, unquestionably, it would be, but its position of dominance in the overall legislative framework, which Canadians have come to accept, could still be maintained. There are at least three reasons why, in any reconstitution of the upper house, the House of Commons would continue to play its present dominant role. First, by the unwritten convention of responsible government, it would continue to be only a want-of-confidence motion in the lower house which would entail the defeat of the government. Second, the primary function of the new senators would be to represent their home provinces; their purpose is principally to

106

voice the needs of their local constituencies while bearing broader national interests in mind. That being the case, it is envisaged that the prime minister and virtually all of the federal cabinet, and certainly the holders of major portfolios, would continue to be drawn from the House of Commons. This would certainly ensure that the formulation of policy would continue to be the main prerogative of that House. The Senate, however, would be a more powerful watch-dog of regional interests than the present upper house, perhaps forestalling by its mere presence the initiation of ill-advised measures in the Commons. And third, money bills, as at present, would continue to originate only in the lower chamber.

The continuance, therefore, of the present convention of responsible government, and the presence of a powerful cabinet in the House of Commons would ensure that the new parliament would not merely be a pale replica of the American Congress with its more stark separation of powers. While maintaining the traditional dominance and legislative leadership of the House of Commons, the reconstituted Senate would infuse a needed, and now absent, federal balance in the halls of Parliament.

NOTES

1. The three rival plans put forward at the Philadelphia constitutional convention of 1787 are known, respectively, as the Virginia Plan, the New Jersey Plan, and the Connecticut Compromise. The Virginia Plan provided for a bicameral legislature with proportional representation in both houses, with the executive and judicial branches to be chosen by the legislature. The New Jersey Plan provided for a single legislative house with equal representation for each state. The Connecticut Compromise, which was ultimately adopted, provided for equal state representation in the Senate and proportional representation in the House of Representatives. See Madison, *Debates, passim.*

2. Liberal leader George Brown, an influential Father of Confederation, was quite explicit about the role of the Senate as a guardian of local interests, and was quoted by the Supreme Court to that effect, in Authority of Parliament, 67, 102 DLR (3rd) 10: "But the very essence of our compact is that the union shall be federal and not legislative. Our Lower Canadian friends have agreed to give us representation by population in the Lower House, on the express condition that they should have equality in the Upper House. On no other condition could we have advanced a step...."

3. Statistics Canada, and see York A3, and "Taken for a Ride on the CF–18."
4. Pursuant to s. 47(1) of the Constitutional Act, 1982, the Senate cannot veto, but may only delay constitutional amendments for a 180-day period; on re-adoption by the House of Commons after such delay, parliamentary assent thereto is effective.

Running Scared

Anthony King ▪ ▪ ▪ ▪ ▪ ▪ ▪ ▪ ▪ ▪

> Painfully often the legislation our politicians pass
> is designed less to solve problems than to protect
> the politicians from defeat in our never-ending
> election campaigns. They are, in short, too fright-
> ened of us to govern

To an extent that astonishes a foreigner, modern America is *about* the holding of elections. Americans do not
merely have elections on the first Tuesday after the first
Monday of November in every year divisible by four. They
have elections on the first Tuesday after the first Monday
of November in every year divisible by two. In addition,
five states have elections in odd-numbered years. Indeed,
there is no year in the United States — ever — when a major statewide election is not being held somewhere. To this
catalogue of general elections has of course to be added an
equally long catalogue of primary elections (for example,
forty-three presidential primaries last year). Moreover, not
only do elections occur very frequently in the United
States but the number of jobs legally required to be filled
by them is enormous — from the presidency of the United

States to the post of local consumer advocate in New York. It has been estimated that no fewer than half a million elective offices are filled or waiting to be filled in the United States today.

Americans take the existence of their never-ending election campaign for granted. Some like it, some dislike it, and most are simply bored by it. But they are all conscious of it, in the same way that they are conscious of Mobil, McDonald's, *Larry King Live*, Oprah Winfrey, the Dallas Cowboys, the Ford Motor Company, and all the other symbols and institutions that make up the rich tapestry of American life.

To a visitor to America's shores, however, the never-ending campaign presents a largely unfamiliar spectacle. In other countries election campaigns have both beginnings and ends, and there are even periods, often prolonged periods, when no campaigns take place at all. Other features of American elections are also unfamiliar. In few countries do elections and campaigns cost as much as they do in the United States. In no other country is the role of organized political parties so limited.

America's permanent election campaign, together with other aspects of American electoral politics, have one crucial consequence, little noticed but vitally important for the functioning of American democracy. Quite simply, the American electoral system places politicians in a highly vulnerable position. Individually and collectively they are more vulnerable, more of the time, to the vicissitudes of electoral politics than are the politicians of any other democratic country. Because they are more vulnerable, they devote more of their time to electioneering, and their conduct in office is more continuously governed by electoral considerations. I will argue that American politicians' constant and unremitting electoral preoccupations have deleterious consequences for the functioning of the American system. They consume time and scarce resources. Worse, they make it harder than it would otherwise be for the system as a whole to deal with some of America's most pressing problems. Americans often complain that their system is not sufficiently democratic. I will argue that, on the contrary, there is a sense in which the system is too democratic and ought to be made less so.

Although this article is written by a foreigner, a Canadian citizen who happens to live in Great Britain, it is not written in any spirit of moral or intellectual superiority. Americans over the years have had quite enough of Brits and others telling them how to run their affairs. I have no wish to prolong their irritation. What follows is the reflections of a candid friend.

FEAR AND TREMBLING

Politics and government in the United States are marked by the fact that U.S. elected officials in many cases have very short terms of office *and* face the prospect of being defeated in primary elections *and* have to run for office more as individuals than as standard-bearers for their party *and* have continually to raise large sums of money in order to finance their own election campaigns. Some of these factors operate in other countries. There is no other country, however, in which all of them operate, and operate simultaneously. The cumulative consequences, as we shall see, are both pervasive and profound.

The U.S. Constitution sets out in one of its very first sentences that "the House of Representatives shall be composed of members chosen every second year by the people of the several states." When the Founding Fathers decided on such a short term of office for House members, they were setting a precedent that has been followed by no other major democratic country. In Great Britain, France, Italy, and Canada the constitutional or legal maximum for the duration of the lower house of the national legislature is five years. In Germany and Japan the equivalent term is four years. Only in Australia and New Zealand, whose institutions are in some limited respects modeled on those of the United States, are the legal maximums as short as three years. In having two-year terms the United States stands alone.

Members of the Senate are, of course, in a quite different position. Their constitutionally prescribed term of office, six years, is long by anyone's standards. But senators' six-years terms are not all they seem. In the first place, so pervasive is the electioneering atmosphere that even newly elected senators begin almost at once to lay plans for their re-election campaigns. Senator Daniel Patrick Moynihan, of New York, recalls that when he first came to the Senate, in 1977, his colleagues when they met over lunch or a drink usually talked about politics and policy. Now they talk about almost nothing but the

111

latest opinion polls. In the second place, the fact that under the Constitution the terms of a third of the Senate end every two years means that even if individual senators do not feel themselves to be under continuing electoral pressure, the Senate as a whole does. Despite the Founders' intentions, the Senate's collective electoral sensibilities increasingly resemble those of the House.

Most Americans seem unaware of the fact, but the direct primary — a government-organized popular election to nominate candidates for public office — is, for better or worse, an institution peculiar to the United States. Neither primary elections nor their functional equivalents exist anywhere else in the democratic world. It goes without saying that their effect is to add a further dimension of uncertainty and unpredictability to the world of American elective politicians.

In most other countries the individual holder of public office, so long as he or she is reasonably conscientious and does not gratuitously offend local or regional party opinion, has no real need to worry about renomination. To be sure, cases of parties refusing to renominate incumbent legislators are not unknown in countries such as France, Germany, and Canada, but they are relatively rare and tend to occur under unusual circumstances. The victims are for the most part old, idle, or alcoholic.

The contrast between the rest of the world and the United States could hardly be more striking. In 1978 no fewer than 104 of the 382 incumbent members of the House of Representatives who sought re-election faced primary opposition. In the following three elections the figures were ninety-three out of 398 (1980), ninety-eight out of 393 (1982), and 130 out of 409 (1984). More recently, in 1994, nearly a third of all House incumbents seeking re-election, 121 out of 386, had to face primary opposition, and in the Senate the proportion was even higher: eleven out of twenty-six. Even those incumbents who did not face opposition could seldom be certain in advance that they were not going to. The influence — and the possibility — of primaries is pervasive. As we shall see, the fact that incumbents usually win is neither here nor there.

To frequent elections and primary elections must be added another factor that contributes powerfully to increasing the electoral vulnerability of U.S. politicians: the relative lack of what we might call "party cover." In most democratic countries the fate of most politicians depends not primarily on their own endeavors but on the fate — locally, regionally, or nationally — of their party. If their party does well in an election, so do they. If not, not. The individual politician's interests and those of his party are bound together.

In contrast, America's elective politicians are on their own — not only in relation to politicians in most other countries but also in absolute terms. Party is still a factor in U.S. electoral politics, but it is less so than anywhere else in the democratic world. As a result, American legislators seeking re-election are forced to raise their own profiles, to make their own records, and to fight their own re-election campaigns.

If politicians are so vulnerable electorally, it may be protested, why aren't more of them defeated? In particular, why aren't more incumbent congressmen and senators defeated? The analysis here would seem to imply a very high rate of turnover in Congress, but in fact the rate — at least among incumbents seeking re-election — is notoriously low. How can this argument and the facts of congressional incumbents' electoral success be reconciled?

This objection has to be taken seriously, because the facts on which it is based are substantially correct. The number of incumbent congressmen and senators defeated in either primary or general elections *is* low. But to say that because incumbent members of Congress are seldom defeated, they are not really vulnerable electorally is to miss two crucial points. The first is that precisely because they are vulnerable, they go to prodigious lengths to protect themselves. Like workers in nuclear-power stations, they take the most extreme safety precautions, and the fact that the precautions are almost entirely successful does not make them any less necessary.

Second, congressmen and senators go to inordinate lengths to secure re-election because, although they may objectively be safe (in the view of journalists and academic political scientists), they do not *know* they are safe — and even if they think they are, the price of being wrong is enormous. The probability that anything will go seriously wrong with a nuclear-power station may approach zero, but the stations tend nevertheless to be built away from the centers of large cities. A congressman or a senator may believe that he is reasonably safe, but if he wants to be re-elected, he would be a fool to act on that belief.

113

HOW THEY CAME TO BE VULNERABLE

American politicians run scared — and are right to do so. And they run more scared than the politicians of any other democratic country — again rightly. How did this come to be so?

The short answer is that the American people like it that way. They are, and have been for a very long time, the Western world's hyperdemocrats. They are keener on democracy than almost anyone else and are more determined that democratic norms and practices should pervade every aspect of national life. To explore the implications of this central fact about the United States, and to see how it came to be, we need to examine two different interpretations of the term "democracy." Both have been discussed from time to time by political philosophers, but they have never been codified and they certainly cannot be found written down in a constitution or any other formal statement of political principles. Nevertheless, one or the other underpins the political practice of every democratic country — even if, inevitably, the abstract conception and the day-to-day practice are never perfectly matched.

One of these interpretations might be labeled "division of labor." In this view, there are in any democracy two classes of people — the governors and the governed. The function of the governors is to take decisions on the basis of what they believe to be in the country's best interests and to act on those decisions. If public opinion broadly supports the decisions, that is a welcome bonus. If not, too bad. The views of the people at large are merely one datum among a large number of data that need to be considered. They are not accorded any special status. Politicians in countries that operate within this view can frequently be heard using phrases like "the need for strong leadership" and "the need to take tough decisions." They often take a certain pride in doing what they believe to be right even if the opinion of the majority is opposed to it.

The function of the governed in such a system, if it is a genuine democracy, is very important but strictly limited. It is not to determine public policy or to decide what is the right thing to do. Rather, it is to go to the polls from time to time to choose those who will determine public policy and decide what the right thing is: namely, the governors. The deciding of issues by the electorate is secondary to the election of the individuals who are to do the deciding. The analogy is with choosing a doctor. The patient certainly chooses which doctor to see but does not normally decide (or even try to decide) on the detailed course of treatment. The division of labor is informal but clearly understood.

It is probably fair to say that most of the world's major democracies — Great Britain, France, Germany, Japan — operate on this basis. The voters go to the polls every few years, and in between times it is up to the government of the day to get on with governing. Electing a government and governing are two different businesses. Electioneering is, if anything, to be deplored if it gets in the way of governing.

This is a simplified picture, of course. Democratically elected politicians are ultimately dependent on the electorate, and if at the end of the day the electorate does not like what they are doing, they are dead. Nevertheless, the central point remains. The existing division of labor is broadly accepted.

The other interpretation of democracy, the one dominant in America, might be called the "agency" view, and it is wholly different. According to this view, those who govern a country should function as no more than the agents of the people. The job of the governors is not to act independently and to take whatever decisions they believe to be in the national interest but, rather, to reflect in all their actions the views of the majority of the people, whatever those views may be. Governors are not really governors at all; they are representatives, in the very narrow sense of being in office solely to represent the view of those who sent them there.

In the agency view, representative government of the kind common throughout the democratic world can only be second-best. The ideal system would be one in which there were no politicians or middlemen of any kind and the people governed themselves directly; the political system would take the form of more or less continuous town meetings or referenda, perhaps conducted by means of interactive television. Most Americans, at bottom, would still like to see their country governed by a town meeting.

WHY THEIR VULNERABILITY MATTERS

In this political ethos, finding themselves inhabiting a turbulent and torrid electoral environment, most American elective officials respond as might be expected: in an almost Darwinian way. They adapt their behavior — their roll-call votes, their introduction of bills, their committee assignments, their phone calls, their direct-mail letters, their speeches, their press releases, their sound bites, whom they see, how they spend their time, their trips abroad, their trips back home, and frequently their private and family lives — to their environment: that is, to their primary and overriding need for electoral survival. The effects are felt not only in the lives of individual officeholders and their staffs but also in America's political institutions as a whole and the shape and content of U.S. public policy.

It all begins with officeholders' immediate physical environment: with bricks, mortar, leather, and wood paneling. The number of congressional buildings and the size of congressional staffs have ballooned in recent decades. At the start of the 1960s most members of the House of Representatives contented themselves with a small inner office and an outer office; senators' office suites were not significantly larger. Apart from the Capitol itself, Congress was reasonably comfortably housed in four buildings, known to Washington taxi drivers as the Old and New House and Senate Office Buildings. The designations Old and New cannot be used any longer, however, because there are now so many even newer congressional buildings.

Congressional staffs have grown at roughly the same rate, the new buildings have been built mainly to house the staffs. In 1957 the total number of people employed by members of the House and Senate as personal staff was 3,556. By 1991 the figure had grown to 11,572 — a more than threefold increase within the political lifetime of many long-serving members. Last year the total number of people employed by Congress in all capacities, including committee staffs and the staffs of support agencies like the Congressional Research Service, was 32,820, making Congress by far the most heavily staffed legislative branch in the world.

Much of the growth of staff in recent decades has been in response to the growth of national government, to Congress's insistence on strengthening its policymaking role in the aftermath of Vietnam and Watergate, and to decentralization within Congress, which has led subcommittee chairmen and the subcommittees themselves to acquire their own staffs. But there is no doubt that the increase is also in response to congressional incumbents' ever-increasing electoral exposure. Congress itself

116

has become an integral part of America's veritable "elections industry."

One useful measure of the changes that have taken place — and also an important consequence of the changes — is the increased proportion of staff and staff time devoted to constituent service. As recently as 1972 only 1,189 House employees — 22.5 percent of House members' personal staffs — were based in home-district offices. By 1992 the number had more than doubled, to 3,128, and the proportion had nearly doubled, to 42.1 percent. On the Senate side there were only 303 state-based staffers in 1972, making up 12.5 percent of senators' personal staffs, but the number had more than quadrupled by 1992 to 1,368, for fully 31.6 percent of the total. Since a significant proportion of the time of Washington-based congressional staffs is also devoted to constituent service, it is a fair guess that more than half of the time of all congressional staffs is now given over to nursing the district or state rather than to legislation and policymaking.

Much constituent service is undoubtedly altruistic, inspired by politicians' sense of duty (and constituents' understandable frustration with an unresponsive bureaucracy); but at the same time nobody doubts that a large proportion of it is aimed at securing re-election. The statistics on the outgoing mail of members of Congress and their use of the franking privilege point in that direction too. Congressional mailings grew enormously in volume from some 100 million pieces a year in the early 1960s to more than 900 million in 1984 — nearly five pieces of congressional mail for every adult American.) New restrictions on franking introduced in the 1990s have made substantial inroads into that figure, but not surprisingly the volume of mail emanating from both houses of Congress is still invariably higher in election years.

The monetary costs of these increases in voter-oriented congressional activities are high: in addition to being the most heavily staffed legislative branch in the world, Congress is also the most expensive. But there is another, non-monetary cost: the staffs themselves become one of the congressman's or senator's constituencies, requiring management, taking up time, and always being tempted to go into business for themselves. American scholars who have studied the burgeoning of congressional staffs express concern about their cumulative impact on Congress as a deliberative body in which face-to-face communication between members, and between members and their constituents, facilitates both mutual understanding and an understanding of the issues. Largely in response to the requirements of electioneering, more and more congressional business is conducted through dense networks of staffers.

One familiar effect of American politicians' vulnerability is the power it accords to lobbyists and special-interest groups, especially those that can muster large numbers of votes or have large amounts of money to spend on campaigns. Members of Congress walk the electoral world alone. They can be picked off one by one, they know it, and they adjust their behavior accordingly. The power of the American Association of Retired Persons, the National Rifle Association, the banking industry, and various veterans' lobbies is well known. It derives partly from their routine contributions to campaign funds and the quality of their lobbying activities in Washington, but far more from the votes that the organizations may be able to deliver and from congressmen's and senators' calculations of how the positions they take in the present may affect their chances of re-election in the future — a future that rarely is distant. Might a future challenger be able to use that speech against me? Might I be targeted for defeat by one of the powerful lobbying groups?

A second effect is that American politicians are even more likely than those in other countries to engage in symbolic politics: to use words masquerading as deeds, to take actions that purport to be instrumental but are in fact purely rhetorical. A problem exists; the people demand that it be solved; the politicians cannot solve it and know so; they engage in an elaborate pretense of trying to solve it nevertheless, often at great expense to the taxpayers and almost invariably at a high cost in terms of both the truth and the politicians' own reputations for integrity and effectiveness. The politicians lie in most cases not because they are liars or approve of lying but because the potential electoral costs of not lying are too great.

At one extreme, symbolic politics consists of speechmaking and public position-taking in the absence of any real action or any intention of taking action; casting the right vote is more important than achieving the right outcome. At the other extreme, symbolic politics consists of whole government programs that are ostensibly designed to achieve one set of objectives but are actually designed to achieve other objectives (in some cases simply the re-election of the politicians who can claim credit for them).

Take as an example the crime bills passed by Congress in the 1980s and 1990s, with their mandatory-minimum sentences, their three-strikes-and-you're-out provisions, and their extension of the federal death penalty to fifty new crimes. The anti-drug and anti-crime legislation, by the testimony of judges and legal scholars, has been at best useless and at worst wholly pernicious in its effects, in that it has filled prison cells not with violent criminals but with drug users and low-level drug pushers. As for the death penalty, a simple measure of its sheer irrelevance to the federal government's war on crime is easily provided. The last federal offender to be put to death, Victor H. Feguer, a convicted kidnapper, was hanged in March of 1963. By the end of 1995 no federal offender had been executed for more than thirty years, and hardly any offenders were awaiting execution on death row. The ferocious-seeming federal statutes were almost entirely for show.

The way in which the wars on drugs and crime were fought cannot be understood without taking into account the incessant pressure that elected officeholders felt they were under from the electorate. As one former congressman puts it, "Voters were afraid of criminals, and politicians were afraid of voters." This fear reached panic proportions in election years. Seven of the years from 1981 to 1994 were election years nationwide; seven were not. During those fourteen years Congress passed no fewer than seven major crime bills. Of those seven, six were passed in election years (usually late in the year). That is, there was only one election year in which a major crime bill was *not* passed, and only one non-election year in which a major crime bill *was* passed.

Another effect of the extreme vulnerability of American politicians is that it is even harder for them than for democratically elected politicians in other countries to take tough decisions: to court unpopularity, to ask for sacrifices, to impose losses, to fly in the face of conventional wisdom — in short, to act in what they believe to be their constituents' interest. Timothy J. Penny, a Democrat who left the House of Representatives in 1994, put the point starkly, perhaps even too harshly, in *Common Cents* (1995).

Voters routinely punish lawmakers who try to do unpopular things, who challenge them to face unpleasant truths about the budget, crime, Social Security, or tax policy. Similarly, voters reward politicians for giving them what they want — more spending for popular programs — even if it means wounding the nation in the long run by creating more debt.

America's enduring budget deficit offers a vivid, almost textbook illustration. For nearly a generation — ever since the early 1980s — American politicians have bemoaned the deficit and exhorted themselves to do something about it. However, they have never done nearly enough, even in their own eyes. Why? Part of the answer undoubtedly lies in genuine ideological differences that make it hard for conservatives and liberals to compromise; but much of the answer also lies in the brute fact that every year in the United States is either an election year or a pre-election year, with primaries and threatened primaries intensifying politicians' electoral concerns. In 1985 Senator Warren Rudman, of New Hampshire, reckoned that he and other senators who had voted for a bold deficit-reduction package had flown a "kamikaze mission." One of his colleagues said they had "jumped off a cliff." Twelve years later, not surprisingly, the federal budget remains in deficit.

MORE DEMOCRACY, MORE DISSATISFACTION

Numerous opinion polls show that millions of Americans are profoundly dissatisfied with the functioning of their political system. Consequently, there is a widespread disposition in the United States — at all levels of society, from the grass roots to the editorial conference and the company boardroom — to want to make American democracy "work better," and concrete proposals abound for achieving this goal.

The proposed reforms can be grouped loosely under four headings. First come those that if implemented would amount to the creation of electronic town meetings, taking advantage of technological developments such as CD-ROM, interactive cable systems, electronic mail, and the Internet. *The Wall Street Journal* referred in this general connection to "arranging a marriage of de Tocqueville and technology."

Second, and related, are proposals for promoting democratic deliberation and citizen participation. The Kettering Foundation and the Public Agenda Foundation already organize National Issues Forums that embrace some 3,000 educational and civic groups across America. David Mathews, the president of the Kettering Foundation, considers these modern forums to be directly linked to America's ancient "town meeting tradition." Benjamin R. Barber, a political philosopher at Rutgers University, would go further and create a nationwide network of neighborhood assemblies that could take actual decisions on strictly local matters and also debate and lobby on broader national questions. James S. Fishkin, a political scientist at the University of Texas, likewise seeks to leap the modern barriers to face-to-face democracy by means of what he calls "deliberative opinion polls" (which have been tried, with considerable success, in England).

The third group of proposed reforms is equally radical but more old-fashioned. This group seeks to complete the work of Progressive Era reformers by extending to the federal level the characteristic state-level reforms that were introduced in that period: the referendum, the initiative, and the recall. The political analyst Kevin Phillips, for example, suggests that "the United States should propose and ratify an amendment to the Constitution setting up a mechanism for holding nationwide referendums to permit the citizenry to supplant Congress and the president in making certain categories of national decisions." He would also like to see congressmen and senators be subject to popular recall once they have been in office for a year. Certainly proposals of this kind have broad public support. Depending on the precise wording of the question, more than 50 percent of Americans support the idea of national referenda and more than 80 percent support both the initiative and the recall.

Finally, many commentators — and the majority off the American public — strongly back the newest and most fashionable item on the "making democracy work better" agenda: the imposition of term limits on both state and federal elected officials, notably members of Congress. But the great majority of those who favor terms limits, true to the American democratic tradition, are less concerned with good government and the public interest as such than with the present generation of politicians' alleged lack of responsiveness to the mass of ordinary people. At the center of this argument is the idea that the United States is now governed by an unresponsive, self-perpetuating, and increasingly remote class of professional politicians, a class that ought to be replaced as soon as possible by "citizen legislators" — men and women who will serve the people simply because they *are* the people. As one advocate of term limits puts it, ordinary people — the proposed citizen legislators of the future — "know things about life in America that people who have lived as very self-important figures in Washington for thirty years have no way of knowing or have forgotten."

Some of the items on this four-part shopping list of reforms are intrinsically attractive, or at least a good case can be made for them. Nevertheless, taken as a whole, the mainstream reformist agenda, with its traditional American emphasis on agency democracy and its view of politicians as mere servants of the people's will, rests on extremely tenuous conceptual foundations and, more important, is almost certainly inappropriate as a response to the practical needs of turn-of-the-century America. America's problem of governance is not insufficient responsiveness on the part of its elected leaders. On the contrary, America's problem is their hyper-responsiveness. Politicians do not need to be tied down still further, to be subjected to even more external pressures than they are already. Rather, they need to be given just a little more political leeway, just a little more room for policy maneuver. Reforms should seek to strengthen division-of-labor democracy, not to create a still purer form of American-style agency democracy.

THE USUAL SUSPECTS

If the reformist prescriptions are bad ones, there may be something wrong with the reformist diagnoses on which they are based. What *are* the principal sources of dissatisfaction with the current state of American democracy?

Many commentators have gotten into the habit of blaming Americans' dissatisfaction, in an almost knee-jerk fashion, on "the Vietnam War and Watergate." It is certainly the case that evidence of widespread dissatisfaction began to appear during and shortly after Vietnam and Watergate. *Post hoc, ergo propter hoc?* Maybe. But in the first place, Vietnam and Watergate led to a flowering of idealism as well as cynicism (and to the election, in 1974, of the "Watergate babies," one of the most idealistic and public-spirited cohorts ever to be elected to Congress). And in the second place, it seems strange to attribute the dissatisfactions of the 1990s to events that took place in the 1960s and early 1970s. That distance in time is roughly that between the two world wars; most of today's college students were not yet born when President Richard Nixon resigned. To be sure, subsequent scandals have undoubtedly (and deservedly) damaged the reputations of the White House and Congress, but at least some of the sleaze of recent years has come about because politicians need such enormous sums to finance their re-election campaigns. Two other hypotheses can be dismissed, or at least assigned little importance. One is that politicians today are a poor lot compared with the intellectual and moral giants of the past. It probably is the case that having to run scared all the time has tended to drive some able people out of politics and to discourage others from coming in. But the phenomenon is a relatively recent one, and for the time being there is no reason to think that the average congressman or senator is in any way inferior to his or her predecessors. The quality of America's existing political class is at most a small part of the problem.

The same is almost certainly true of the idea that divided government — in which one party controls one or both houses of Congress while the other controls the presidency — is to be preferred. Divided government has characterized America for most of the past thirty years, and it has been associated with some of the more spectacular political and policy failures of that period — the Iran-contra scandal of the 1980s (which arose out of a Republican Administration's desire to circumvent a Democratic Congress), and successive shut-downs of parts of the government as Presidents and Congress have failed to agree on timely taxing and spending measures. Other things being equal, divided government is probably to be regretted.

All the same, it is hard to credit the idea that Americans' disillusionment with their politics would be significantly less today if party control had been mainly undivided over the past thirty years. On the one hand, recent periods in which the government has not been divided (the Carter years, 1977–1980, and the first two Clinton years, 1993–1994) were not notably successful (Carter never surmounted the energy crisis, and Clinton failed to reform America's health-care system even though that

123

reform had figured prominently in his campaign promises). On the other hand, as David R. Mayhew, a political scientist at Yale University, has shown, periods of divided government have often been extremely productive in legislative terms. On balance, divided government appears to be more of a nuisance and a distraction than a root cause of either the government's difficulties or the public's disillusionment.

The idea that the system suffers from the excessive power of interest groups, however, needs to be taken seriously. Jonathan Rauch, in his recent book *Demosclerosis*, argues persuasively that America's interest groups have become larger, more numerous, and more powerful over the past three decades, to the point that they now have the capacity to prevent the government from doing almost anything that would disadvantage or offend any of the clients they represent — taking in, as it happens, virtually the whole American population.

Rauch is probably right; but one needs to go on to ask, as he himself does, what the power of these pullulating and all-encompassing lobby groups is based on. The answer is straightforward: their power depends ultimately on their money, on their capacity to make trouble for elected officials, on the votes of their members (the AARP has more than 30 million members), and on elective politicians' fear of not being re-elected. The groups' power, in other words, depends on politicians' electoral vulnerability; and America's interest groups are peculiarly powerful in large measure because America's elective politicians are peculiarly vulnerable. It is not quite as simple as that — but almost.

It is also important to note the precise timing of the developments described by Rauch and by almost everyone else who has written on this subject. Nearly all these developments date, almost uncannily, from the past thirty years: the rise in the number of interest groups, the growth in their membership and power, the decline in the public's trust in government officials, and the increased sense among voters that who they are and what they think do not matter to politicians and officials in Washington. In other words, the origins of the present era of democratic discontent can be traced to the end of the 1960s and the beginning of the 1970s. It was then that people began to think something was wrong not with this or that aspect of the system but with the system itself.

What happened at that time? It is hard to escape the conclusion that the crucial developments, largely provoked by the Vietnam War and Watergate, were the attempts from 1968 onward to open up the American system, to make it more transparent, to make it more accessible, to make it, in a word, more "democratic." These attempts led to an increase in the number of primary elections, to a further weakening of America's already weak political parties, to increases in the already high costs of electoral politics, and to the increasing isolation, in an increasingly hostile environment, of elective officials. In short, the post-Vietnam, post-Watergate reforms led, as they were meant to lead, to increased vulnerability to their electorates on the part of individual American officeholders.

The paradox that has resulted is obvious and easily stated. Recent history suggests that when large numbers of Americans become dissatisfied with the workings of their government, they call for more democracy. The more they call for more democracy, the more of it they get. The more of it they get, the more dissatisfied they become with the workings of their government. The more they become dissatisfied with the workings of their government, the more they call for more democracy. The cycle endlessly repeats itself.

WHAT, IF ANYTHING, MIGHT BE DONE?

Precisely because American politicians are so exposed electorally, they probably have to display — and do display — more political courage more often than the politicians of any other democratic country. The number of political saints and martyrs in the United States is unusually large.

There is, however, no special virtue in a political system that requires large numbers of politicians to run the risk of martyrdom in order to ensure that tough decisions can be taken in a timely manner in the national interest. The number of such decisions that need to be taken is always likely to be large; human nature being what it is, the supply of would-be martyrs is always likely to be small. On balance it would seem better not to try to eliminate the electoral risks (it can never be done in a democracy) but to reduce somewhat their scale and intensity. There is no reason why the risks run by American politicians should be so much greater than the risks run by elective politicians in other democratic countries.

How, then, might the risks be reduced? What can be done? A number of reforms to the existing system suggest themselves. It may be that none of them is politically feasible — Americans hold tight to the idea of agency democracy — but in principle there should be no bar to any of them. One of the simplest would also be the most radical: to lengthen the terms of members of the House of Representatives from two years to four. The proposal is by no means a new one: at least 123 resolutions bearing on the subject were introduced in Congress in the eighty years from 1885 to 1965, and President Lyndon B. Johnson advocated the change in his State of the Union address in January of 1966.

A congressman participating in a Brookings Institution round table held at about the time of Johnson's message supported the change, saying, "I think that the four years would help you to be a braver congressman, and I think what you need is bravery. I think you need courage." Another congressman on the same occasion cited the example of another bill that he believed had the support of a majority in the House. "That bill is not going to come up this year. You know why it is not coming up?...Because four hundred and thirty-five of us have to face election....If we had a four-year term, I am as confident as I can be the bill would have come to the floor and passed."

A similar case could be made for extending the term of senators to eight years, with half the Senate retiring or running for re-election every four years. If the terms of members of both houses were thus extended and made to coincide, the effect in reducing America's never-ending election campaign would be dramatic.

There is much to be said, too, for all the reasons mentioned so far, for scaling down the number of primary elections. They absorb extravagant amounts of time, energy, and money; they serve little democratic purpose; few people bother to vote in them; and they place additional and unnecessary pressure on incumbent officeholders. Since the main disadvantage of primaries is the adverse effect they have on incumbents, any reforms probably ought to be concerned with protecting incumbents' interests.

At the moment, the primary laws make no distinction between situations in which a seat in the House or the Senate is already occupied and situations in which the incumbent is, for whatever reason, standing down. The current laws provide for a primary to be held in either case. An incumbent is therefore treated as though the seat in question were open and he or she were merely one of the candidates for it. A relatively simple reform would be to distinguish between the two situations. If a seat was open, primaries would be held in both parties, as now; but if the incumbent announced that he or she intended to run for re-election, then a primary in his or her party would be held only if large numbers of party supporters were determined to have one — that is, were determined that the incumbent should be ousted. The obvious way to ascertain whether such determination existed would be by means of a petition supervised by the relevant state government and requiring a considerable number of signatures. The possibility of a primary would thus be left open, but those who wanted one would have to show that they were both numerous and serious. A primary would not be held simply because an ambitious, possibly demented, possibly wealthy individual decided to throw his or her hat into the ring.

Any steps to strengthen the parties as institutions would be desirable on the same grounds. Lack of party cover in the United States means that elective officeholders find it hard to take tough decisions partly because they lack safety in numbers. They can seldom, if ever, say to an aggrieved constituent or a political-action committee out for revenge, "I had to vote that way because my party told me to," or even "I had to vote that way because we in my party all agreed that we would." Lack of party cohesion, together with American voters' disposition to vote for the individual rather than the party, means that congressmen and senators are always in danger of being picked off one by one.

BALLOT FATIGUE

What might be done to give both parties more back-bone? Clearly, the parties would be strengthened — and elective officeholders would not need to raise so much money for their own campaigns — if each party organization became a major source of campaign funding. In the unlikely event (against the

127

background of chronic budget deficits) that Congress ever gets around to authorizing the federal funding of congressional election campaigns, a strong case could be made for channeling as much of the money as possible through the parties, and setting aside some of it to cover their administrative and other ongoing costs.

The party organizations and the nexus between parties and their candidates would also be strengthened if it were made easier for ordinary citizens to give money to the parties and for the parties to give money to their candidates. Until 1986, when the program was abolished, tax credits were available for taxpayers who contributed small sums to the political parties. These credits could be restored. Larry J. Sabato, a political scientist at the University of Virginia, has similarly suggested that citizens entitled to a tax refund could be allowed to divert a small part of their refund to the party of their choice. Such measures would not, however, reduce candidates' dependence on donations from wealthy individuals and PACs unless they were accompanied by measures enabling the parties to contribute more generously to their candidates' campaigns. At the moment there are strict legal limits on the amount of money that national or state party organizations can contribute to the campaigns of individual candidates. The limits should be raised (and indexed to inflation). There is even a case for abolishing them altogether.

All that said, there is an even more straightforward way of reducing incumbents' dependence on campaign contributors. At present incumbents have to spend so much time raising funds because the campaigns themselves are so expensive. They could be made cheaper. This, of course, would be one of the effects of making U.S. elections less numerous and less frequent than they are now. Another way to lower the cost of elections would be to provide candidates and parties with free air time on television and radio.

THE CASE FOR SWANS

Clearly, the idea of term limits also needs to be taken seriously. After all, if American politicians are excessively vulnerable at the moment, one way of rendering them invulnerable would be to prevent them from running for re-election — no impending election contest, no need to worry overmuch about the voters.

As is evident, much of the actual campaigning in favor of term limits takes the form of ranting — against big government, against Washington, against "them," against taxes, against the deficit. Much of the rhetoric of term-limiters is sulfurous, and their principal motive often seems to be revenge. They claim that members of Congress are insufficiently responsive to their constituents, when the evidence suggests that, on the contrary, they are far too responsive. The term-limits movement is of a piece with previous outbursts of frustrated American populism, including the Know-Nothing movement of the 1850s — an essay, as one historian has put it, in "the politics of impatience."

Nevertheless, there is an alternate case for term limits, based not on American politicians' alleged lack of responsiveness to the voters but on their alleged overresponsiveness to the voters and interest groups in order to secure their own re-election. The most persuasive and subtle advocate of this line of argument is the political commentator George F. Will. His goal, Will says partway through his book *Restoration* (1992), "is deliberative democracy through representatives who function at a constitutional distance from the people." He reiterates the point about distance in his final paragraphs: "Americans must be less demanding of government. They must give to government more constitutional space in which to think, more social distance to facilitate deliberation about the future."

The case for giving American politicians more space and distance is undoubtedly a strong one, but assuming these objectives are desirable, it is still not clear that term limits are a suitable means for achieving them. Three questions arise. Would term limits achieve the desired objectives? Would they do so at an acceptable cost in terms of other American goals and values? Might the desired objectives not be better achieved by other means? The first question is strictly empirical. The other two mix the empirical and the moral.

One way in which term limits might promote deliberation is by causing some incumbent legislators — namely those serving out their final term under term limits — to think, speak, and vote differently from the way they would have thought, spoken, and voted if they had been eligible and running for re-election. In addition, for term limits to affect the behavior not just of certain individuals but of Congress as a whole, it would be necessary for any given Congress to contain a significant number of these final-term members. In other words, congressional lame ducks would have to quack differently from other ducks, and there would have to be a fair number of them on the pond.

It is impossible to be sure, but it seems unlikely that term limits would have significant effects along these lines. In the first place, existing research (along with most human experience) suggests that a final-term congressman or senator, after eleven or twelve years on Capitol Hill, would be unlikely to alter his pattern of behavior in any radical way. he might send out fewer pieces of franked mail and make fewer trips back home, but he would probably not execute many U-turns in the way he spoke and voted. In the second place, although the proportion of senators who would be in their final term under term limits would normally be large (possibly half if senators were restricted to two terms), the proportion of lame-duck congressmen would normally be much smaller (an average of sixty to seventy out of 435 if House members were limited to six terms). The cumulative impact of the lame ducks would thus be much greater in the Senate than in the House, and in both houses it would probably be felt mainly at the margins (though of course the margins can, on occasion, be important).

But those who advocate term limits in fact build very little of their case on the expected future behavior of lame ducks. Rather, they are seeking to create a wholly new class of elected representatives. George Will holds out the prospect that mandatory term limits would have the effect of replacing today's political careerists with noncareerists — in other words, of replacing today's ducks with creatures more closely resembling swans. The new legislators, because they were not careerists, would not be driven by the need to secure re-election, and for that reason they would be more likely to concern themselves with the national interest. Also because they were not political careerists, they would be more likely to have some personal, hands-on understanding of America and its real concerns.

The prospect is undoubtedly attractive. But is it realistic? Would term limits in fact diminish the number of careerists and produce legislators who were more national-minded and disinterested?

The most important difficulties with Will's hypothesis are twofold. One is that modern politics at all levels, local and state as well as national, is an immensely time-consuming, energy-consuming activity that demands enormous commitment from those who are attracted to it. Legislative sessions are long, constituents' demands are exigent, policy problems are increasingly complicated. As a result, politics all over the world, not just in the United States, is becoming professionalized. Men and women in all countries increasingly choose a political career at an early age and then stick with it. It seems likely that even under term limits the great majority of congressmen and senators would be drawn from this professional political class, which has not only the commitment to politics but also the requisite patience, skills, and contacts. To be sure, people's political careers would take a different shape; but they would still be political careers. The other difficulty is the reverse of the first. Just as politics is becoming more professionalized, so is almost every other occupation. As many women in particular know to their cost, it is becoming harder and harder to take career breaks — those who jump off the ladder in any profession find it increasingly hard to jump back even to the level they were on when they left, let alone the level they would have attained had they stayed. For this reason it is hard to imagine that many upwardly mobile corporate executives or successful professionals or small-business owners would take time off to serve in Congress on a citizen-legislator basis. The citizens who sought to serve on this basis would probably be largely the rich and the old.

VOTER-PROOFING

Despite their differences, term limits and the proposals offered here have in common the fact that they seek major changes in America's political institutions — in some cases involving an amendment to the Constitution. But of course America's politicians are free to alter the way they behave in the context of the country's existing institutions. They can try to find alternative ways of insulating at least some aspects of policymaking from the intense campaigning and electioneering pressures they are now under.

Short of taking difficult issues out of electoral politics altogether, there are tactics that could be employed. Most of them are out of keeping with the contemporary American preferences for direct democracy, high levels of political participation, and the maximum exposure of all political processes to the public gaze; but that is precisely their strength. Bismarck is reputed to have said that there are two things one should never watch being make: sausages and laws. Both should be judged more by the end result than by the precise circumstances of their manufacture.

One available tactic might be called "the collusion of the elites." There may be occasions on which the great majority of America's politicians, in both the executive and legislative branches, are able to agree that an issue is of such overriding importance to the nation that it must be dealt with at almost any cost; that the politicians involved must therefore be prepared to set aside their ideological and other differences in the interests of finding a workable solution; and that having found a solution, they must stick together in presenting it to what may well be a disgruntled or even hostile electorate. In order to be successful, the collusion-of-elites tactic requires not only a substantial degree of bipartisanship (or, better still, nonpartisanship) but also unusually small terms of negotiators, complete secrecy (not a single ray of "sunshine" must penetrate the proceedings), and the presentation to Congress and the public of a comprehensive, all-or-nothing, take-it-or-leave-it proposal.

The number of occasions on which politicians will be prepared to set aside their ideological differences and pool their political risks in this fashion will inevitably be small. There were no signs that such a spirit might prevail when President Clinton and the Republican majorities in Congress wrangled over how to cut the budget deficit last winter. But there have been instances of the successful collusion of elites, even in relatively recent times.

One of them occurred in 1983, when representatives of President Reagan and the two party leaderships on Capitol Hill colluded to save the Social Security system, which at that time was in imminent danger of bankruptcy. Paul Light's classic account of the 1983 Social Security reform, *Artful Work* (1985), is in effect a case study of how to conduct collusion-of-elites politics and of the circumstances in which it may succeed. The so-called Gang of Seventeen that was originally put together to hammer out a deal (and was later reduced to a Gang of Nine) excluded all the more-extreme ideologues and met in circumstances of great secrecy, even using, according to one participant, "unmarked limos."

Of the Gang of Seventeen's activities, Light writes,

The meetings seemed to inaugurate a new form of presidential-congressional government. The meetings were secret. There were no minutes or transcripts. All conversations were strictly off the record. The gang was free to discuss all of the options without fear of political retaliation. It...[existed] completely outside of the constitutional system.

Ultimately, as Light relates, the "secret gang built a compromise, wrapped it in a bipartisan flag, and rammed it through Congress. There was no other way to move. It was government by fait accompli." It was also successful government — and none of the participants suffered electoral damage.

Another possible tactic, with many similarities to the collusion of elites, might be called "putting it into commission." If taking tough decisions is too risky politically, then get someone else to take them. If someone else cannot be found to take them, then make someone else *appear* to take them. The someone else need not be but usually will be a bipartisan or nonpartisan commission of some kind.

Such a commission, the National Commission on Social Security Reform, played a role in the passage of the 1983 act, but an even better example was the procedure adopted by Congress in 1990 for closing redundant military bases. Earlier practice had been almost a caricature of Congress's traditional decision-making process. The Secretary of Defense would propose a program of base closures. Senators and congressmen would immediately leap to the defense of targeted bases in their home states or districts. They of course had the support of their colleagues, who were threatened with or feared base closures in *their* home states or districts. Almost never did anyone manage to close any bases.

Realizing that the process was absurd and that huge sums of taxpayers' money were being wasted in keeping redundant bases open, Congress decided to protect itself from itself. It established the Defense Base Closure and Realignment Commission, which employed an extraordinarily simple formula. The Defense Secretary every two years published a list of the bases he proposed to close, together with a statement of criteria he had used in compiling his list. The commission then examined the list in light of the criteria, held public hearings, and recommended a modified list (with additions as well as deletions) to the President. The President was obliged to accept the commission's list as a whole or reject it as a whole. If, as invariably happened, he accepted it, Congress could intervene only if within forty-five legislative days it passed a bill overriding the President's decision and rejecting the whole list. This it never did.

The formula was a near miracle of voter-proofing. Members of Congress were left free to protest the closure of bases in their home districts or states, but the decision was ultimately taken by the President, who could nonetheless ascribe all blame to the commission, and all Congress had to do for the President's decision to take effect was to do nothing. In the event, hundreds of bases were closed and millions of dollars saved, but no member of Congress ever had to vote — and be seen by his constituents to be voting — in favor of closing a base near home. Beyond any question the results were in America's national interest.

It is not wholly fantastic to suppose that the President in odd-numbered years might, on the basis of advice received from a bipartisan commission, announce a list of "program eliminations," which Congress could countermand only by voting to reject the list as a whole. Presidents would probably prefer to put forward such lists at the beginning of their first term in office — or at any time during their second term — when they, at least, were not up for re-election.

A final tactic, which could also be adopted without major institutional change, might be described as "thinking big." Proposals that are put forward on a piecemeal basis can also be opposed, and in all probability defeated, on a piecemeal basis. In contrast, large-scale, broad-based proposals may have a better chance of success simply by virtue of their comprehensiveness. They can provide something for everyone — conservatives as well as liberals, deficit cutters as well as program defenders, residents of the Sun Belt as well as of the Rust Belt. Gains as well as losses can be broadcast widely. The 1983 Social Security reform and the 1986 tax reform were certainly "big thoughts" of this general type. So, in its way, was the recent base-closure program.

Tactics like these — the collusion of elites, putting issues into commission, and thinking big — all have their virtues, but they also suffer from being tactics in the pejorative as well as the descriptive sense. At bottom they are somewhat cynical devices for getting around the real difficulty, which is the hyper-responsiveness of American politicians that is induced by their having to run scared so much of the time. Although it would be harder, it would be better over the long term to confront this problem directly and try to bring about at least some of the fundamental institutional changes proposed here. The American people cannot govern themselves. They therefore need to find appropriate means of choosing representatives who can do a decent job of governing on their behalf, and that means giving the people's representatives space, time, and freedom in which to take decisions, knowing that if they get them wrong, they will be punished by the voters. In twentieth-century America the airy myths of agency democracy are precisely that: myths. What America needs today, though it does not seem to know it, is a more realistic and down-to-earth form of division-of-labor democracy.

THE CONSTITUTIONAL FRAMEWORK

Introduction to
the Constitutional Framework

James C. Simeon

C anada's hybrid Constitution is the main focus of this section that includes the most pertinent parts of the Constitution Acts, 1867 and 1982, along with a summary of recent constitutional events. Constitutional reform has been an intensive and ongoing preoccupation of Canadian governments for at least the last forty years. On October 26, 1992 Canada held a national referendum to determine whether governments in Canada should proceed with ratification of the Charlottetown Accord. It failed to receive an overall national majority, and failed to carry, most notably, in Quebec, Alberta, and British Columbia. The defeat of the Charlottetown Accord reflected the clear lack of consensus in Canada on issues of constitutional reform. Canada's so-called, constitutional "crisis" will continue, so it seems, for the foreseeable future. The Canadian Constitution, both its written and unwritten components, is the foundation of our federal system of government. It also provides the preconditions for the theory and practice of public administration in Canada.

The Constitution Act, 1867, As Amended

Government of Canada

An Act for the Union of Canada, Nova Scotia, and New Brunswick, and the Government thereof; and for Purposes connected therewith.
(*29th March, 1867.*)

Preamble

WHEREAS the Provinces of Canada, Nova Scotia and New Brunswick have expressed their Desire to be federally united into One Dominion under the Crown of the United Kingdom of Great Britain and Ireland, with a Constitution similar in Principle to that of the United Kingdom:

And whereas such a Union would conduce to the Welfare of the Provinces and promote the Interests of the British Empire:

And whereas on the Establishment of the Union by Authority of Parliament it is expedient, not only that the Constitution of the Legislative Authority in the Dominion be provided for, but also that the Nature of the Executive Government therein be declared:

And whereas it is expedient that Provision be made for the eventual Admission into the Union of other Parts of British North America:

. . . .

Executive Power

9. The Executive Government and Authority of and over Canada is hereby declared to continue and be vested in the Queen.

10. The Provisions of this Act referring to the Governor General extend and apply to the Governor General for the Time being of Canada, or other the Chief Executive Officer or Administrator for the Time being carrying on the Government of Canada on behalf and in the Name of the Queen, by whatever Title he is designated.

11. There shall be a Council to aid and advise in the Government of Canada, to be styled the Queen's Privy Council for Canada; and the Persons who are to be Members of that Council shall be from Time to Time chosen and summoned by the Governor General and sworn in as Privy Councillors, and Members thereof may be from Time to Time removed by the Governor General.

. . . .

Legislative Power

17. There shall be One Parliament for Canada, consisting of the Queen, an Upper House styled the Senate, and the House of Commons.

. . . .

The Senate

. . . .

26. If at any Time on the Recommendation of the Governor General the Queen thinks fit to direct that Four or Eight Members be added to the Senate, the Governor General may by Summons to Four or Eight qualified Persons (as the Case may be), representing equally the Four Divisions of Canada, add to the Senate accordingly.

27. In case of such Addition being at any Time made, the Governor General shall not summon any Person to the Senate, except on a further like Direction by the Queen on the like

Recommendation, to represent one of the Four Divisions until such Division is represented by Twenty-four Senators and no more.

28. The Number of Senators shall not at any Time exceed One Hundred and twelve.

. . . .

Money Votes: Royal Assent

. . . .

53. Bills for appropriating any Part of the Public Revenue, or for imposing any Tax or Impost, shall originate in the House of Commons.

54. It shall not be lawful for the House of Commons to adopt or pass any Vote, Resolution, Address, or Bill for the Appropriation of any Part of the Public Revenue, or of any Tax or Impost, to any Purpose that has not been first recommended to that House by Message of the Governor General in the Session in which such Vote, Resolution, Address or Bill is proposed.

55. Where a Bill passed by the Houses of the Parliament is presented to the Governor General for the Queen's Assent, he shall declare, according to his Discretion, but subject to the Provisions of this Act and to Her Majesty's Instructions, either that he assents thereto in the Queen's Name, or that he withholds the Queen's Assent, or that he reserves the Bill for the Signification of the Queen's Pleasure.

56. Where the Governor General assents to a Bill in the Queen's Name, he shall by the first convenient Opportunity send an authentic Copy of the Act to One of Her Majesty's Principal Secretaries of State, and if the Queen in Council within Two Years after Receipt thereof by the Secretary of State thinks fit to disallow the Act, such Disallowance (with a Certificate of the Secretary of State of the Day on which the Act was received by him) being signified by the Governor General, by Speech or Message to each of the Houses of the Parliament or by Proclamation, shall annul the Act from and after the Day of such Signification.

. . . .

DISTRIBUTION OF LEGISLATIVE POWERS

Powers of the Parliament

Legislative Authority of Parliament of Canada

91. It shall be lawful for the Queen, by and with the Advice and Consent of the Senate and House of Commons, to make Laws for the Peace, Order, and good Government of Canada, in relation to all Matters not coming within the Classes of Subjects by this Act assigned exclusively to the Legislatures of the Provinces; and for greater Certainty, but not so as to restrict the Generality of the foregoing Terms of this Section, it is hereby declared that (notwithstanding anything in this Act) the exclusive Legislative Authority of the Parliament of Canada extends to all Matters coming within the Classes of Subjects next hereinafter enumerated; that is to say —

1. Repealed.
1A. The Public Debt and Property.
2. The Regulation of Trade and Commerce.
2A. Unemployment insurance.
3. The raising of Money by any Mode or System of Taxation.
4. The borrowing of Money on the Public Credit.
5. Postal Service.
6. The Census and Statistics.
7. Militia, Military and Naval Service, and Defence.
8. The fixing of and providing for the Salaries and Allowances of Civil and other Officers of the Government of Canada.
9. Beacons, Buoys, Lighthouses, and Sable Island.
10. Navigation and Shipping.
11. Quarantine and the Establishment and Maintenance of Marine Hospitals.
12. Sea Coast and Inland Fisheries.
13. Ferries between a Province and any British or Foreign Country or between Two Provinces.
14. Currency and Coinage.
15. Banking, Incorporation of Banks, and the Issue of Paper Money.
16. Savings Banks.
17. Weights and Measures.
18. Bills of Exchange and Promissory Notes.
19. Interest.

20. Legal Tender.
21. Bankruptcy and Insolvency.
22. Patents of Invention and Discovery.
23. Copyrights.
24. Indians, and Lands reserved for the Indians.
25. Naturalization and Aliens.
26. Marriage and Divorce.
27. The Criminal Law, except the Constitution of Courts of Criminal Jurisdiction, but including the Procedure in Criminal Matters.
28. The Establishment, Maintenance, and Management of Penitentiaries.
29. Such Classes of Subjects as are expressly excepted in the Enumeration of the Classes of Subjects by this Act assigned exclusively to the Legislatures of the Provinces.

And any Matter coming within any of the Classes of Subjects enumerated in this Section shall not be deemed to come within the Class of Matters of a local or private Nature comprised in the Enumeration of the Classes of Subjects by this Act assigned exclusively to the Legislatures of the Provinces.

Exclusive Powers of Provincial Legislatures

Subjects of Exclusive Provincial Legislation

92. In each Province the Legislature may exclusively make Laws in relation to Matters coming within the Classes of Subject next hereinafter enumerated; that is to say —

1. Repealed.
2. Direct Taxation within the Province in order to the raising of a Revenue for Provincial Purposes.
3. The borrowing of Money on the sole Credit of the Province.
4. The Establishment and Tenure of Provincial Offices and the Appointment and Payment of Provincial Officers.
5. The Management and Sale of the Public Lands belonging to the Province and of the Timber and Wood thereon.
6. The Establishment, Maintenance, and Management of Public and Reformatory Prisons in and for the Province.
7. The Establishment, Maintenance, and Management of Hospitals, Asylums, Charities, and Eleemosynary Institutions in and for the Province, other than Marine Hospitals.

143

8. Municipal Institutions in the Province.
9. Shop, Saloon, Tavern, Auctioneer, and other Licences in order to the raising of a Revenue for Provincial, Local, or Municipal Purposes.
10. Local Works and Undertakings other than such as are of the following Classes: —
    (a) Lines of Steam or other Ships, Railways, Canals, Telegraphs, and other Works and Undertakings connecting the Province with any other or others of the Provinces, or extending beyond the Limits of the Province;
    (b) Lines of Steam Ships between the Province and any British or Foreign Country;
    (c) Such Works as, although wholly situate within the Province, are before or after their Execution declared by the Parliament of Canada to be for the general Advantage of Canada or for the Advantage of Two or more of the Provinces.
11. The Incorporation of Companies with Provincial Objects.
12. The Solemnization of Marriage in the Province.
13. Property and Civil Rights in the Province.
14. The Administration of Justice in the Province, including the Constitution, Maintenance, and Organization of Provincial Courts, both of Civil and of Criminal Jurisdiction, and including Procedure in Civil Matters in those Courts.
15. The Imposition of Punishment by Fine, Penalty, or Imprisonment for enforcing any Law of the Province made in relation to any Matter coming within any of the Classes of Subjects enumerated in this Section.
16. Generally all Matters of a merely local or private Nature in the Province.

Non-Renewable Natural Resources, Forestry Resources and Electrical Energy

Laws Respecting Non-Renewable Natural Resources, Forestry Resources, and Electrical Energy

92A.(1) In each province, the legislature may exclusively make laws in relation to
    (a) exploration for non-renewable natural resources in the province;

(b) development, conservation and management of non-renewable natural resources and forestry resources in the province, including laws in relation to the rate of primary production therefrom; and

(c) development, conservation and management of sites and facilities in the province for the generation and production of electrical energy.

Export from Provinces of Resources

(2) In each province, the legislature may make laws in relation to the export from the province to another part of Canada of the primary production from non-renewable natural resources and forestry resources in the province and the production from facilities in the province for the generation of electrical energy, but such laws may not authorize or provide for discrimination in prices or in supplies exported to another part of Canada.

Authority of Parliament

(3) Nothing in subsection (2) derogates from the authority of Parliament to enact laws in relation to the matters referred to in that subsection and, where such a law of Parliament and a law of a province conflict, the law of Parliament prevails to the extent of the conflict.

Taxation of Resources

(4) In each province, the legislature may make laws in relation to the raising of money by any mode or system of taxation in respect of

(a) non-renewable natural resources and forestry resources in the province and the primary production therefrom, and

(b) sites and facilities in the province for the generation of electrical energy and the production therefrom, whether or not such production is exported in whole or in part from the province, but such laws may not authorize or provide for taxation that differentiates between production exported to another part of Canada and production not exported from the province.

"Primary Production"

(5) The expression "primary production" has the meaning assigned by the Sixth Schedule.

Existing Powers or Rights

(6) Nothing in subsections (1) to (5) derogates from any powers or rights that a legislature or government of a province had immediately before the coming into force of this section.

Education

Legislation Respecting Education

93. In and for each Province the Legislature may exclusively make Laws in relation to Education, subject and according to the following Provisions: —

(1) Nothing in any such law shall prejudicially affect any Right or Privilege with respect to Denominational Schools which any Class of Persons have by Law in the Province at the Union:

(2) All the Powers, Privileges, and Duties at the Union by Law conferred and imposed in Upper Canada on the Separate Schools and School Trustees of the Queen's Roman Catholic Subjects shall be and the same are hereby extended to the Dissentient Schools of the Queen's Protestant and Roman Catholic Subjects in Quebec:

(3) Where in any Province a System of Separate of Dissentient Schools exists by Law at the Union or is thereafter established by the Legislature of the Province, an Appeal shall lie to the Governor General in Council from any Act or Decision of any Provincial Authority affecting any Right or Privilege of the Protestant or Roman Catholic Minority of the Queen's Subjects in relation to Education.

(4) In case any such Provincial Law as from Time to Time seems to the Governor General in Council requisite for the due Execution of the Provisions of this Section is not made, or in case any Decision of the Governor General in Council on any Appeal under this Section is not duly executed by the proper Provincial Authority in that Behalf, then and in every such Case, and as far only as the Circumstances of each Case require,

the Parliament of Canada may make remedial Laws for the due Execution of the Provisions of this Section and of any Decision of the Governor General in Council under this Section.

Uniformity of Laws in Ontario, Nova Scotia and New Brunswick

Legislation for Uniformity of Laws in Three Provinces

94. Notwithstanding anything in this Act, the Parliament of Canada may make Provision for the Uniformity of all or any of the Laws relative to Property and Civil Rights in Ontario, Nova Scotia, and New Brunswick, and of the Procedure of all or any of the Courts in Those Three Provinces, and from and after the passing of any Act in that Behalf the Power of the Parliament of Canada to make Laws in relation to any Matter comprised in any such Act shall, notwithstanding anything in this Act, be unrestricted; but any Act of the Parliament of Canada making Provision for such Uniformity shall not have effect in any Province unless and until it is adopted and enacted as Law by the Legislature thereof.

Old Age Pensions

Legislation Respecting Old Age Pensions and Supplementary Benefits

94A. The Parliament of Canada may make laws in relation to old age pensions and supplementary benefits, including survivors, and disability benefits irrespective of age, but no such law shall affect the operation of any law present or future of a provincial legislature in relation to any such matter.

Agriculture and Immigration

Concurrent Powers of Legislation Respecting Agriculture, etc.

95. In each Province the Legislature may make Laws in relation to Agriculture in the Province, and to Immigration into the Province; and it is hereby declared that the Parliament of

Canada may from Time to Time make Laws in relation to Agriculture in all or any of the Provinces, and to Immigration into all or any of the Provinces; and any Law of the Legislature of a Province relative to Agriculture or to Immigration shall have effect in and for the Province as long and as far only as it is not repugnant to any Act of the Parliament of Canada.

. . . .

Judicature

96. The Governor General shall appoint the Judges of the Superior, District, and County Courts in each Province, except those of the Courts of Probate in Nova Scotia and New Brunswick.

. . . .

101. The Parliament of Canada may, notwithstanding anything in this Act, from Time to Time provide for the Constitution, Maintenance, and Organization of a General Court of Appeal for Canada, and for the Establishment of any additional Courts for the better Administration of the Laws of Canada.

. . . .

Revenues; Debts; Assets; Taxation

. . . .

121. All Articles of the Growth, Produce, or Manufacture of any one of the Provinces shall, from and after the Union, be admitted free into each of the other Provinces.

. . . .

Miscellaneous Provisions

. . . .

132. The Parliament and Government of Canada shall have all Powers necessary or proper for performing the Obligations of Canada or any Province thereof, as Part of the British Empire, towards Foreign Countries, arising under Treaties between the Empire and such Foreign Countries.

. . . .

ADDITIONS TO THE CONSTITUTION ACT, 1867, MADE BY THE CONSTITUTION ACT, 1982

Part I: Canadian Charter of Rights and Freedoms

Whereas Canada is founded upon principles that recognize the supremacy of God and the rule of law:

Guarantee of Rights and Freedoms

1. The *Canadian Charter of Rights and Freedoms* guarantees the rights and freedoms set out in it subject only to such reasonable limits prescribed by law as can be demonstrably justified in a free and democratic society.

Fundamental Freedoms

2. Everyone has the following fundamental freedoms:
   (a) freedom of conscience and religion;
   (b) freedom of thought, belief, opinion and expression, including freedom of the press and other media of communications
   (c) freedom of peaceful assembly; and
   (d) freedom of association.

Democratic Rights

3. Every citizen of Canada has the right to vote in an election of members of the House of Commons or of a legislative assembly and to be qualified for membership therein.

4.(1) No House of Commons and no legislative assembly shall continue for longer than five years from the date fixed for the return of the writs of a general election of its members.

(2) In time of real or apprehended war, invasion or insurrection, a House of Commons may be continued by Parliament and legislative assembly may be continued by the legislature beyond five years if such continuation is not opposed by the votes of more than one-third of the members of the House of Commons or the legislative assembly, as the case may be.

5. There shall be a sitting of Parliament and of each legislature at least once every twelve months.

Mobility Rights

6.(1) Every citizen of Canada has the right to enter, remain in and leave Canada.

(2) Every citizen of Canada and every person who has the status of a permanent resident of Canada has the right
    (a) to move to and take up residence in any province; and
    (b) to pursue the gaining of a livelihood in any province.

(3) The rights specified in subsection (2) are subject to
    (a) any laws or practices of general application in force in a province other than those that discriminate among persons primarily on the basis of province of present or previous residence; and
    (b) any laws providing for reasonable residency requirements as a qualification for the receipt of publicly provided social services.

(4) Subsections (2) and (3) do not preclude any law, program or activity that has as its object the amelioration in a province of conditions of individuals in that province who are socially or economically disadvantaged if the rate of employment in that province is below the rate of employment in Canada.

Legal Rights

7. Everyone has the right to life, liberty and security of the person and the right not to be deprived thereof except in accordance with the principles of fundamental justice.

8. Everyone has the right to be secure against unreasonable search or seizure.

9. Everyone has the right not to be arbitrarily detained or imprisoned.

10. Everyone has the right on arrest or detention
    (a) to be informed promptly of the reasons therefor;
    (b) to retain and instruct counsel without delay and to be informed of that right; and

(c) to have the validity of the detention determined by way of *habeas corpus* and to be released if the detention is not lawful.

11. Any person charged with an offence has the right
  (a) to be informed without unreasonable delay of the specific offence;
  (b) to be tried within a reasonable time;
  (c) not to be compelled to be a witness in proceedings against that person in respect of the offence;
  (d) to be presumed innocent until proven guilty according to law in a fair and public hearing by an independent and impartial tribunal;
  (e) not to be denied reasonable bail without just cause;
  (f) except in the case of an offence under military law tried before a military tribunal, to the benefit of trial by jury where the maximum punishment for the offence is imprisonment for five years or a more severe punishment;
  (g) not to be found guilty on account of any act or omission unless, at the time of the act or omission, it constituted an offence under Canadian or international law or was criminal according to the general principles of law recognized by the community of nations;
  (h) if finally acquitted of the offence, not to be tried for it again and, if finally found guilty and punished for the offence, not to be tried or punished for it again; and
  (i) if found guilty of the offence and if the punishment for the offence has been varied between the time of commission and the time of sentencing, to the benefit of the lesser punishment.

12. Everyone has the right not to be subjected to any cruel and unusual treatment or punishment.

13. A witness who testifies in any proceedings has the right not to have any incriminating evidence so given used to incriminate that witness in any other proceedings, except in a prosecution for perjury or for the giving of contradictory evidence.

14. A party or witness in any proceedings who does not understand or speak the language in which the proceedings are conducted or who is deaf has the right to the assistance of an interpreter.

Equality Rights

15.(1) Every individual is equal before and under the law and has the right to the equal protection and equal benefit of the law without discrimination and, in particular, without discrimination based on race, national or ethnic origin, colour, religion, sex, age or mental or physical disability.

(2) Subsection (1) does not preclude any law, program or activity that has as its object the amelioration of conditions of disadvantaged individuals or groups including those that are disadvantaged because of race, national or ethnic origin, colour, religion, sex, age or mental or physical disability.

Official Languages of Canada

16.(1) English and French are the official languages of Canada and have equality of status and equal rights and privileges as to their use in all institutions of the Parliament and government of Canada.

(2) English and French are the official languages of New Brunswick and have equality of status and equal rights and privileges to their use in all institutions of the legislature and government of New Brunswick.

(3) Nothing in this Charter limits the authority of Parliament or a legislature to advance the equality of status or use of English and French.

17.(1) Everyone has the right to use English or French in any debates and other proceedings of the legislature of New Brunswick.

(2) Everyone has the right to use English or French in any debates and other proceedings of the legislature of New Brunswick.

18.(1) The statutes, records and journals of Parliament shall be printed and published in English and French and both language versions are equally authoritative.

(2) The statutes, records and journals of the legislature of New Brunswick shall be printed and published in English and French and both language versions are equally authoritative.

19.(1) Either English or French may be used by any person in, or in any pleading in or process issuing from, any court established by Parliament.

(2) Either English or French may be used by any person in, or in any pleading in or process issuing from, any court of New Brunswick.

20.(1) Any member of the public in Canada has the right to communicate with, and to receive available services from, any head or central office of an institution of the Parliament or government of Canada in English or French, and has the same right with respect to any other office of any such institution where
> (a) there is a significant demand for communications with and services from that office in such language; or
> (b) due to the nature of the office, it is reasonable that communications with and services from that office be available in both English and French.

(2) Any member of the public in New Brunswick has the right to communicate with, and to receive available services from, any office of an institution of the legislature or government of New Brunswick in English or French.

21. Nothing in sections 16 to 20 abrogates or derogates from any right, privilege or obligation with respect to the English and French languages, or either of the, that exists or is continued by virtue of any other provision of the Constitution of Canada.

22. Nothing in sections 16 to 20 abrogates or derogates from any legal or customary right or privilege acquired or enjoyed either before or after the coming into force of this Charter with respect to any language that is not English or French.

Minority Language Educational Rights

23.(1) Citizens of Canada
> (a) whose first language learned and still understood is that of the English or French linguistic minority population of the province in which they reside, or
> (b) who have received their primary school instruction in Canada in English or French and reside in a province where the language in which they received that

instruction is the language of the English or French linguistic minority population of the province,

have the right to have their children receive primary and secondary instruction in that language in that province.

(2) Citizens of Canada of whom any child has received or is receiving primary or secondary school instruction in English or French in Canada, have the right to have all their children receive primary and secondary school instruction in the same language.

(3) The right of citizens of Canada under subsections (1) and (2) to have their children receive primary and secondary school instruction in the language of the English or French linguistic minority population of a province

  (a) applies wherever in the province the number of children of citizens who have such a right is sufficient to warrant the provision to them out of public funds of minority language instruction; and

  (b) includes, where the number of those children so warrants, the right to have them receive that instruction in minority language educational facilities provided out of public funds.

Enforcement

24.(2) Anyone whose rights or freedoms, as guaranteed by this Charter, have been infringed or denied may apply to a court of competent jurisdiction to obtain such remedy as the court considers appropriate and just in the circumstances.

(2) Where, in proceedings under subsection (1), a court concludes that evidence was obtained in a manner that infringed or denied any rights or freedoms guaranteed by this Charter, the evidence shall be excluded if it is established that, having regard to all the circumstances, the admission of it in the proceedings would bring the administration of justice into disrepute.

General

25. The guarantee in this Charter of certain rights and freedoms shall not be construed so as to abrogate or derogate from any aboriginal, treaty or other rights or freedoms that pertain to the aboriginal peoples of Canada including

(a) any rights or freedoms that have been recognized by the Royal Proclamation of October 7, 1763; and

(b) any rights or freedoms that now exist by way of land claims agreements or may be so acquired.

26. The guarantee in this Charter of certain rights and freedoms shall not be construed as denying the existence of any other rights or freedoms that exist in Canada.

27. This Charter shall be interpreted in a manner consistent with the preservation and enhancement of the multicultural heritage of Canadians.

28. Notwithstanding anything in this Charter, the rights and freedoms referred to in it are guaranteed equally to male and female persons.

29. Nothing in this Charter abrogates or derogates from any rights or privileges guaranteed by or under the Constitution of Canada in respect of denominational, separate or dissentient schools.

30. A reference in this Charter to a Province or to the legislative assembly or legislature of a province shall be deemed to include a reference to the Yukon Territory and the Northwest Territories, or to the appropriate legislative authority thereof, as the case may be.

31. Nothing in this Charter extends the legislative powers of any body or authority.

Application of Charter

32.(1) This Charter applies

(a) to the Parliament and Government of Canada in respect of all matters within the authority of Parliament including all matters relating to the Yukon Territory and Northwest Territories; and

(b) to the legislature and government of each province in respect of all matters within the authority of the legislature of each province.

(2) Notwithstanding subsection (1), section 15 shall not have effect until three years after this section comes into force.

33.(1) Parliament or the legislature of a province may expressly declare in an Act of Parliament or of the legislature, as the case may be, that the Act or a provision thereof shall operate not-withstanding a provision included in section 2 or sections 7 to 15 of this Charter.

(2) An Act or a provision of an Act in respect of which a declaration made under this section is in effect shall have such operation as it would have but for the provision of this Charter referred to in the declaration.

(3) A declaration made under subsection (1) shall cease to have effect five years after it comes into force or on such earlier date as may be specified in the declaration.

(4) Parliament or the legislature of a province may re-enact a declaration made under subsection (1).

(5) Subsection (3) applies in respect of a re-enactment made under subsection (4).

Citation

34. This Part may be cited as the *Canadian Charter of Rights and Freedoms.*

. . . .

Part V: Procedure for Amending Constitution of Canada

38.(1) An amendment to the Constitution of Canada may be made by proclamation issued by the Governor General under the Great Seal of Canada where so authorized by
    (a) resolutions of the Senate and House of Commons; and
    (b) resolutions of the legislative assemblies of at least two-thirds of the provinces that have, in the aggre-gate, according to the then latest general census, at least fifty per cent of the population of all the provinces.

(2) An amendment made under subsection (1) that derogates from the legislative powers, the proprietary rights or any other

rights or privileges of the legislature or government of a province shall require a resolution supported by a majority of the members of each of the Senate, the House of Commons and the legislative assemblies required under subsection (1).

(3) An amendment referred to in subsection (2) shall not have effect in a province the legislative assembly of which has expressed its dissent thereto by resolution supported by a majority of its members prior to the issue of the proclamation to which the amendment relates unless that legislative assembly, subsequently, by resolution supported by a majority of its members, revokes its dissent and authorizes the amendment.

(4) A resolution of dissent made for the purposes of subsection (3) may be revoked at any time before or after the issue of the proclamation to which it relates.

39.(1) A proclamation shall not be issued under subsection 38(1) before the expiration of one year from the adoption of the resolution initiating the amendment procedure thereunder, unless the legislative assembly of each province has previously adopted a resolution of assent or dissent.

(2) A proclamation shall not be issued under subsection 38(1) after the expiration of three years from the adoption of the resolution initiating the amendment procedure thereunder.

40. Where an amendment is made under subsection 38(1) that transfers provincial legislative powers relating to education or other cultural matters from provincial legislatures to Parliament, Canada shall provide reasonable compensation to any province to which the amendment does not apply.

41. An amendment to the Constitution of Canada in relation to the following matters may be made by proclamation issued by the Governor General under the Great Seal of Canada only where authorized by resolutions of the Senate and House of Commons and of the legislative assembly of each province:
- (a) the office of the Queen, the Governor General and the Lieutenant Governor of a province;
- (b) the right of a province to a number of members in the House of Commons not less than the number of Senators by which the province is entitled to be represented at the time this Part comes into force;

(c) subject to section 43, the use of English or the French language;

(d) the composition of the Supreme Court of Canada; and

(e) an amendment to this Part.

42.(1) An amendment to the Constitution of Canada in relation to the following matters may be made only in accordance with subsection 38(1):

(a) the principle of proportionate representation of the provinces in the House of Commons prescribed by the Constitution of Canada;

(b) the powers of the Senate and the method of selecting Senators;

(c) the number of members by which a province is entitled to be represented in the Senate and the residence qualification of Senators;

(d) subject to paragraph 41(d), the Supreme Court of Canada;

(e) the extension of existing provinces into the territories; and

(f) notwithstanding any other law or practice, the establishment of new provinces.

(2) Subsections 38(2) to (4) do not apply in respect of amendments in relation to matters referred to in subsection (1).

43. An amendment to the Constitution of Canada in relation to any provision that applies to one or more, but not all, provinces, including

(a) any alteration to boundaries between provinces, and

(b) any amendment to any provision that relates to the use of the English or the French language within a province,

may be made by proclamation issued by the Governor General under the Great Seal of Canada only where so authorized by resolutions of the Senate and House of Commons and of the legislative assembly of each province to which the amendment applies.

44. Subject to sections 41 and 42, Parliament may exclusively make laws amending the Constitution of Canada in relation to the executive government of Canada or the Senate and House of Commons.

45. Subject to section 41, the legislature of each province may exclusively make laws amending the constitution of the province.

46.(1) The procedures for amendment under sections 38, 41, 42 and 43 may be initiated either by the Senate or the House of Commons or by the legislative assembly of a province.

(2) A resolution of assent made for the purposes of this Part may be revoked at any time before the issue of a proclamation authorized by it.

47.(1) An amendment to the Constitution of Canada made by proclamation under section 38, 41, 42 or 43 may be made without a resolution of the Senate authorizing the issue of the proclamation if, within one hundred and eighty days after the adoption by the House of Commons of a resolution authorizing its issue, the Senate has not adopted such a resolution and if, at any time after the expiration of that period, the House of Commons again adopts the resolution.

(2) Any period when Parliament is prorogued or dissolved shall not be counted in computing the one hundred and eighty day period referred to in subsection (1).

48. The Queen's Privy Council for Canada shall advise the Governor General to issue a proclamation under this Part forthwith on the adoption of the resolutions required for an amendment made by proclamation under this Part.

49. A constitutional conference composed of the Prime Minister of Canada and the first ministers of the provinces shall be convened by the Prime Minister of Canada within fifteen years after this Part comes into force to review the provisions of this Part.

. . . .

Part VII: General

52.(1) The Constitution of Canada is the supreme law of Canada, and any law that is inconsistent with the provisions of the Constitution is, to the extent of the inconsistency, of no force or effect.

(2) The Constitution of Canada includes
    (a) the *Canada Act 1982*, including this Act;
    (b) the Acts and orders referred to in the schedule; and
    (c) any amendment to any Act or order referred to in paragraph (a) or (b).

(3) Amendments to the Constitution of Canada shall be made only in accordance with the authority contained in the Constitution of Canada.

Summary of
Constitutional Events

*Janice E. Nicholson
and Diane Jurkowski*

The exclusion of Quebec from the final agreement on the Constitution Act of 1982 led during the past decade to an attempt to remedy a situation in which Quebec regarded itself as excluded from the most important constitutional event in the history of Canadian federalism. In particular, it was concerned to establish five minimum conditions for its participation in the 1982 Constitution Act. These were:

1. recognition of Quebec's distinctive political and cultural nature;
2. limitation of the federal government's spending power;
3. an adoption of the unanimity rule for all constitutional amendments (Section 41 of the 1982 Constitution Act);
4. greater powers for Quebec on immigration;
5. participation in the appointment of judges to the Supreme Court of Canada.

The eleven first ministers accepted these conditions at Meech Lake on April 30, 1987. They were ratified in their legal form in June 1987. However, Section 41 of the Constitution Act, *1982* specified that the Accord had to be ratified by the Parliament of Canada and all the provincial legislatures within three years.

By the end of June 1990, two provinces, Manitoba and Newfoundland, had failed to ratify the Accord, and the process to amend the Constitution Act of 1982 to make it acceptable to Quebec had failed.

On September 4, 1990, a Commission on the Political and Constitutional Future of Quebec was created under legislation adopted unanimously by all political parties in the Quebec National Assembly. It was given a mandate to study and analyze the political and constitutional status of Quebec and to make recommendations. Its membership included the Premier of Quebec, Mr. Robert Bourassa, and the leader of the official Opposition, Mr. Jacques Parizeau. This commission (The Bélanger-Campeau Commission) submitted its report on March 27, 1991.

Prior to this, in March 1990, the Quebec Liberal Party formed a Constitutional Committee chaired by Jean Allaire. The committee began its first working sessions in April 1990, but after the failure of the Meech Lake Accord in June 1990, the committee increased its activities and tabled a report with the Executive Committee of the Quebec Liberal Party by the end of January 1991. The report of the Constitutional Committee (Allaire Report) was adopted by the Quebec Liberal Party at its convention on March 9, 1991.

Essentially both reports recommended major constitutional changes and a complete restructuring of the relationship of Quebec and Canada. The Allaire Report, adopted by the Quebec government, proposed three major areas of reform:

1. political autonomy of Quebec, which will be achieved by Quebec assuming a far wider range of powers including taxation and revenue, immigration, foreign policy, and native affairs. Quebec would share these powers with the federal government. The only exclusive powers the federal government would have would be in the areas of defence, customs and tariffs, management of the common debt, currency and equalization payments.

2. formation of a Quebec-Canadian economic union which would guarantee free movement of persons, goods, and

capital. Reduction in the size of the federal government and restrictions on the taxation powers of the federal government.

3. the establishment of a new Quebec-Canada structure including a new constitution, the maintenance of a common Parliament, the abolition of the Senate and reform of the Bank of Canada.

The Quebec government passed legislation to ensure that a referendum would be held by the autumn of 1992. The purpose of this referendum was to either ratify the agreement with Canada on the proposed reforms, or to ratify Quebec's assumption of sovereign statehood along with an offer to form an economic union with Canada.

The reaction of the federal government and the various provincial legislatures was to establish their own commissions and committees. The most publicized being the Citizens' Forum chaired by Mr. Keith Spicer. This commission had the mandate to hear from citizens and groups across the country on constitutional issues. It reported at the end of June 1991. Essentially, it reflected the deep disillusionment of the citizens on the current state of affairs: lack of confidence with political parties and politicians, concern for the economic problems, and bewilderment regarding the restructuring of the Quebec-Canada relationship. The report recommended that special constitutional arrangements should be made for Quebec to allow it the freedom and the means to be itself. The report also recommended native self-government for the aboriginal peoples, shorter parliamentary sessions, more free votes, and a fundamental reform of the Senate.

Among the many commissions, committees and hearings was the House of Commons/Senate committee known as the Committee for a Renewed Canada or the Beaudoin-Dobbie Committee. It issued its report in the first week of March 1992. Among its recommendations was a Canada clause that states the nation's principles and values. In addition it recommended the "promotion of Quebec as a distinct society." Other recommendations included:

i) the inherent right of aboriginal peoples to self-government;
ii) property rights be included in the Charter of Rights and Freedoms;

163

iii) election of senators on the basis of proportional representation;

iv) the power of the Senate should be similar to the House
of Commons except on supply (money) bills;

v) an expansion of provincial powers;

vi) an economic union which could disallow provincial restrictions on the movement of goods, services, people, and
capital;

vii) a social covenant which would commit governments to
fostering comprehensive and universal social and health
services, education, unionization, and preserving the environment.

This report formed the basis for the discussions between the
federal minister responsible for constitutional affairs, Mr. Joe
Clarke, the provincial premiers, including Quebec, territorial
leaders, and the native leaders. Throughout the summer of 1992
these discussions continued with many trials, tribulations, and
doubts. It frequently looked as if no agreement would be
reached.

At last on August 28, 1992, an agreement was reached at
Charlottetown, PEI. The agreement had a considerable resemblance to the Beaudoin-Dobbie Committee recommendations.

It was recommended that there would be:

i) a Canada clause;

ii) a social and economic union;

iii) Quebec recognized as a distinct society;

iv) recognition of the inherent right of self-government for
aboriginal peoples:

v) a reformed Senate;

vi) greater degree of federal/provincial power sharing.

However, there were differences, and it was some of these
differences that became the focus of controversy in the debate
leading up to the referendum.

It was proposed that:

1. The Senate should have six elected senators from each
province and one senator for each territory, aboriginal representation in the Senate should be guaranteed by the
Constitution.

But the Senate would not be allowed to block money bills and it could not defeat a government with a majority in the House of Commons on any legislation. Therefore, this was not a Triple E Senate, as the Senate was not as powerful as the House of Commons. Thus, this part of the agreement was unpopular in the West.

Additionally, Quebec was guaranteed 25 percent of the seats in the House of Commons regardless of its population size. This was also greatly resented in the West.

2. A greater sharing of power between the federal government and the provinces was indicated, but some people in Quebec considered this insufficient.

3. The inherent right to self-government for aboriginal people was recognized and it was recommended that the Constitution Act, *1982* should be changed to recognize this right. However, this was opposed by some aboriginal leaders, especially women, who were opposed to traditional forms of Native government, since they considered that women were put in a subordinate role in such a traditional society.

4. Finally, the amending formula was to be altered so that in some areas a unanimity rule would apply, that is, the unanimous agreement of Parliament and the provinces. These areas would be:
   (a) amendments relating to any changes in the Senate (once it was reformed);
   (b) amendments affecting the House of Commons including Quebec's guarantee of 25 percent of the seats;
   (c) matters affecting the creation of new provinces. Critics argued that the introduction of a unanimity rule into the amending formula made it virtually impossible to change the Constitution once it was amended along the lines of the Charlottetown Accord.

Before the federal referendum, the Quebec government withdrew the legislation requiring that a referendum be held in Quebec by the autumn of 1992, since the federal government had agreed to a federal referendum on the Charlottetown Accord.

Despite strenuous campaigning on the part of the federal government and some provincial premiers, the Charlottetown Accord was defeated in the October 26, 1992 referendum. In order to pass, the accord required a majority of affirmative votes in all the provinces. In fact, a number of provinces voted against the accord including Quebec, British Columbia, and Alberta. In several provinces, including Ontario, the vote was very close.

As a result of this defeat, it is thought that the federal government will not pursue any further constitutional initiatives before the next federal election.

Separatists had received a boost from the election of the Parti Québécois to form the provincial government in Quebec in September 1994. The Parti Québécois was committed to Quebec sovereignty. This was the second occasion on which the issue would be placed before the electorate as a referendum. In the 1980 referendum, Quebecers had rejected independence by a 60 to 40 percent margin. But the Parti Québécois was resolved to try again. If they were successful in the 1995 referendum, the government would then enter into negotiations with the rest of Canada to work out a new political and economic partnership.

On October 30, 1995, a referendum was held in Quebec. The question asked Quebecers:

"Do you agree that Quebec should become sovereign, after having made a formal offer to Canada for a new economic and political partnership, with the scope of the bill respecting the future of Quebec and of the agreement signed on June 12, 1995?"

The recorded vote was:

No:	50.6%	(2,631,526)
Yes:	49.4%	(2,308,028)

The referendum results were perceived as a narrow win of 50,000 for the federal government. The sovereignist forces vowed that they would not stop until they had a nation. A third referendum is planned by the Parti Québécois in two years. However, Quebec law states that two referenda cannot be held within the same mandate of a government. A provincial election is scheduled in 1998.

In response to the Quebec referendum, in September 1996, the justice minister sought a ruling from the Supreme Court to clarify the rules of separation. The federal government asked the court three questions:

- Can the government of Quebec take the province of Quebec out of Canada unilaterally?
- Is there a right of self-determination under international law?
- If there is a conflict between domestic and international law on the question, which one takes precedence in Canada?

On February 3, 1996, Bill C-110 passed Parliament and received royal assent granting veto power to Quebec, Ontario, and British Columbia. In addition, any two prairie provinces with 50 percent of the regional population or any two Atlantic provinces with 50 percent of the regional population, can now veto any constitutional amendment. The law effectively creates four classes of provinces. The new formula for gaining the federal government's approval is an addition to the existing constitutional amending formula, which requires seven provinces with 50 percent of the population to approve most amendments. However, the constitutional validity is in question when a simple act of Parliament can amend the Constitution Act without applying the existing constitutional amending formula.

In February 1997, the federal government filed a brief in the Supreme Court stating that Quebec has no right under domestic or international law to secede unilaterally from Confederation. However, the brief further stated that Quebec could secede through a constitutional amendment only after holding discussions with the federal and provincial governments. The case is expected to be heard in fall 1997.

Quebec has refused to participate in the court hearings, maintaining the Quebec independence will only be settled by the people through a democratic vote in a referendum. Thus, the federal government has asked the Supreme Court to appoint legal representation on Quebec's behalf.

What Does It Mean for the Nation: Death of a Political Era

Thomas J. Courchene

As the No vote gained momentum last night, with results rolling in from east to west, we Canadians were not merely rejecting the Charlottetown accord. We were asserting in no uncertain terms that the conceptions and traditions which dominated Canadian governance during the past 125 years were no longer appropriate to the Canada of today and tomorrow.

The print and electronic media will focus *ad nauseam* on why the accord went down to defeat. These post-mortems are of course appropriate and, in any event, inevitable. But they are not the essence of what is happening, since most of the elements of the accord will now begin to be implemented through the political rather than the constitutional route.

Instead, this was a referendum on the perceived legitimacy of our system and the accord as a product of this system.

From *The Globe and Mail*, October 27, 1992. Reprinted by permission of the author.

Not only were both found wanting, but the very fact that the accord was the culmination of a truly monumental exercise in consultative and executive federalism, and had the full backing of virtually all the traditional elites, means that we have seen the passing of the old political order. Long after we have forgotten the details of the accord, yesterday's date will live in the annals of our history as a defining moment of the new order.

In strict constitutional terms, what has happened is that we Canadians have completed the patriation process that began in 1982 by altering, de facto, the amending formula. The Constitution of Canada now belongs to the people of Canada and it can never be amended without our direct consent, whatever the Constitution may say on this subject. In a sense this is our Gettysburg — we now have a Constitution of, by and for the people and the unfolding task will be to transfer these principles to our governance. This is the project that was launched last night.

To understand what tomorrow will bring requires that we likewise understand the series of recent societal changes, both institutional and attitudinal, that led ultimately to the rejection of the accord. At the core of these changes is the demise of the two-founding-nations/elite-accommodation approach to governing the federation.

What made this system so effective in its heyday, when political and economic power resided in the centre, was how well it meshed with our practice of parliamentary federalism — including national parties, strict party discipline and the evolution of executive federalism. Even the existing Senate fits fully in this model, given the distribution of seats, the method of selection and the total domination by the two traditional national parties.

The impressive accomplishments of this system of governance are often taken for granted. For example, we pride ourselves on having national social programs that are far more generous than those of the United States. But how does this square with the fact that we are also far more decentralized? The answer lies in the genius of the underlying elite-accommodation system, and particularly in the fact that one of the two founding nations was a have-not province, desirous of greater autonomy.

The two-nations concept came to an abrupt end in 1982 when Quebec found out that the most significant amendment to

169

the Constitution did not require the consent of one of the founding nations. That year was also an important milestone for interpreting the Constitution as a compact among provinces.

The requirement for unanimity in the 1987–90 Meech Lake process then led to the notion of a compact among *equal* provinces. Thus symmetry became the new constitutional buzzword, almost to the point of ignoring the fact that asymmetry was one of the cornerstones of the previous order.

This was the death knell of constitutional special status, in any of its variants. What did not die at that point was the belief that elite accommodation (through top-down executive federalism) was the way to bring Quebec back into the Canadian constitutional family. Yet last night it perished, along with the notion that the Constitution is a compact among equal provinces. Provinces may continue to be conceived in terms of equality, but the constitutional compact is among citizens.

However, by far the most significant feature of 1982, and by far the most fundamental factor in undermining the existing conception of governance, was the Charter of Rights and Freedoms. This set in motion not only the process of democratizing the Constitution, but also that of undermining parliamentary government and redefining the essence of what it means to be a Canadian.

Under the Charter, rights were to be pan-Canadian in nature, not subject to the whims of provincial legislatures. Almost immediately we were faced with two profoundly different conceptions of our nation. One was federal in nature, where the cleavages were territorial: federal-provincial and interprovincial. The other was inherently non-territorial, pitting pan-Canadian Charter-rights groups against powerful vested interests.

It was also non-federal, in that the inherent dynamic was to extend Charter-type rights to ensure entitlements in other areas such as social policy, where any resulting programs must be national and uniform. Whereas opting out was an integral element in our success over our first century, almost overnight it came to symbolize what was wrong with our federation.

More disturbing, particularly for Quebeckers, is that implicit in the rhetoric of equality is the revisionist notion that our nation was always based on equality of citizens and provinces. This is the real threat to Canadian unity.

Although the Charter embodied some collective rights, it was basically an individual-rights document grounded in British common law and incorporating the due-process aspects of the *U.S. Bill of Rights*. This provided yet another vehicle for levying a broadside against the more collective visions of both the Quebecois and aboriginal societies.

No matter that the first Europeans to come to our shores marvelled at the free democratic societies of our first nations — a degree of individual freedom and democracy that was unimaginable in the Europe of the day. Our evolution of freedom and democracy, some of it modelled if not borrowed from the first nations, tends now to be intolerant of their traditional ways.

These were among the competing visions, often diametrically opposed visions, that the orchestrators of the Charlottetown accord had to grapple with. We are too close to the process to evaluate what they accomplished. However, I am willing to forecast that historians will eventually marvel at the incredible balancing act embodied in the accord.

For better or worse, however, the particulars of the deal were largely irrelevant. There is not and never will be a comprehensive compromise package that will meet with the approval of all Canadians. The more critical issue is that the package was devised within the context of a political environment and conception that had lost all legitimacy for Canadians.

There is a tendency across our land to associate this lack of legitimacy with the Prime Minister and the ruling Tories. Obviously, there is considerable truth to this. But the reality goes much deeper. On a whole host of fronts, we have become a nation of uncompromising special interests, of entitlement seekers.

While the world around us integrated and restructured, we Canadians were bent on looking inward and engaging in a negative-sum, redistributional game over entitlements, powers and transfers. Canada's domestic and international debt/deficit overhang is testimony to our catering to this process and, in the larger context, is testimony to the inability of our parliamentary system to make the shift from dealing with accommodating elites to dealing with special interest.

Beyond this, what we could not get through the market or the normal political process we aggressively pursued through a veritable constitutional feeding frenzy. Thus constitution-making ceased to be an exercise in statecraft and degenerated into a process of brokering among uncompromising and unreconcilable special interests, whose measure of success in the process

171

tended to be not what they gained in absolute terms but how they fare in relation to other special interests.

Once it was obvious that the accord was in trouble, the referendum exercise took on a life of its own. It became a costless way to vent our wrath on our system and on our leaders. There may have been a point early on in the campaign when the Yes side could have made some inroads. This would have been an attempt to level with Canadians and to sell the package on its merits. Instead — outside of Quebec, in any event — it resorted to alternating visions of national unity and fear. In a sense the Yes rhetoric became an embodiment of the problem, not of the solution. And when Yes leaders dragged in other elites, such as members of the Business Council on National Issues, they merely gave the No side a chance to vent its disillusionment concerning another topic: the Canada-U.S. free-trade agreement.

Yogi Berra was wrong; it was over before it was over!

In the aftermath of the No vote, Canadians are naturally concerned with a number of immediate issues. Will the gnomes of Zurich and the bond-rating agencies lower the boom on the Canadian dollar? Can the Prime Minister hold the Tories together? Will Robert Bourassa follow Rene Levesque in losing the referendum but winning the next election?

The manner in which these issues play out will obviously have an impact on our political and economic evolution. However, my interest is in the longer-term dynamics that are likely to flow from the No vote. Likewise, I shall sidestep the national-unity question. I am making the heroic assumption that the No vote in Quebec is sufficiently cathartic and/or symbolic so as not to lead immediately to a secessionist initiative. The issue then becomes: how will the political economy of Canada evolve, given that the constitutional status quo remains intact?

The first observation is that we have seen the end of comprehensive constitutional compromises and of the incredible notion that constitutional amendment is the preferred solution to every societal issue. This never was the Canadian way.

We were able as a society to manoeuvre brilliantly within the framework of the *British North America Act*. Without changing the written constitutional word, we went through cycles of decentralization and centralization as circumstances required. We utilized an impressive array of instruments (tax-point transfers, opting out, intergovernmental transfers, federal spending power) to achieve the goals we set for ourselves, again without formal constitutional amendment.

Moreover, Quebec was able to usher in two societal evolutions without the benefit of any constitutional favours from the rest of us. Now that the constitutional amendment route is blocked, we have no choice except to fall back on our ingenuity. This is the good news. Unfortunately, there are a few new constraints in our path.

The most important of these relates to the evolution of the global economy. Economic space is transcending political space because it is the private sector not the public sector, that is integrating globally. The economic nation-state is countering by passing some functions upward through free-trade agreements such as the Canada-U.S. pact or the European accord, or by an increase in supranational regulation.

At the same time, subnational units are now able to latch on to these agreements and pursue aspects of what we in Canada would call distinct societies. Thus, what is emerging in Europe, for example, is a regional-international rather than a national-international conception of decision-making. In order words, what we are seeing is an integrating global economy and a fragmenting global policy.

This has important implications for the economic regions of Canada. Increasingly, trade is moving away from an East-West axis and toward a North-South axis. As a result, what binds Canadians together East-West is more and more a social-policy railway, rather than an economic-policy railway. The Charlottetown accord attempted to accommodate this by transferring some economic functions (mining, forestry) downward in return for a greater federal or national role in the evolution of social policy. The challenge remains: how do we mount an East-West transfer system over a North-South trading system?

This is further complicated by the fact that:

- We are faltering economically;
- Our debt and deficit overhang has already led to an erosion of the social envelope;
- A No vote will presumably exacerbate both of the above.

The third general observation relates to the political-institutional ramifications of the No vote. One aspect of this is that there is, for the immediate future, no unifying vision of who we are as a nation or society.

Another is that Canadians sent a clear message to their elected representatives that henceforth they should pay more attention to constituency and less to party. It may be possible that we can unite behind some party or some philosophy, but the likelihood is a fragmentation of parties, none national in nature.

A final aspect here is that we have also sent our politicians a message about process. An executive-federalism, top-down approach is no longer acceptable. This is a significant shift for Canadians since, unlike Americans, we have always put more emphasis on goals than on means. This is yet another bit of the American creed creeping into our society.

What do these observations imply about the manner in which our political economy might unfold? The first point to be made is that much of what failed constitutionally will now begin to be implemented politically. For example, the existing Constitution provides an eminently workable framework for aboriginal self-government; negotiations which are continuing quite independently of the Charlottetown accord are ample testimony to this. The distinct-society provision will not be enshrined, but it will surely be factored into court decisions.

Moreover, some devolution of powers is inevitable in the context of globalization. Consider the most controversial of these devolutions, namely labour-market training. We have made a mess of training in this country. It is clear that training has to be integrated with areas like apprenticeship programs, postsecondary institutions, and the incentives in welfare programs and unemployment insurance.

Since the provinces control most of these areas, a good case can be made for devolution. Indeed, provisions are already in place for Ontario to co-ordinate more than $1 billion of training money. Quebec will surely need flexibility too, given the obvious link between human-capital development and language. And on this and other matters, British Columbia will also need flexibility as it integrates further with the Pacific Rim.

This is not a power grab by the provinces. It is the emerging economic reality, given that the needs and challenges of a Great Lakes economy are not the same as the needs and challenges of a Pacific Rim economy. The only way Ottawa can stave this off is to devise framework policies so that there is

174

flexibility for the regional economies to pursue their economic interests. If Canada is more decentralized by 2002, it will have more to do with effective policy-making in the light of the global and North American economies than with what we did or did not enshrine in 1992.

Not all areas of the accord will fare as well in the political arena. The social envelope is a case in point. The Social Charter is gone. So is the Triple-E Senate which, with more than 70 per cent of senators from have-not provinces, would probably have mounted a legislative program driven by interregional equity. And there is now no special spending-power provision, so that Ottawa will be subject to court challenge if it attempts to design programs in provincial jurisdiction.

To this one must add the fact that, short of some miracle, the Commons will be fragmented in terms of both parties and vision. If there is added pressure from the international sector because of the failure of the accord, it is not hard to envision that aspects of the social envelope will become a hard sell.

The reality is that we have gone too far in the direction of a transfer economy. Transfers designed to accommodate "place prosperity" are in obvious trouble, but I think our sharing principles remain sufficiently intact to be generous on the "people prosperity" front. Nonetheless, it is evident that efforts toward economic union will intensify in the Maritimes and will surface in the Prairies as well.

The impact on central institutions is less clear. The complications that arose from marrying a Charter of Rights with a parliamentary system will be exacerbated with a fragmentation of parties and an erosion of party discipline. Whether this will tilt the balance in the direction of a more republican approach to governance will depend, among other things, on the evolution of the Senate.

However, if the House of Commons becomes characterized by gridlock, the likely result will be a significant devolution of effective powers to the provinces. A weakened central government would find it difficult to withstand concerted demands from the likes of Quebec, Ontario and British Columbia. In this case, not only would the federation become asymmetric, since not all provinces would want or be able to handle new powers, but Quebec would acquire the powers that it was denied under the Charlottetown accord. Quebec may accomplish through the political route what it was unable to do constitutionally.

This may or may not be a likely scenario. But the general point is that the failure of the accord will not lead to the old status quo. One reason is that much of what the accord was up to was enshrining continuing trends and/or processes; these will now be pursued politically. Another is that our prolonged focus on the constitutional dossier masked the reality of the global economy.

Both of these factors would appear to point toward a more economically oriented evolution of the federation. Complicating all of this is that the status quo on the political front is equally under siege. Here Yogi was right: if you don't know where you're going you may end up somewhere else.

[The National Referendum on the Charlottetown Accord held on October 26, 1992, provided the following results:]

	% YES	% NO
Newfoundland	62.9	36.5
P.E.I.	73.6	25.9
Nova Scotia	48.5	51.0
New Brunswick	61.4	38.0
Quebec	42.4	55.4
Ontario	49.8	49.6
Manitoba	38.1	61.5
Saskatchewan	44.4	55.2
Alberta	39.5	60.3
British Columbia	31.8	67.8
Yukon	44.2	55.3
N.W.T.	59.2	40.1
Canada	45.2	53.7

Source: Canadian Press, *Globe & Mail*, October 27, 1992.

Post-Meech Constitutional Options: A Brief Survey

Dwight Herperger and R.L. Watts

The following analysis of basic options both for the constitutional renewal process and for future institutional structures has been taken from Dwight Herperger and R.L. Watts, *Looking Forward, Looking Back: constitutional proposals of the past and their relevance in the post-Meech era*, pp. 4–8, prepared for the Council of Canadian Unity, November 1990.

OPTIONS FOR THE CONSTITUTIONAL RENEWAL PROCESS

General Issues

If the Meech Lake process has taught us anything, it is that Canadians are overwhelmingly dissatisfied with existing processes of constitutional reform. Often throughout the debate the question was asked, "What right do eleven

From *The Network*, January, 1991, 1(1): 4–6. Reprinted by permission of the Council of Canadian Unity, Communication Department, Montreal, Quebec.

men, locked in a room in secrecy, have to change *my* Constitution?" Clearly, many groups and indeed the general public felt frozen out of the process. The practice of "Executive Federalism" which effected constitutional and other reforms in recent decades has been seriously discredited. The public has made it eminently clear that they expect more extensive consultation in the process earlier on and assurances that their participation will have an impact on final outcomes. The longer-term implications of these demands are that the process will inevitably become more complex as it is further democratized.

Another consideration is the scope of constitutional reform which should be attempted. The Meech Lake Accord was an attempt to deal with the singular concern of the failure to achieve Quebec's signature to the *Constitution Act, 1982*. The underlying assumption of the strategy to achieve the Accord was that incremental reform, with a focused and more manageable agenda, would have a greater chance of success than would more comprehensive initiatives (witness for example the experiences of the Swiss federation where incremental constitutional reform has been frequent, but the recent effort at comprehensive reform was a total failure). However, the Meech Lake exercise demonstrated the difficulty of isolating specific constitutional issues from other concerns. The entrenchment of a Charter of Rights in 1982 has inspired a host of new constitutional actors who now actively seek to protect their particular constitutional identities, regardless of the agenda agreed upon by First Ministers.

The existing legal requirements for the adoption of constitutional amendments adopted in 1982 raise major difficulties for any process of constitutional reform. The requirement of legislative approval for constitutional amendments was an innovation introduced in the 1982 Constitution Act, and the Meech Lake Accord was the first major constitutional proposal to test these procedures. As became evident in the process to ratify the Accord, ratification by provincial legislatures under a three-year allowable time limit can significantly affect the momentum and dynamics of support for a constitutional proposal. Moreover, the unanimity provisions for certain kinds of amendments (Canada is unique among federations in having such a requirement) proved to be too difficult a requirement to effect constitutional change in this particular instance.

Basic Options

Status Quo

This would envision a new round of multilateral negotiations facilitated by a series of First Ministers' Conferences. Any agreed upon proposals for constitutional amendment would then follow the ratification procedures established in the *Constitution Act, 1982*. In technical terms, this would be a repeat of the process associated with the Meech Lake Accord. The Quebec government has indicated that it will not submit itself to such a process again; moreover, public reaction to the Meech Lake fiasco has made it evident that this process is no longer perceived as legitimate.

Constitutional Commissions

This option of course has already been taken up. Preceding or paralleling any substantive initiatives for reform, the federal and several provincial governments, and even non-governmental organizations, have established commissions to survey the public's views on constitutional options.

Bilateral Negotiations

The federal and Quebec governments could pursue direct bilateral negotiations as provided for under section 43 of the 1982 Constitution Act, but the potential scope for extensive constitutional modification under these provisions is rather limited. Other provincial governments may also decide to pursue direct negotiations with the federal government in tandem with an Ottawa-Quebec process.

Two-stage Process

Acknowledging the difficulties inherent in the existing amendment procedures, one approach is to undertake a two-stage process for constitutional reform. The first stage would deal only with matters relating to constitutional amendment procedures, and the second would use the revised amendment procedure to undertake reforms pertaining to institutional structures and basic rights in the federation. In any event, the first stage would require a round of multilateral negotiations and would be subject to the strictures of the existing unanimity provisions.

Unilateral Initiatives

The most dramatic of the options being considered, this approach would see Quebec or any other government present a *fait accompli*, unilaterally declaring its decision to follow a particular course of constitutional action such as separation. This would effectively raise the stakes of the debate over constitutional reform to a zero-sum dimension. While this might force other participants to accede to more substantial compromise solutions, in the resulting heat and tension it could just as easily result in the ultimate disintegration of the federation.

OPTIONS FOR FUTURE INSTITUTIONAL STRUCTURES

Basic Options

Status Quo

This would imply the continuation of the existing Canadian federal structure without consideration of any constitutional or institutional reforms in the immediate future. Given the increasing tensions and rising uncertainties witnessed during and after the Meech Lake exercise, this option appears untenable for anything but the short term. Moreover, the Quebec government has officially rejected the status quo, committing itself to a process for substantive reforms.

Adjustments of Jurisdictions within the Existing Federal Structure

Canadian federalism might be made more effective if the powers of the central government were increased in some areas and decreased in others. Federal jurisdiction might be enhanced to ensure the freer movement of people, goods and services (the European Community is often cited, even in Quebec, as a superior example in this respect). At the same time, jurisdiction over some other areas where centralization is not a prerequuisite for effectiveness might be devolved, going a significant distance towards meeting the concerns of Quebec and some other provinces.

General Decentralization of the Existing Federal Structure

This would involve a general devolution of powers from the federal to the provincial governments in a range of program areas designed to meet the demands of some provinces for increased legislative authority and autonomy without any counterbalancing allocation of additional powers to the central government. While this option has the advantage of some continuity from the present structure, it also is unlikely to garner much support from smaller provinces which significantly rely upon redistribution programs associated with a more centralized federal structure.

Asymmetrical Federation

This option would provide for an asymmetrical federal structure whereby one province, presumably Quebec, would be allocated a wider range of autonomous jurisdiction than that assigned to the other constituent units of the federation. The *British North America Act, 1867* provided for some elements of asymmetry vis-à-vis Quebec in its original assignment of powers. Indeed, one possible approach might be to adopt a form of "Section 94 Federalism" by expanding upon these powers in the Constitution to achieve the desired level of asymmetry. This option, however, poses special problems regarding the appropriate role of the representatives of such a province in central institutions in relation to those federal policies which do not apply to it.

Confederalism of Regions

Such an approach might envision a loose confederation of four or five regional units. The principal purpose of this grouping would be to introduce a greater level of symmetry amongst the constituent members of the federation. By establishing a stronger degree of self-sufficiency within these regional units, they would presumably be more capable of exercising their increased jurisdictional authority inherent in a confederal arrangement. Naturally, the prospects for such an arrangement are dependent on the willingness of smaller provinces to coalesce, but it is interesting to note that more modest versions of this approach have been recently suggested by an Atlantic and some Western Canadian premiers.

Sovereignty Association

This solution assumes a bipolar central structure combining two constituent units: Quebec and an English-Canadian federal or unitary state. Critical elements include the powers to be maintained by the central structure and the nature of the relationship of that structure with its two constituent components. As experience with bipolar structures elsewhere has shown, the existence of only two constituent units makes almost inevitable the preponderance of deadlocks in deciding upon common affairs.

Common Markets

This alternative provides for the establishment of a common market of anywhere up to ten individual units which would maintain only minimal central institutions. Association is almost exclusively for the purposes of establishing a free and common market, effectively precluding nationally coordinated programs in the social and cultural fields, for example.

Separation

The establishment of complete economic and political independence for Quebec is the most radical of the alternative structures considered. It would require, among other things, negotiations over a broad range of issues including the appropriate assumption of national debt, arrangements for transborder communications and transportation, etc. Moreover, it should be noted that within the rest of Canada it would result in a federation dominated by Ontario, which has virtually half the population and more than half of the GNP.

THE CANADIAN LEGAL SYSTEM

Introduction to
the Legal Environment

■　■　■　■　■　■　■　■ *Victor S. MacKinnon*

This section discusses the structures of the legal and constitutional system within which any administrator must work. This administrator may be a part of the apparatus of the state which regulates the activities of the citizen, or may be one who is on the receiving end of that regulation. In either case, it behooves the administrator to be aware of the legal foundations of, and limitations on, administrative power. A more individualistic form of protection of the citizen has recently been introduced in the form of the Canadian Charter of Rights and Freedoms, to which a portion of this discussion is devoted. Finally, an extract is given from a leading case decided by the Supreme Court of Canada in the area of the relationship between the individual and the state. This illustrates that even prior to the Charter, the courts have considered the Canadian legal and constitutional system to contain inherent principles of fairness which protect the individual citizen from possible oppression by the state.

Theories and Principles

Victor S. MacKinnon

CONCEPTS OF LAW

Law as the administrator, public or private, encounters it is a social phenomenon. For the administrator, the term "the law" means the system of rules which a group of people adopt to regulate their relationships with each other.

The group may be as small as, say, a bowling club, in which case its rules will be few in number and small in significance for the rest of the human race, or it may be as large as an entire nation, in which case the rules will be more complex and of concern not only to the members of that nation but possibly to other nations of the world as well.

The term "law" can be used in other applications also. We can, and do, speak of the "laws of physics" or the "laws" (or "rules") of various sports, or of the "moral law" or even the "law of nature." The term "laws of physics" refers to our perception that certain processes in the world of matter appear to occur universally and invariably. The "laws" or "rules" of baseball or football denote the practices which must be followed for the activity to exist at all. The "law of nature" describes the basis on which the universe appears to be constructed. The "moral law" describes the way in which we consider people ought to behave so as to be in harmony with the way the world is constructed.

185

Many people would consider that the world was constructed by God, and that "moral law" is therefore constituted by the rules prescribed by religion. Others, who do not believe in the existence of God, would nevertheless consider that there are certain rules to which human conduct should conform, i.e., they consider that the world is constructed on certain standards. Still others would assert that "natural law" has no relation to either a God or to moral rules and standards. This viewpoint is, perhaps, closer to acceptance of the "law of the jungle" as the basis of the natural order.

When we say that law in the legal sense is a social phenomenon, all this means is that it occurs in human society. The concepts incorporated in legal rules may reflect social, political, economic, philosophical or even religious concepts. This is not to say, however, that law is merely a branch of sociology, or political science, or economics or the dogmas of a particular church. (This can, of course, be the case on occasion. The twentieth century legal system of the Soviet Union is dominated by Marxian economics; the legal and governmental system of Iran of the 1990s is dominated by Islamic fundamentalist religious views.)

Western legal systems, to an increasing extent, at least seek to acknowledge their awareness of the influence of these various doctrines, and to moderate the power of any one doctrine to dominate to the exclusion of others. Thus, capitalist views of the rights of employers and socialist views of the rights of trade unions are both incorporated to varying degrees in the labour laws of various Western countries. Similarly, moral or religious views as to the sanctity of human life and egocentric views as to the rights of the person over one's own body are both incorporated to varying degrees in the abortion laws of various Western countries.

It is clear, therefore, that we can make a distinction between "what the law is" and "what the law ought to be." There is an overlap between the two, inasmuch as large portions of the law consist of prescribing patterns of behaviour to which people are expected to conform. This creates a desire to define "law" in practical terms, and that in turn gives rise to what are called "positivist" schools of thought as regards the nature of law. Thus, the nineteenth century English scholar John Austin, one of the early positivists, writing in his "Lectures on Jurisprudence," defined law as "a rule laid down for the guidance

186

of an intelligent being by an intelligent being having power over him."

This affirms the distinction to be made between what we may call "positive law" on the one hand, and "ideal law" or "ethics" or "justice" or "what the law ought to be," on the other hand. The essence of law, in the positivist view therefore, is that it is a command, addressed by an identifiable "law-giver" (usually called "the sovereign" or "sovereign power"), accompanied by the threat of a sanction if that command is disobeyed.

Concentration on the element of "sanction" leads those positivists who form what is called the "realist" school of thought to emphasise "enforceability" as the hallmark of what should be recognized as "law" in the practical sense (as distinguished from the theoretical sense). Thus "moral law," which many people consider they *ought* to follow in the conduct of their personal lives is not, from the standpoint of a realist, to be considered as "law" in the *legal* sense, since it is not systematically enforced by any of the agencies of the State.

While the shades of difference between "positivists" in general and "realists" in particular are many and varied, we may for our purposes here summarise the issue by saying that for positivists as such, the role of the legislature (the modern "law-giver" or "sovereign") and the influences upon it, are the key elements, while for the realists as such, the role of the courts as the ultimate *enforcers* of the law, and what influences the judges in arriving at their decisions, are the crucial areas. (We can also add here that the modern development of administrative tribunals as resolvers of disputes brings them within the category of "courts," while at the same time some of those administrative tribunals also have the function of being "law-givers," e.g., the Canadian Radio-television and Telecommunications Commission, the Atomic Energy Control Board, Labour Relations Boards, etc.)

The positivist (including the realist) approach to legal analysis tends to be the most prevalent one at the present day. Adherents of the "natural law" school, i.e., those who believe that "the law" derives from a balanced natural order inherent in the structure of the world and which may be discovered by the rational intelligence of mankind, are fewer in number than they were in less cynical times. "Law and order" on the one hand, and "justice" on the other hand, are currently viewed by many as being not necessarily synonymous and possibly even as mutually antagonistic.

SYSTEMS OF LAW

There are three principal systems of law which survive today: Islamic Law; Roman Law; and Anglo-American Common Law. (Although the Soviet Union and China contain a large proportion of the world's population, their legal systems are not sufficiently distinctive in substance or in procedural rules as to constitute completely separate "systems." Their main differentiation is as regards their being so completely within the continuous control of one particular political party.)

The common law originated in England, principally during the reign of Henry II (1154–1189). In earlier medieval England, law was localised, and tended to follow the old political boundaries such as those of the formerly separate Anglo-Saxon kingdoms such as Wessex and Mercia. The most durable result of Henry's reign was that the whole of English law was centralised and unified by the institution of a permanent court of professional judges. This sat mainly at Westminster but there were also itinerant judges who systematically visited the various counties of England and who eventually replaced the local courts presided over by the local nobility. The law thus became "common" in the sense of its being uniform. Even before the end of the twelfth century the judicial rolls contain many accounts of law-suits about very small pieces of land between persons of lowly rank. In the seventeenth-century struggles between King and Parliament the common law finally emerged as the bastion of defence against the arbitrary exercise of executive power by the Crown.

British settlers who colonised various areas around the world including those territories which eventually became Canada and the United States of America, took with them English common law. This became the foundation of the legal system in those colonies, almost all of which are now sovereign independent members of the international family of nations. The development of this system of law which has occurred outside England itself, particularly in the United States, is such as to justify adoption of the name "Anglo-American common law" to refer to it.

188

SOURCES OF LAW

At the earliest stages of social life, "justice" means not much more than a system of order imposed by someone with the authority to do so. In such a context "authority" can broadly be equated with "power." It is not until later in societal development that we take practical account of conflicts between positive law and justice, arising mainly out of abuses of authority. This problem of the relation between positive law and justice is of major, perhaps supreme importance, but this is not the place to discuss it. We are concerned here only with positive law, the law as we find it.

Accordingly we may confine ourselves to a consideration of law in its earliest forms as being based on custom, on usages and practices, on traditions. In various parts of the world, as for example on the African continent, we still find substantial portions of the legal system comprised of "customary law." Knowledge of the customs of the societal group is usually entrusted to some well-respected members of it, for example the tribal elders. This knowledge also usually entitles these elders to resolve disputes which may arise among other members of the tribal unit. Knowledge of the customs i.e., the "laws" is usually handed down from father to son, orally, and the resolution of a major dispute is, like the law itself, stored in memory, not written down.

The establishment of permanent courts, such as the common law courts of twelfth-century England referred to above, can be viewed as a formal institutionalization of the dispute-resolution process. The *source* of the law remains custom, usages, practices. The more these customs and usages, and the solutions to disputes about them, are recorded in writing however, the more these records become the source of the law, rather than the actual customs themselves. When this happens, we say that what started off as a custom or usage, has now "hardened" into law in the legal sense. It has become a "rule of common law." We preserve the connection with the original customs and practices by asserting that judges do not "make" the law, but simply "declare" what it is. They attach the necessary stamp to a particular customary practice, so that from here on we know for certain that that customary practice is "law." (A famous American judge, Mr. Justice Cardozo, once described this as "the process by which forms of conduct are stamped in the judicial mint as law, and thereafter circulate freely as part of the coinage of the realm.")

Before leaving the topic, mention should be made of two other sources of common law — Roman Law and Canon Law. Canon Law is ecclesiastical or church law. For many centuries after the birth of Christ, the prevailing church in Western countries was the Roman Catholic church. The law of this church, the Canon Law, was based in large part on Roman Law, and, inasmuch as the church was, in this period, the principal source of the educational system, many of the royal judges were themselves clerics. These judges therefore were familiar with these other bodies of law on which they could draw to provide a problem-solving principle in situations where custom and usage gave them no answer.

In the early development of the common law, Roman Law concepts were therefore influential, but as the role of the clerics declined in later centuries, so also the influence of Roman Law diminished and the common law developed along its own separate and special path. The influence of canon law persisted the longest in the areas of the law of marriage, and succession to property, and as regards the regulation of the conduct of members of the clergy.

The other main source of law in the modern era is legislation, that is, the rules made by the organ of government known as the "legislature."

At the same time as it performs its function of making laws, the legislature also performs the function of being the vehicle through which are made known the views of the individual citizens in society as to how they should be governed. This is described as the "democratic" function, from the Greek words "demos" meaning "people" and "kratein" meaning "to rule" or "kratos" meaning "authority." It took thousands of years for the concept that the authority to rule a society should be derived from the people forming that society, to become fully developed. Consequently the decisions of the courts administering the common law were, for many centuries, the most important source of our law. In the last hundred and fifty years or so, however, the growing strength of the principles of democracy and the rapidly increasing complexity of modern societies have made legislation, produced by elected legislatures, far and away the pre-eminent source of new law.

SOME BASIC LEGAL TERMINOLOGY

We have already introduced two important terms — *common law* and *legislation*. Common law is the law declared to be such by the courts and is therefore sometimes referred to as *judge-made law*. The judges perform this function in the disputes or cases which come before them for resolution, and therefore another term used in this regard is *case law*. Decided cases are frequently referred to as *precedents* for the case currently before the court. When the decisions (precedents) in a number of cases on related points of law are assembled together, we frequently find a more general principle or rule emerging, a *rule of common law*. This occurs, therefore, through a process of inductive reasoning, an inferring of general law from particular instances. This is in contrast to the deductive reasoning used when we apply a statute and draw an inference from the general to the particular.

Once a court has laid down a principle of law as applicable to a certain set of facts, it will adhere to that principle and apply it to all future cases where the factual situation is substantially the same, even although the parties involved are different. Courts of equivalent rank are not absolutely bound to follow each other's decisions, but usually do so. Lower courts are considered to be bound by the decisions of higher courts. All of this is described as the principle of *stare decisis*.

The term *statute* just employed above is one of a number of more or less interchangeable terms used to describe the end product of the work of a *legislature*. Legislature is a generic term (derived from the Latin word "lex" meaning "law") used to describe the modern organ of government which affords the general mass of citizens a degree of participation in the process of government. This occurs by virtue of the fact that in modern times the legislature in most of the countries of the world is elected by the citizens. The legislature therefore acquires two principal functions (a) that of *representing the interests of the people* and (b) making laws. As we have already noted, in modern times the laws made by the legislature have surpassed the laws declared by the courts in volume and in significance.

There are specific names for the legislature in various countries. In Canada the federal legislature is called *Parliament*, which copies British usage. (The word "Parliament" is derived from the French word "parler" meaning "to speak." The French

191

legislature is thus called *le Parlement*.) The legislatures of the Provinces of Canada are most commonly called *Legislative Assembly*, the principal exception being Quebec, where it is called the *National Assembly* (l'Assemblee Nationale) for reasons of history and politics.

The legislature of the United States is called *Congress*. It is divided into houses or chambers called the *House of Representatives* and the *Senate*. The Parliament of Canada also has two chambers, the *House of Commons* and the *Senate*. The two chambers of the British Parliament are called the House of Commons and the *House of Lords*. Many legislatures have only one chamber however. This is the case with the Legislative Assembly of all ten Canadian Provinces, the national legislature of Israel (the *Knesset*) and the national legislature of Sweden (the *Riksdag*).

Another word used to describe what a legislature produces is *Act* — Act of Parliament, Act of the Legislative Assembly, Act of Congress, etc. Individual statutes will have names such as the Labour Relations Act, the Finance Act, and so on. More generally we can speak of *enacted law* or *enactment*, or alternatively, *statute law*, or *legislation*.

While a statute is still in process of being enacted, i.e., while it is still passing through the various procedures employed by the legislature concerned, and has not yet become a completed Act of that legislature, it is referred as a *Bill*.

It is also open to a legislature to group together the various common law rules which have been developed in this or that area of the law, and to re-enact them in a comprehensive form as legislation. The word commonly used to describe the result is *Code*. In Canada we can find both federal and Provincial examples of this e.g., the Canadian Criminal Code (federal) or the Quebec Civil Code. The latter is a Canadian adaptation of the older Napoleonic Code of France, which was a major restatement and revision of the numerous customary laws existing rather chaotically in France prior to the reign of the Emperor Napoleon Bonaparte. A codification need not necessarily bear the label of "code" e.g., the Sale of Goods Act enacted in 1893 by the British Parliament is a codification of the case law on this topic. All of the Provinces of Canada except Quebec have done the same thing in this area of the law.

The law can be classified in a variety of ways. A contrast is usually made between *civil law* and *criminal law*. Basically, civil law is everything which is not criminal. Criminal law deals with the commission of offences which have a typically criminal purpose and which lead to the imposition of some kind of punishment. (The definition of what is a "typically criminal purpose" can present the courts with difficulty from time to time.)

A specialised use of the term *civil law* may be noted here. In the Roman Empire the term *ius civile* denoted the general law which was applicable to, and available only to, Roman citizens. (Where non-citizens were involved in a dispute, the applicable law was the *ius gentium*, the "law of peoples" or the "law of nations." It is from this latter body of principles that portions of modern international law are derived.) In countries where the legal system is based on Roman law, the term *civil law* usually refers to *that* fact. Thus as regards, say, France, or Germany or the Canadian Province of Quebec we commonly say that these jurisdictions each have a civil law system, meaning that their law derives principally from the Roman law system, not the common law system.

Another contrast frequently made is that between *private law* and *public law*.

Private law sub-divides into a number of separately distinguishable topics. The law of *Contracts* regulates the manner in which binding agreements are made between or among individuals, and how these are enforced if necessary. The law of *Torts* deals with civil, as distinct from criminal, wrongs. (The word itself is simply the French word for "wrong.") Thus if I unintentionally, but negligently, knock you down with my automobile and injure you, the law requires me to make good to you this non-criminal wrong that I have done you. The most common form of reparation is by payment of a sum of money, called *damages*, by the negligent person to the injured person. The law recognises a substantial number and range of torts.

The law of *Marriage and Divorce* regulates this very personal set of relationships — how does one get married, what are the rights and duties of the partners during the subsistence of the marriage, and how does one terminate the legal status of being married. This is a branch of the broader topic of *Family Law*, under which the rights of the children of a marriage are also dealt with. *Property Law* deals with how you acquire legal rights to all kinds of property, both tangible (e.g., automobiles, land and buildings) and intangible (shares in a company, rights

193

under an insurance policy) and how those rights may be sold or otherwise transferred.

On your death your property will pass to somebody else and this is regulated by the law of *Wills and Succession,* dealing with the way in which you can personally control what is to happen to your property by drawing up a document called a will, or the general rules for identifying the persons who will succeed to your property in the event that you die without leaving any personal instructions in the form of a will. *Company (Corporation) Law* and the *Law of Partnerships* will deal with these particular ways of carrying on a business and *Bankruptcy Law* provides the rules for dealing with a situation where your business has failed.

Public Law involves the regulation of relationships between individual citizens and the state or its organs of government. It too can be sub-divided. *Constitutional Law* lays down the structure of the governmental system, specifying the organs of government and their powers. Frequently also, as is now the case in Canada since 1982, it will regulate the political and human rights of the individual citizen vis-à-vis the state. *Administrative Law* is the law regulating the dealings of the individual citizen with the bureaucracy i.e., the "public service" or "civil service," as distinct from the "politicians." *Criminal Law*, as defined earlier, deals with the commission of offences which have a typically criminal purpose and which lead to the imposition of some kind of punishment. It falls under the heading of public law because in modern societies the state has taken over the vindication of criminal violations of the rights of individual citizens. The majority of crimes are committed by individuals against individuals, but we no longer allow self-help in such situations. We do not allow the injured party to take revenge on the offending party. Instead, the state acts in the public interest, on behalf of us all, in seeking to punish the guilty. *International Law* is the most obviously "public" of these various areas. It regulates the dealings of countries (nations) with one another and with international organizations such as the United Nations.

In this regard we may also mention the *Law of Evidence* and the *Law of Procedure*. These are in a sense neutral topics, in that they are neither specifically private nor specifically public in their reach. Their adjunct nature leads to their being described on occasion as *Adjectival Law*. We may also note, however, that in certain circumstances they may become

194

substantive in character, for example, where refusal to admit a particular piece of evidence, or a failure to observe minimum procedural standards might lead to the individual citizen thus affected making a claim that rights guaranteed by the constitution were being infringed.

Finally the term *jurisdiction* should be noted. In general terms this refers to the legal power possessed by a judge, or a court or other tribunal to inquire into a matter and to make a decision upon it. We can also note some more specific usages. *Original jurisdiction* is possessed by the tribunal where you are entitled to commence your case. If you are dissatisfied with the original decision, and if the law so permits, then you may appeal to a higher tribunal in an effort to get that decision altered. This second tribunal is said to have *appellate jurisdiction*. A court or tribunal will usually have limits on its *territorial jurisdiction*. The courts of the Province of Ontario have no jurisdictional power to decide cases which arise in Manitoba. The Supreme Court of Canada cannot decide cases which arise in Italy. Lastly, courts may have specialised powers as regards their *substantive jurisdiction*. For example, some courts may have power only in criminal cases, while similarly, other courts may have only civil jurisdiction. In the lower levels of courts we may find those which deal only with road traffic matters, or only with family law disputes. A rapidly developing modern phenomenon is the growth of administrative tribunals which deal, somewhat more informally than a regular common law court, with disputes arising in particular areas of administrative law, for example, a labour relations board or a municipal assessment appeals tribunal.

THE CONSTITUTION AND THE LAW

The constitution of a country is sometimes referred to as a "higher law." The extent to which this is true relates to the extent to which that constitution is enforceable in the courts or through some other institution.

For example, the former Soviet Union had quite a lengthy and complex written constitution, but no procedure existed whereby an individual citizen could compel the government to observe any provision of that document. Again, it is frequently said that Britain has an "unwritten" constitution. What this

195

really means is that there is no one single document that can be pointed to as "the British constitution," although there exist several individual documents which are of constitutional significance in Britain. Again, apart from a few procedural rights, there is no procedure for individual citizens to achieve enforcement of constitutional principles. Indeed, one of the most cherished principles of the British constitution is the complete authority of the legislature or, as it is more usually expressed, "the sovereignty of Parliament." This refers to the inability of any other institution of government in Britain to contradict what Parliament says, leading to the situation where, as is often said, "In Britain, the constitution is what Parliament says it is." (This position has been somewhat modified in recent years by Britain's membership of the European Common Market.)

The preamble to the Canadian Constitution expresses Canada's desire to have "a Constitution similar in principle to that of the United Kingdom." Consequently, in broad principle, this "sovereignty of Parliament" or "legislative supremacy" is a feature of the Canadian constitution also.

However, this principle has to be modified in Canada to take account of the fact that Canada also has a "federal" system of government. This means that we have a duplication of the organs of government — legislature, executive and judiciary — i.e., not *one* set of each, as in a "unitary" state such as Britain, but *two* sets each. One set comprises the national, central or "federal" organs of government, situated in Ottawa, and the other set is divided into ten units, comprising the organs of government of each of the ten member units (called "Provinces") which together form the Canadian federal union. Governmental power is therefore *distributed* between the federal legislature and cabinet in Ottawa on the one hand and the ten legislatures and cabinets in each of the ten Provincial capitals (Toronto, Fredericton, Winnipeg, etc.) on the other hand. There is an analogous distribution as regards judicial power.

In Canada, therefore, we describe the federal organs and the provincial organs as "each being supreme within its own sphere." Putting them all together, we have the *totality* of Canadian governmental power, as viewed from the outside. Viewed from the inside, however, we see a provincial sphere and a federal sphere of power.

The written constitution of Canada makes a formal distribution of powers between those two spheres. (See Sections 91 and

196

92 of the Constitution particularly.) Consequently, if the federal government seeks to exercise powers which the constitution allocates to the sphere of power of the Provincial governments — or vice versa — then it is acting beyond its powers or, as we more usually say, using a Latin phrase, it is acting *ultra vires*. If a challenge is made in the courts, the courts have the power to declare the action to be of no force and effect, to be null and void, on the ground that the action is *ultra vires*. Conversely, after detailed scrutiny of the action involved, the courts may declare that the government concerned has acted *within* its sphere of power, that it has acted *intra vires*. The power of the courts to do this is referred to as the power of judicial review.

Until 1982, the ground of *ultra vires* was the only ground on which Canadian legislation, federal or Provincial, could be invalidated. In that year some major amendments were made to the Canadian constitution.

When the constitution was first enacted in 1867 it was entitled the British North America Act, but in 1982 it and all the amendments made to it between 1867 and 1982 were re-named the "Constitution Act, 1867, as amended." A new procedure for future amendments was added, but perhaps the most significant addition to the original constitution was 34 new sections collectively forming the Canadian Charter of Rights and Freedoms. (Note that what occurred in 1982 was the making of substantial additions and amendments to the 1867 constitution which, nonetheless survived intact in large measure. Canada did *not*, in 1982, receive a *new* constitution, although one occasionally still sees loose and wholly inaccurate statements to that effect.)

The Charter of Rights and Freedoms inserted into the constitution various principles such as freedom of speech and press, the right to vote, the right to enter and leave Canada, the right not to be arbitrarily detained or imprisoned, and so on and so forth.

This is not to say that such rights and freedoms did not exist in Canada prior to 1982. Most of them did in some form or other, but they were not formally incorporated into the text of the constitution. Rather, the same view was taken in Canada as still prevails in Britain today, that, as the noted English legal scholar A.V. Dicey expressed it, "most of these rights are consequences of the more general law or principle that no man can be punished except for direct breaches of law (i.e., crimes) proved in the way provided by law (i.e., before the courts of the realm)."

Section 52(1) of the 1982 Constitution Act declares that "The Constitution of Canada is the supreme law of Canada, and any law that is inconsistent with the provisions of the Constitution is, to the extent of the inconsistency, of no force or effect."

The result is that, since 1982, legislation which is *intra vires* as regards its falling within the sphere of power assigned by the constitution to the legislature which enacted it, may nevertheless be declared by the courts to be *unconstitutional* and therefore of no force or effect, on the ground that it conflicts with one of the rights or freedoms contained in the Charter of Rights and Freedoms. (It continues also to be possible to invalidate legislation on the ground that it is *ultra vires*.)

(For the sake of completeness, there must also be mentioned the Canadian Bill of Rights Act, 1960. Under this, the courts could declare legislation "inoperative" if it offended against certain principles enunciated in that Act. The Act applied to federal legislation only, and it did not form part of the constitution itself. Its precise role and status were therefore somewhat obscure. While it has not been repealed, it is more relevant for our purposes here to concentrate on the Charter of Rights and Freedoms.)

ADMINISTRATIVE LAW

It has already been indicated above that Administrative Law is that branch of public law which regulates the relationships between the individual and the state, while Constitutional Law deals with the rules, practices and institutions which *constitute* the state. Let us now explain the scope of administrative law a little further.

From a descriptive point of view, administrative law involves noting the various government institutions which the citizen may encounter. The most comprehensive of these is the 'Ministry' or 'Department', a division of the government, usually under the charge of a politician — or 'Minister' — who is a member of the political executive branch i.e., of the government for the time being. In conjunction with these Ministries or Departments we find a large array of other bodies with lesser powers and more narrowly specialized functions. These go under a wide variety of names, with no particular reason for the selection of one title rather than another. Thus we find an 'Agency' or 'Board' or 'Commission' or 'Tribunal' or 'Bureau' of this, that or the other, to mention only some of the more common names found.

From another descriptive point of view we might say that a study of administrative law involves a study of the actual rules, decisions and policies that administrators make. Those are a matter of content and substance, and many scholars prefer to refer to them as 'regulatory law' and to reserve the label 'administrative law' for the *procedures* for making policies. Professor Lief H. Carter has expressed it as that "Administrative law refers to the way the legal system, primarily the courts, translates the philosophy of the rule of law into controls on bureaucratic power." (Administrative Law and Politics, 1983, p. 35).

There are many ways in which administrative functions may be classified. Perhaps the simplest and certainly the broadest is to break them down into 'economic regulation' and 'benefit distribution'. The former would include such bodies as the federal Canadian Radio-television and Telecommunications Commission (CRTC), provincial egg marketing boards, professional organizations such as law societies or colleges of physicians, labour relations boards both federal and provincial, and so on. The latter would include a range of agencies administering various forms of health care and of income support and other social welfare benefits. Some bodies would straddle the two areas, such as agencies dealing with pollution control or wildlife protection.

Again as already mentioned, the courts are the principal agency through which controls over the administrative process are exercised. The courts have, on certain terms and conditions (which are themselves part of the substance of administrative law) the power of 'judicial review' over the propriety of administrative actings.

In the first place, they may examine the validity of the delegation, by the legislature to an administrative agency, of the power to act — the extent and nature of the grant and conditions under which it is granted; are these authorized by other principles of law, including the law of the constitution itself, or has there been an excessive or inappropriate delegation of power. Next the courts may inquire into what is called the 'rule-making process', if the particular agency has been given this quasi-legislative power — has the agency exercised this power to make rules of general application within the terms of the power delegated to it or has it exceeded them. Finally the courts may examine the propriety of the way in which the administrative agency has exercised what is called its 'adjudicative power', its power to make decisions involving individual citizens — has the agency observed the general rules which apply in this area.

Over a long period of time, sometimes stretching over centuries, the courts have developed a number of principles to which they require administrative bodies to conform when they act in ways which affect the rights of individual citizens. Many of these principles are comprehended within the concept of 'the principles of natural justice'. They have, for example, upheld the doctrine of *audi alteram partem* — that the individual must be given an opportunity to represent his or her side of the issue, whether this be done by means of a formal hearing or by some other process. Involved in these processes are the right to be represented by legal counsel (not always granted); to be given adequate advance notice of any proceedings and disclosure of what the state proposes say on the matter; to cross-examine witnesses (again, not always granted); and the right to have one's representations considered by an un-biased adjudicator. Increasingly in recent years the courts have expanded the 'principles of natural justice' and developed a concept of 'fairness' as their yardstick for assessing administrative action. They have also expanded the range of persons and organizations which they will consider to have 'title' or 'standing' to bring actions.

The courts have also developed the principles upon which they will, or will not, overturn an administrative decision or acting because it is based upon an error of law, or an error of fact, or is based upon inadequate evidence, and upon which they will decline to intervene at all because they consider that the administrative side of government must be allowed a certain amount of latitude or discretion to act untrammelled.

Lastly, the courts will have to consider the remedy which they will provide to the aggrieved citizens if successful in his or her case before them. The court may 'quash' the administrative decision or acting which has been challenged. This may lead to the particular administrative decision or acting being repeated in revised form so as to take account of the court's criticism, or, quite frequently, to the decision or acting simply being abandoned. The court may issue an order to a public authority compelling it to take some action which it has failed to take, or forbidding it from taking some action which it ought not to take. Another alternative is for a court to issue an order declaratory of the rights of the parties, which can pave the way for a variety of other solutions to the problem at hand.

The Canadian Charter of Rights and Freedoms

Victor S. Mackinnon

Canada has a federal form of constitutional structure, and, as is common, includes as part of that structure, the principle of judicial review of the constitutional validity of legislation. From the outset, therefore,[1] Canada's courts have had the power to declare Acts of the federal parliament and of the legislative assemblies of the ten provinces which make up the Canadian federation, to be of no force and effect.

From 1867 until 1960, however, the only basis on which the courts would invalidate legislation was the principle of *ultra vires*. Section 92 of the constitution enumerates the specific legislative powers of the provincial legislatures, and by section 91 the residue of legislative power belongs to the federal parliament.[2] We can, therefore, speak of there being two spheres' of legislative power, and of each legislature, federal or provincial, being 'supreme within its own sphere'. Put another way, each legislature possesses only those powers which are conferred upon it by the constitution. If, say, the federal parliament seeks to exercise a power which the constitution confers upon a provincial legislature, then it has moved out of its own sphere and into the sphere in which it has no power, i.e., it is acting *ultra vires*.[3] In such circumstances the courts will declare the federal statute null and void. The same would apply to attempted invasion of the federal legislative sphere by a provincial legislature.

Until 1960, therefore, the courts looked at any piece of legislation which was challenged before them, solely in terms of whether there was power in the legislature concerned to pass it. If the court concurred that such power did indeed exist at the time of enactment, then that was an end of the inquiry. There was no further analysis to see whether the statute concerned e.g., offended against some general principle of federalism[4] and certainly no invalidation on any such grounds. The statute was either *ultra vires* or *intra vires*.

The Canadian courts were fortified in taking such a 'narrow' (in the technical legal sense) approach to constitutional interpretation by the fact that until 17 April 1982, the text of the Canadian constitution contained no statements of principle which could serve to invalidate legislation which was otherwise *intra vires* the enacting legislature.[5]

With the enactment of the Constitution Act 1982, however, there was added[6] *inter alia* to the constitution, the Canadian Charter of Rights and Freedoms.

Section 52 of this Act states

> **52.**(1) The Constitution of Canada is the supreme law of Canada, and any law that is inconsistent with the provisions of the Constitution is, to the extent of the inconsistency, of no force or effect.

Section 24 makes the various rights and freedoms specified in sections 2 to 23 of the Charter justiciable

> **24.**(1) Anyone whose rights or freedoms, as guaranteed by this Charter, have been infringed or denied may apply to a court of competent jurisdiction to obtain such remedy as the court considers appropriate and just in the circumstances.

These rights and freedoms of the charter are grouped into *Fundamental Freedoms* (s. 2) comprising the standard rights of freedom of speech, press, assembly, association and religion; *Democratic Rights* (s. 3 to 5) covering franchise rights; *Mobility Rights* (s. 6) concerning the rights to move freely from province to province for the purposes of residence and/or employment; *Legal Rights* (s. 7 to 14) conferring standard procedural rights in criminal proceedings; *Equality Rights* (s. 15) guaranteeing no discrimination by law on grounds of race, ethnic origin, colour, religion, sex, age or mental and physical disability;[7] and *Language Rights* (s. 16 to 23). After some further sections dealing with *General* matters and *Application of the Charter*, section 34 concludes this Part of the *Constitution Act* 1982 by declaring

> **34.** This part may be cited as the Canadian Charter of Rights and Freedoms.

Since 1982, therefore, legislation enacted by the federal parliament or by the provincial legislature, can be declared 'unconstitutional',[8] on the ground that even although it is *intra vires* the enacting legislature in terms of the powers conferred upon it by section 91 or section 92 of the constitution respectively, it nevertheless offends against one or other of the principles contained in the Charter of Rights and Freedoms.

We may now remind ourselves that Canada, as well as having a federal form of constitution, also adopts the (Westminster) parliamentary form of government in both the federal and provincial spheres. We should note here the gesture of acknowledgement in the direction of the 'sovereignty of parliament' made by section 33 of the Canadian Charter of Rights and Freedoms, in providing

> **33.**(1) Parliament or the legislature of a Province may expressly declare in an Act of Parliament or of the legislature, as the case may be, that the Act or a provision thereof shall operate notwithstanding a provision included in section 2 or sections 7 to 15 of this Charter.

Section 33 goes on to provide that such declarations shall expire after five years (or earlier if so specified) but may be re-enacted.

The Canadian experience may be of even further interest here, in particular as regards the period between 1960 and the introduction of the Charter of Rights and Freedoms in 1982.

In 1960 the federal parliament of Canada enacted the Canadian Bill of Rights Act.[9] As the contents of this statute would have affected the constitutional powers of the provinces if applied to them, the *making* of it applicable to the provinces would have required an amendment to the constitution, an amendment of a nature which, at that time, in terms of section 91(1) of the constitution, would have required to be enacted by the *British* parliament. A request to the British parliament to enact such an amendment would have required provincial consultation and consent. For a variety of political reasons it was not desired to set this process in motion, and the Canadian Bill of Rights Act 1960, was therefore made applicable to the federal organs of government only. This enabled it to be enacted by the federal parliament unilaterally.

A further consequence of this mode of enactment was that the Canadian Bill of Rights Act 1960, although it had what may be termed constitutional 'significance' or 'import', did not, in law, form part of the text of the constitution itself. As a result it was possible for judges of the Supreme Court of Canada to refer to it as being "little more than a rule of construction"[10] and as "an Act that is not of a constitutional character."[11]

The 1960 Bill of Rights Act also contained, in section 2, the progenitor of the 'express derogation' provision mentioned above as being contained in section 33(1) of the subsequent charter of 1982, and without the latter's limitation as to duration.

The effect of the 1960 Bill of Rights Act on federal statutes which might appear inconsistent with its terms, hinged on the effect to be given to section 2 thereof, stating

> **2.** Every law of Canada shall, unless it is expressly declared by an Act of the Parliament of Canada that it shall operate notwithstanding the Canadian Bill of Rights, be so construed and applied as not to abrogate, abridge or infringe or to authorize the abrogation, abridgement or infringement of any of the rights or freedoms herein recognised and declared...

The issue became — did this section mean

1. If a statute conflicted with this Bill of Rights Act and the conflict could not be avoided by interpretation, did the statute then have to be 'applied' by the court, despite the conflict?

2. If the court could not 'construe' the statute concerned, so as to avoid a conflict with the Bill of Rights Act, did the court then have to hold the statute 'inoperative'?

There were no cases on the matter until 1969 when the leading case of *R. v. Drybones*[12] held that section 2 of the Bill of Rights Act had the effect of overriding inconsistent federal statutes, by rendering them 'inoperative'. There was soon something of a retreat from this position, however, and acceptance of the second viewpoint above as being completely definitive could perhaps be considered somewhat tenuous.[13]

The first of the above two viewpoints has been described as making this kind of a provision a form of 'indirect judicial review'[14] or of 'judicial braking'[15], by treating it as an 'interpretative statute'.[16]

NOTES

1. Federal union was inaugurated in Canada in 1867 by the enactment by the Westminster parliament of the *British North America Act* 30 & 31 Vict c. 3. Britain terminated its residual involvement in the procedures for amending Canada's constitution by enacting the *Canada Act* 1982, 30 & 31 Eliz II c. 11. The *Canada Act* incorporated and enacted on Canada's behalf the *Constitution Act* 1982. The *Constitution Act* 1982, re-named the *British North America Act* 1867, as amended, as the *Constitution Act* 1867, as amended. The *Constitution Act* 1982, also includes procedures for henceforth amending the Canadian constitution solely by Canadian procedures, without any resort whatsoever to the British parliament. See note 8, *infra*.

2. Substantial confusion has been caused in judicial interpretation of the constitution over the years, by the well-meaning but misguided attempt of the founding fathers to introduce what they though would be "greater certainty" as to how far the residual powers extend, by listing some twenty-nine items which are specifically to be included under the otherwise general, residual power of the federal parliament. This textual complexity does not, however, entail any derogation from the applicability of the standard federal principle in Canada, *viz.*, that there are two 'spheres' of legislation, one enumerated, and one residual, with the two together comprising the totality of the legislative sovereignty of Canada.

3. *Cf. Home Office v. Dorset Yacht Co.* (1970), 2 All ER 294 332 *per* Lord Reid, on "...the public law concept of *ultra vires*..." as applied in England to executive actions.

4. *Cf.* the Australian case of *City of Melbourne v. The Commonwealth* 74 Common LR 31 81 *per* Dixon J. "The federal system itself is the foundation of the restraint upon the use of the power to control the States."

5. The only guarantees of fundamental rights of the individual contained in the original text of the Canadian constitution are (1) as regards the right to use either the French or the English language — but enjoyment of this right is limited to the arenas of the

Federal and Quebec courts and legislatures. See the *Constitution Act* 1867 as amended section 133(b) as regards preservation of denominational schools — and even there, the remedy provided is by way of appeal to the Governor-General in Council, not to the courts. See the *Constitution Act* 1867 as amended section 93.

6. Many people in Canada and elsewhere were (and some still are) under the misapprehension that the *Constitution Act* of 1982 gave Canada an entirely 'new' constitution. It did no such thing. The main features of the original constitution remain intact, subject to certain additions made by the 1982 Act, the principal one of which is discussed here.

7. Under section 32(2) of the 1982 Act, these section 15 rights did not come into effect until after 17 April 1985.

8. There was considerable procedural difficulty prior to the enactment of the *Canada Act* 1982, which contained the *Constitution Act* 1982. There was no express provision whatsoever in the original constitution, the *British North America Act* 1867, as to how it should be amended. As it was a British statute, it was simply assumed that the appropriate manner of amending it would be the enactment of a subsequent British statute. Uniquely among the constitutions of the world, this was indeed the sole manner of amendment until the passage by the Westminster Parliament of the *British North America (No. 2) Act* 1949, 13 Geo VI c. 81. This added a new section 91(1) to the original constitution, empowering the Canadian federal parliament to amend most of the constitution. Certain matters were, however, excluded from this additional power, notably for our purposes here, amendments which would affect the rights and powers of the provinces. As the Charter of Rights and Freedoms, and other portions of the *Constitution Act* 1982 — such as the addition of a new, wholly Canadianised procedure for constitutional amendments — clearly affect the rights and powers of the provinces, the *Constitution Act* 1982, had, therefore, to be enacted by the British parliament on Canada's behalf, under the name of the *Canada Act* 1982. The issue which then caused difficulty was the degree of provincial consultation and/or consent required before the British parliament could be requested to act on Canada's behalf on this one last occasion before the new amendment procedures freed her of that responsibility. Again because of the lack of any express mention of provincial involvement in constitutional amendment in either in 1867 or the 1949 Acts, this issue had from the outset been regulated entirely by constitutional convention. The limits of this convention were a little uncertain. Thus the federal Prime Minister, Mr. P.E. Trudeau, at one point threatened to make the request to Britain unilaterally if an acceptable measure of provincial agreement could not be obtained. Reaction to his threat led to

litigation culminating in the decision by the Supreme Court of Canada in *Reference re Amendment of the Constitution of Canada Nos. 1, 2 and 3* 1981, 125 DLR (3d) 1. The Supreme Court held that while unilateral action by the federal government would be "legal" it would nevertheless be "unconstitutional." This use of the term 'unconstitutional' to describe a flouting of a constitutional convention is both interesting and uncommon.

9. Now RSC 1970 Appendix III. It is interesting that, somewhat anomalously, this 1960 statute, despite the subsequent enactment of the Canadian Charter of Rights and Freedoms in 1982, has not been formally repealed. This raises a further interesting questions as to whether rights of private property, protection of which was removed from the original drafts of the Charter as a means of getting support for it from the New Democratic Party (a mildly left-wing party) can still be asserted under the 1960 Act section 1(a).

10. *R. v. Drybones* (1969), 9 DLR (3d) 473 491 *per* Pigeon J. (dissenting).

11. *Curr v. The Queen* (1972), 26 DLR (3d) 603 613 *per* Laskin J. For a fuller discussion of this whole issue see MacKinnon "Booze, Religion, Indians and the Canadian Bill of Rights" 1973 *Public Law* 295.

12. *Supra*, note 13.

13. See e.g., *AG for Canada v. Lavell* (1973), 38 DLR (3d)a 481. The constitutional issue involved in this case, which concerned the requirement of section 12(1)(b) of the *Indian Act* that an Indian woman marrying a non-Indian man be de-registered as an Indian, may or may not have to be retried with the coming into delayed effect as from 17 April 1985, of section 15 of the Charter of Rights and Freedoms forbidding discrimination on grounds of, *inter alia*, sex. This will depend on the outcome of on-going discussions which may result in a major reform of the whole *Indian Act* regime.

14. J. Jaconelli *Enacting a Bill of Rights* (1980) 34.

15. *Ibid.*, quoting E. McWhinney *Judicial Review* (4th ed., 1968) 13.

16. *Id.* at 62 quoting D.A. Schmeiser *Civil Liberties in Canada* (1964) 52. Jaconelli himself uses the term "the interpretation Act variant" *id.* at 42.

THE CANADIAN POLITICAL INSTITUTIONS

Introduction to Canadian Political Institutions and the Canadian Policy Process

James C. Simeon

Political institutions are the channels through which the political process flows. Parliament is the symbolic centre of our system of government. It is the public battle field among the major informal institutional contenders of the political process: political parties, pressure groups, and the media. These contests and encounters are reported in minute detail by the mass media, whether it is the electric media of the parliamentary channels of Cable TV or the print media of the major daily newspapers. The public bureaucracy also has it part to play in Canada's premier formal political institution of Parliament. The Auditor General, along with the other officers of Parliament, constantly scrutinize the work of government departments and public servants. Public servants often accompany their ministers to defend and support their actions and requests for public funds or to account for the use of these public funds.

It is generally acknowledged that the public bureaucracy in Canada plays a central role in the public policy process. The public bureaucracy not only formulates public policies, but it is responsible for their effective and efficient implementation; that is, administration. This section also covers a number of diverse aspects of the Canadian public policy process and how it impinges on public administration. This section begins with an examination of theories of government and the provision of public goods. It includes the presentation of a model for assessing government intervention in society. A chapter on the Immigration and Refugee Board, Canada's largest administrative tribunal, outlines how the technique of focus groups was employed to discern this organization's core values within a broader project of administrative renewal. Finally, Eleanor Glor examines the various dimensions and aspects of foster innovation within the public sector in Canada.

Representative Government and the Provision of Public Goods

Janice E. Nicholson

> [The governments of all parties] have managed to create a tax and social security system of such complex detail that they could not possibly understand it. The only explanation for their achievement is that it happened piecemeal, each change being made in pursuit of the latest fashion, social purpose or whim. (*Economist*, October 1983)

In the continuing debate surrounding the imperfections of the social security systems in developed countries two themes emerge: the application of the market concept to the provision of public goods, and the role of the state in providing a rational planned approach in both the provision of public goods and the establishment of priorities concerning them.

Both themes trace their roots to the Classical Economists of the eighteenth and nineteenth centuries, and the fundamental issues raised by these political theorists have remained unresolved.

The emphasis of the Classical Economists upon free enterprise and the market was a result of their rejection of the Mercantilist State. They were suspicious of state intervention which had served the interests of special groups by providing protection for their various economic interests. They wished to see the social and economic system cleared of abuses. They argued that the people are more ardent and skilful in the defence of their own interests than the state would be. Thus the state should remove itself as far as possible from the economic sphere, so that the individual in pursuing his own interests will in the end, pursue the interests of society.

However, Robbins argues that their attachment to the laissez-faire principle has been exaggerated. While they did have a general presumption of free economic activity, they were not opposed to state activity per se. Their principle was utility and they did not think that wide state activity led to utility. On the other hand, they were not so naive as to believe that the establishment of complete economic freedom would lead to harmony among different economic interests.

> The most that can be said of the Classical Economists in this respect is that they believed that in a world of free enterprise, certain relationships would arise which were of a mutually advantageous kind to the individuals concerned and superior to those resulting from alternative systems.[1]

Within this framework the state was given a limited role. Adam Smith saw the state performing three main functions: external defence, protection of the individual from injustice at the hand of any other member of society, and some public works.[2] Smith perceived education and justice as the chief public functions. But Jeremy Bentham and John Stuart Mill extended the role of the state. They believed that public goods should be financed as 'collateral aids', which private enterprise would not provide, but which would create improved economic and social conditions so that the individual could pursue his enlightened self-interest.

At this point, the line becomes blurred. It is no longer possible to distinguish between those social goods that the individual is responsible for providing for himself via the market place, and those that the state should provide as 'collateral aids'.

This ambiguity is reflected in the work of Jeremy Bentham. In some of his work, Bentham does have a general presumption against government activity. In his "Institute of Political Economy" he outlines a general rule:

Nothing ought to be done or attempted by government for the purpose of causing an augmentation to take place in the national mass of wealth, with a view to increase of the means of either subsistence or enjoyment without some special reason.[3]

But he was also capable of arguing that a group of individuals acting in their own best interests could not alone bring about the end of maximizing happiness:

that the uncoerced and unenlightened propensities and powers of individuals are not adequate to the end without the control and guidance of the legislator is a matter of fact of which the evidence of history, the nature of man, and the existence of political society are so many proofs.[4]

He appeared to pursue this point further when he went on to outline several ends of economic activity. He refers to these ends of subsistence, security, opulence and equality as subordinate ends, but it is implied in his analysis that they are in fact components of the ultimate end of the greatest happiness of the greatest number. Once Bentham outlined a multiplicity of ends for society, he implied a broadening of state intervention. Although he asserts that government activity may not be necessary in the spheres of 'subsistence' and 'equality', the possibility arises that with a multiplicity of ends government intervention may be necessary to deal with conflicts in the pursuit of different ends.

The work of Bentham highlights the problems which arise once a move is made away from individual freedom to choose in an open marketplace. Once the assumption is made that the state has an obligation to provide some social goods, the question arises as to which social goods should be provided, at what cost and to what end.

The Utilitarians tended to answer that question by reference back to the principle of utility. This principle can be defined in terms of either individual self interest or social stability, or by the Benthamite terms of the greatest happiness of the greatest number. However, whichever way it is defined, it does not provide a guide as to the means society should take either individually or collectively to pursue such a goal. As long as the individual is perceived as being best able to determine his own needs, then social goals remain an aggregate of individual choices. Once this view is abandoned and the state is seen as having an obligation to pursue certain ends for the benefit of society, then choices must be made between both different means and ends. But the question recurs: on the basis of what criteria and what values shall these choices be made?

> The welfare and happiness of millions cannot be measured on a single scale of less or more.... It cannot be adequately expressed as a single end, but only as a hierarchy of ends, a comprehensive scale of value in which every need of every person is given its place.[5]

But how is the state to construct this hierarchy of ends? On what basis can it assess the every need of every person?

One answer to this question is to see societal values in a constant state of evolution. Gradually the norms and values of the society emerge and can be translated into state action. Thus Edward Burke saw government conducted by the leadership of a public spirited minority which the country would be willing to follow since it understood and expressed the prevailing communal values.[6]

Such a view was unacceptable to the Utilitarians, even those who saw a very limited role for state intervention, since "a policy based on natural evolution is a paralysis of inaction."[7] In this situation the state cannot act until society's norms have evolved to the point where clear messages can be sent to the government.

A compromise was suggested by both John Stuart Mill and Alexis de Tocqueville. Both saw the polity as a product of man, but subject to a series of constraints. Within these constraints policies and institutions can be a matter of choice. The constraints define the scope of ideological or technical possibilities for development.[8]

Within the limits of the present evolved values of society some choices can be made with regard to ends in the provision of public goods. This allows for both evolutionary and planned change. These choices may be influenced by the examples set by other societies when faced with the same challenges. Thus both the constraints and the choices may be partly determined by decisions made outside the society.

But this does not tell us the process by which the society selects certain values and constraints as a basis for action. This process is best described in the discussion of representative and responsible government. Theories of representation attempt to answer the questions of:

- Who has the authority to speak for the whole?
- How is this authority attained?
- Do any particular groups or interests have the right to be heard and to take part in the establishment of that authority?

Much of the work of John Stuart Mill is devoted to the subject of representative government. His views reflect the influence of Utilitarianism, although he differs from his father's theory of representation in several important respects.

Basically, the Utilitarians viewed citizens as politically rational human beings who would exercise their political rights by choosing freely among rival candidates and conflicting policies. They assumed that although men's opinions and personal interests may vary, there were no fundamental conflicts of interest in the society. As the state was assumed to be neutral, minorities would be willing to accept the decision of the majority, since they had the opportunity to convince the majority of the error of their views.

James Mill did not concern himself with the problems arising from the power of the numerical majority as he assumed that the "middle rank" formed the largest proportion of society and that the virtue and wisdom of the "middle rank" would prevail in a representative government. He stressed that the benefits of the representative system were lost, if there was not an identity of interests between the community and the body which chooses the members of Parliament.

However, John Stuart Mill argued that this was not the only aspect on which good government depended, and in any case such an identity of interest could not depend on the conditions of elections alone. But the main difference between John Stuart Mill and his father was that they differed over the end of representative government. For James Mill the most important end was to secure the greatest happiness of the greatest number, for John Stuart Mill it was to secure the intellectual and moral advancement of society.

J.S. Mill bases his argument in favour of representative government on the grounds that a person's interests are only secure when he is able to defend them himself, and it is only when the whole community can play a part that the maximum moral

216

and intellectual improvement occurs. As it is no longer possible for all to participate directly in the political life of the community, then the best alternative is one based on representation.

The best form of representative government is one in which the representative body has the duties of control and criticism, whilst the actual control of affairs is left in the hands of a well trained and intelligent few.

There are two great dangers in representative government. First, there is the danger that the representative body will consist of mainly unintelligent members who are controlled by an equally unintelligent popular opinion. Secondly, the numerical majority will concern itself only with its own interests which will result in a predominance of legislation in its favour. Minority opinion will not be heard and minorities will, in effect, be disenfranchised.

It is of great importance, then, that the representatives are of a high calibre who will be able to take a wider and more informed view than their constituents. Thus, the representative is not a 'delegate' in the sense that he simply reflects the views of the majority of his constituents, he is a more knowledgeable and informed person than his electorate, and thus better able to make decisions regarding their interests.

As Currin Shields argues "this claim implies that standards of political value exist external to and independent from the government; by consulting these objective principles, an elite can determine how authority should be exercised to promote the general interest."[9] Shields accuses Mill of advocating an elitist society where in theory the people are supreme, but in practice they are without power and are ruled by an elite minority which is chosen on the basis of merit. But Mill does not indicate where this elite group will obtain its superior standards and values and why its values will have a greater utility for the society than those of the 'uninformed' majority.

The Utilitarian/Liberal view essentially saw society in terms of individuals presenting their interests to the state, which in turn governed in a way which aided this aggregation of individual interests. The questions was: how best could these individual interests be represented?

But there is an alternative view of representation which sees society divided into strata, or functional groupings. Each of these groupings has a right to be represented, due to their importance to society. This collectivist view of representation may

217

be expressed by those with varying ideological beliefs. Socialists may see society divided into various socio-economic strata. These socioeconomic interests may be best expressed by a party system in a parliamentary democracy. Pluralists see society as being divided among a wide diversity of interests some of which will be expressed via the political party process, but others will need to seek access to the political system by other means. Conservatives may see society in a traditional organic form, with part of that society, the governing elite, being more able to express the will of the society as a whole than any other part. Whatever the ideological approach, however, it is difficult to reconcile these collectivist theories of representation with a system of representation which drew its inspiration from the liberal emphasis on the individual as the basis of society and state.

One way in which this can be done is to perceive the political party as a bridge between the individual voter and the state. The political party expresses both the views of its members via intraparty democracy and at the same time provides alternative policies to the voters at election time. In Schumpeter's terms voter participation in the political process is restricted to choosing between political party contestants at regular intervals.[10] In this sense there is no direct expression of the individual voters interests in the political process. But if the citizen's interests are not expressed via this channel, then he may choose to combine with others of similar interests and form an interest group.

At this point the discussion of representation turns from the contrast of individual versus collectivist theories of representation to a consideration of the potentially harmful effects of powerful interest groups on the political decision making process in contemporary society.

Mill's concerns, that majority views would prevail over those of the minority regardless of the merits of their case, have been replaced by the concern that the views of powerful interest groups will prevail over both individual interests and those of other interest groups.

One possible approach to this problem is to suggest that the methods of representation be brought into line with the actualities of the political process. Representation should be based on the collectivity. Interest groups should be represented in Parliament on the basis of their functional utility to society. There are two problems with this approach: one is the question of who is to decide on the comparative functional utility of each group. The second problem is the dynamic and changing nature of the society itself. Interest groups which would have a 'right' to representation at a certain time may lose their economic and social utility as time passes and need to be replaced by others.

It is difficult to imagine such groups voluntarily relinquishing their representation on the grounds that they no longer have a useful function in society. If it could be shown that their economic utility had waned, they would most likely stake their claim on the basis of social utility — a far more ambiguous category.

Contemporary Western political systems can be seen as a compromise between the nineteenth century liberal theory of representation with its emphasis on individual interests, and a collectivist theory of representation expressed through the activities of interest groups in the political process. This means that we have left unresolved the question of whether the common good is best expressed via an aggregate of individual interests, or whether the common good can only be pursued by collectivities. Both the aggregate of individual interests, as measured by the Gallup polls, and the degree of political pressure exerted by interest groups play a role in determining political outcomes. The result appears to be haphazard, piecemeal, incremental changes in the provision of social goods. This is frequently called "disjointed incrementalism." It is regarded as an irrational and often unpredictable process by which decisions are made in the political system. It is the opposite of the planned rational approach which we tend to regard as desirable in the decision making process. It indicates that within the evolved values of society we face both choices and constraints. These may vary according to both issues, time and place, and may explain why societies differ in the choices they make when faced with similar sets of circumstances.

An example of this process are the problems that most developed countries face in the provision of health care services. They are confronting similar problems: the escalation of costs in technologically sophisticated health care systems, the need to integrate services increasingly fragmented by specialization, and to develop new and more economic ways to provide primary services to the population.

David Mechanic relates these problems to the fact that the systems of rationing in health care systems are in a process of transition. He identifies three rationing systems: rationing by fee, implicit rationing and explicit rationing.[11] At each phase in these rationing systems we move from situations in which choices are made by the individual user — the closest to a free market system, to one where the choice tends to be made by interest groups — a semi market system, until we finally reach the point where most of the important choices are made by the state and rationing is imposed upon both the consumer and the supplier. Under the system of *rationing by fee*, those with the financial means were able to obtain whatever level of health care was available. Those people who did not have sufficient funds were dependent upon whatever services were provided by the government, the philanthropy of the churches and the medical profession. As long as medical technology remained unsophisticated this system worked reasonably well, since health professionals were only able to offer the public a limited range of health services.

Once medical technology and knowledge began to develop more rapidly after the First World War, and far more active medical intervention became possible, the costs of a serious medical episode became much higher. There was a growing demand for a system that would help individuals share the risk. This was expressed through the development of private insurance plans, and as costs mounted, government intervention in the health insurance field was sought. With the introduction of third party payment a system of *implicit rationing* was introduced. Implicit rationing depends upon a queue. Limited resources, facilities and manpower are made available. It is assumed that the medical practitioner will make a rational choice in distributing the limited resources giving the highest priority to those whose health care needs are most acute. But he may have his own biases as to the relative importance of various health needs and, at the same time, some groups of consumers may be more demanding than others.

A contemporary example of implicit rationing is the establishment of pre paid medical plans and Health Maintenance Organizations, especially in the U.S.A. Under these arrangements private insurance companies contract with a group of doctors who agree to provide all outpatient services to a group of patients for a capitation fee. From the monthly premiums it collects the insurance company creates a fund to cover the costs of hospitalization. If the doctors and the affiliated hospitals spend less on hospitalization than the insurance company has earmarked, they may have the opportunity to share the savings. Thus both doctors and hospitals have an incentive to reduce costs. This implies rationing, with both the medical profession and the hospital administrators the main decisionmakers. Certain interest groups the insurance companies, the purchasers of insurance packages (usually large companies), the medical profession and the affiliated hospitals play a major role in deciding the choices and the constraints in the provision of public goods.

As the provision of health care moves from the private sector to the public sector the range of interests involved in the decision making process become much broader. It is at this level that the State has the prime responsibility to reflect the interests of the citizens as a whole. Thus in the face of ever increasing costs it may need to move to a system of *explicit rationing*. Under this system, limits are set on total expenditures for care, and there is an attempt to develop mechanisms to arrive at more rational decisions regarding investments in different types of facilities and manpower. Mechanic argues that the difficulty in establishing priorities and standards in this way is the overall lack of definitive evidence as to which health care practices really make a difference in illness outcomes.[12] Wagner and Zubkoff support this view when they claim that there is mounting evidence that many health services have made little difference in health outcomes. Nonmedical factors appear to have been more important in reducing mortality and morbidity rates over the past fifty years.[13]

Mechanic is searching for a rational planned basis on which to justify explicit rationing of health care by the public sector. This would require a statistical analysis of the health outcomes of specific treatments, an analysis of the extent of iatrogenic disease, especially related to the overuse of certain medical treatments such as prescription drugs, and an evaluation of costs and health outcomes of innovative medical technology. Such a thorough analysis of the health care system in any country seems unlikely. If it was undertaken, it seems probable that its results would be challenged by threatened interest groups.

Thus the question recurs: If decisions cannot be made regarding the provision of public goods on a planned rational basis, how is the decision to be made? It seems the answer lies in most pluralist societies in a balancing, by the political system, of individual and interest group demands and expectations. As a result, countries with similar political systems may supply different answers to the same social question, depending upon the balance of political groups existing at the time crucial decisions were made.

A case in point is the varying approach of the Canadian and Australian federal governments to the question of national health insurance plans. The two countries have many cultural, economic and political similarities, yet their approach on this issue has been different.

Both countries have a federal parliamentary form of government with a political culture strongly influenced by the British. Their economies are heavily depended on natural resources, yet their labour forces are employed primarily in the industrial and service sectors. The majority of the population live in urban areas surrounded by a vast, largely uninhabited, hinterland. In terms of development, standard of living, influence of other English speaking cultures, and activity of interest groups in the political process, both countries have very much in common. They differ in respect to the degree of regionalization.

With two official languages and with, at least, two separate cultures, Canada has a much greater degree of regional heterogeneity. This is not the case in Australia. Both linguistically and culturally there is a high degree of homogeneity in Australia. Each state has a largely urban workforce, and its own natural resource base. In view of the cultural and economic homogeneity of the states it would be assumed that they, and the federal government, would find it easier to reach agreement on social issues than in the more diverse Canadian political system.

In fact the reverse appears to be true, as far as health insurance is concerned. In Canada this issue has been largely resolved for almost 20 years.[14] In Australia there has been continuing controversy and debate, with complete policy reversals occurring as late as the 1970s.

After the Second World War there was a growth of voluntary health insurance plans in Canada and Australia. Although there had been discussion of publicly supported health insurance schemes during the Second World War, they had not been made operational. In Australia the Labour party government adopted a National Health Insurance Plan in 1942. It was incorporated into the necessary legislation, but it was never

222

implemented because of the opposition of the Australian branch of the British Medical Association.[15]

The progress toward a national health insurance programme in Canada was less direct but no more successful. In early 1943 the proponents of such a plan were able to establish a House of Commons Special Committee on Social Security with the responsibility to report on the practical measures required to implement a comprehensive social security plan. The Committee heard the opinions of a number of groups, including the Canadian Medical Association and the Canadian Hospital Council. Both groups supported a national health, although the Canadian Medical Association made it plain that the schedule of fees should be under the complete control of the organized profession in each province.[16]

Despite the support of major interest groups, the proposals to implement a national health insurance plan became a victim of the federal-provincial disputes over taxation changes at the Dominion Provincial Conference in August 1945.

In the ensuing years the voluntary private health insurance plans grew in both countries. By 1952 almost 5.5 million people were insured for hospital benefits in Canada through voluntary and commercial insurance plans. Almost 4 million were insured for medical and/or surgical benefits.[17] The success of the commercial plans probably provoked a reversal of the previous positions of the main interest groups. The Canadian Medical Association abandoned its 1943 policy of support for a national health insurance scheme, and proposed instead the extension of voluntary plans to cover all Canadians. The task of the government would be to pay the premiums for low income and indigent Canadians. The Canadian Hospital Association and the commercial industry supported these proposals.

According to Taylor, the Liberal government under St. Laurent had become reluctant to commit itself to a federally supported national health insurance programme. There were several concerns. In the first place, it was clear that the Canadian Medical Association, the Canadian Hospital Association and the commercial insurance industry were now opposed. There was some concern about the cost of the programme, since a publicly supported plan cannot exclude poor risks. Finally, there was the realization that a high degree of cooperation was required between the federal and provincial levels of government.[18]

On the other hand, there were several provincial health insurance plans. Saskatchewan led the way and Alberta and British Columbia had followed. In Taylor's view the federal government was gradually pushed toward developing a national health insurance plan by Premier Frost of Ontario.[19] As the Ontario government maintained pressure on this issue for several years, the federal government was pushed first to announce a national proposal in January 1956, and then a compromise proposal in early 1957. In April 1957 the legislation was passed, despite the fact that six of the provinces had not indicated that they would be willing to join. By 1961 all provinces had joined and almost the total population of Canada was covered.

Despite the resistance of important interest groups, the unwillingness of some of the provinces, and the reluctance of the federal government, Canada had legislated and implemented a national hospital insurance plan. Taylor explains this success in terms of two major factors: the skill of the Premier of Ontario in pursuing this end and the problems of operating a fragmented system.[20] The Premier had gradually persuaded the provincial interest groups to accept his approach. The Ontario Hospital Association had been drawn into the discussions at an early date. The Ontario Medical Association came to accept the plan tentatively, so long as medical services in the diagnostic field were considered separately from hospital care.

Faced with a similar political and economic situation, the Australian government moved in the opposite direction. In 1953 the Liberal/ Country Party government introduced a Voluntary Health Insurance Plan. It provided a subsidy to those citizens who voluntarily joined private health insurance funds. This scheme persisted without substantial amendments until the late 1960s. However, the programme was regarded as unsatisfactory and this eventually led to the appointment of a Commonwealth Committee of Inquiry under Mr. Justice Nimmo. The Committee found that the programme was unnecessarily complex and beyond the comprehension of many. The benefits received were often much less than the cost of the hospital and medical treatment. The premiums had increased substantially so that it was beyond the capability of lower income groups to pay them. Furthermore, the rules of many of the insurance companies limited claims for particular conditions.[21] The Nimmo Committee visited Canada and they were impressed by the Canadian system. They noted that despite the fact that the Canadian system gave universal and comprehensive coverage, it had been more effective in containing overall health costs than the U.S.A.. This appeared to be due to the lower cost of physician services in Canada and, in particular, to the lower costs of administration.[22]

AUSTRALIAN HEALTH CARE SYSTEM

In the federal election of 1972 the Labour party was returned to office after a long period as the opposition party. During their period in opposition they had developed a comprehensive health insurance program designed to cover the entire population, funded from a health tax and administered by a federal government authority. Attempts to introduce the legislation for this program were strongly opposed by the federal opposition parties, the Australian Medical Association and the voluntary health insurance funds. The legislation to introduce Medibank, as the health insurance program was called, was twice rejected by the Senate. The legislation was only passed after a new election in which the Labour party was once more returned to power.

After considerable negotiation the medical insurance aspects of Medibank were introduced on July 1, 1975 and a federal Health Insurance Commission was established. However, after the election of the Liberal-National party coalition in December 1985, the new government systematically dismantled the main features of Medibank. By 1981 this government had essentially returned to the private voluntary health insurance program. The federal subsidy was payable only to members of voluntary registered health funds.

With another swing of the political pendulum the Labour party was returned to power in 1983. The party reintroduced a system of universal tax funded health insurance administered by a federal Health Insurance Commission. Medicare, as the new plan was called, differed from Medibank mainly in that part of the increased cost to the federal government was met by a one per cent levy on taxable income.

Opposition to the new health insurance program was more subdued on this occasion. The Australian Medical Association indicated that despite its philosophical objections to compulsory health insurance it would not actively oppose the program. However, the Liberal Party, in the 1987 federal election campaign, again indicated its intention to dismantle the principal elements of Medicare. As it has not yet succeeded in defeating the Labour Party, the basic Medicare plan is still in operation as of 1993.

A major point of conflict, since the introduction of Medicare, has been the method of payment to physicians providing medical services to patients in hospitals. Under the original medicare arrangements physicians treating patients in public hospitals were normally paid by the hospital on a part-time salaried (seasonal) basis. Physicians' treatment of private patients in public hospitals was on a fee-for-service basis. Much of the physicians opposition to Medibank and Medicare was based on the expectation that as the number of private patients declined the physicians' incomes would decrease, since sessional payment arrangements were substantially less than the amounts they would receive from fee-for-service.

This was the basis for the doctors' dispute which occurred mainly in New South Wales where many orthopaedic surgeons and ophthalmologists resigned from the public hospital system. Palmer and Short[23] suggest that one possible solution to the problem would be to move to the Canadian practice of permitting physicians to bill on a fee-for-service basis all patients in public hospitals. In this way, there would be no automatic income advantage attached to privately insured patients. This would require an increase in the health tax levy to offset the higher cost of medical services, but it would also mean the removal of a continuing source of irritation among physicians.

It is unlikely that there will be a fundamental change in the Australian health care system, as long as the Labour party continues to control the federal government. However, if the Liberal/National parties had won the 1993 federal election, they may have been tempted to dismantle the present system and proceed once more with a system based upon voluntary private health insurance.

The decision to do this would depend upon a number of factors:

- the length of time the present system has been in place;
- the degree of opposition by the medical profession to the present system;
- the amount of public support for a comprehensive Medicare program.

Over the last four decades, a publicly funded health insurance program has been a far greater political football in Australia than it has been in Canada. While there have been a number of disputes relating to health care in Canada, especially over such issues as extra billing, the fundamental principles of a publicly funded program have not been seriously questioned. In contrast, in Australia, the debate relating to the costs and efficiency of a publicly funded system continued throughout the 1970s, despite the fact that the original Medibank scheme proved to have one third of the administrative costs of the previous fragmented private system.

It is hard to find any fundamental differences in the political, economic, or social environment of Canada and Australia which would explain the difference in public policy direction in the health field. At most, it is possible to point to a higher degree of regionalization in Canada, and to perhaps a slightly more conservative orientation in the Australian political scene. But these two aspects appear to provide an inadequate explanation. Premier Frost headed a Progressive Conservative government in Ontario, and the greater degree of regionalization in Canada would presumably be more of a hindrance to developing a national plan than an aid. In both countries a national health insurance plan had been discussed in detail and even accepted in principle during the Second World War. In both countries private health insurance plans had become well established after the war. Neither the Australian or the Canadian federal governments had shown any particular interest in developing a national health insurance plan in the 1950s.

The difference, if there is one at all, seems to lie in the greater degree of heterogeneity among the Canadian provinces. Since the provinces tend to differ economically, socially and sometimes culturally, this may lay the foundation for a greater degree of experimentation. Taylor regards Saskatchewan's contribution to the establishment of a national health insurance programme as very important. On both occasions, that is, for both hospital and medical insurance, it led the way and demonstrated to the rest of the country that it could be done.[24]

Taylor tends to attribute Saskatchewan's initiative to a combination of characteristics unique to the province:

> the precarious underpinnings of the one crop economy and the severity of the depression; the geography of the province that

yielded a uniformly thin distribution of population in small rural municipalities and urban centres; the high proportion of citizens serving as local government councilors and school trustees together with the extraordinary number of cooperative associations that also contributed to widespread citizen participation in policy making and reinforced an orientation directed to collective action to solve mutual problems....[25]

In other words the dire economic circumstances and the lack of political power within Confederation tended to force Saskatchewan into collective social action and experimentation to find a solution to some of their problems. They demonstrated that publicly funded hospital and medical insurance programmes could work effectively, and a wealthy and powerful province like Ontario could start the move for a national plan and effectively manoeuvre the federal government into supporting it.

Once a programme is securely established, and it is perceived as serving the interests of individual citizens, then it becomes difficult to remove. The balance between the aggregate of individual demands and the demands of affected interest groups shifts in favour of the aggregate of individual citizens. Individual voters can become united around issues that affect their own interests directly. The disadvantages that arise from their lack of organizational unity is offset by their direct access to the vote. Governments respond to them at election time and to the polls which indicate their preferences between elections.

Interest groups, on the other hand, only have indirect access to representation. They may seek to influence the political process by lobbying, and they may threaten to use their power to influence blocks of voters at election time. But they cannot usually directly participate in the political process. If they enjoyed some type of functional representation then presumably they would be able to shift the political decision making process more directly in their favour. While their indirect influence on the decision making process may be useful and very effective on a number of occasions, it is probably ineffective once a substantial proportion of the voting public supports a particular policy or plan of action.

NOTES

1. L. Robbins, *The Theory of Economic Policy in English Classical Political Economy*, p. 28.

2. *Ibid.*, p. 37.
3. Werner Stark, *Jeremy Bentham*, Vol. III, p. 333.
4. T.W. Hutchinson, "Bentham as an Economist," *Economic Journal*, June 1956, p. 303.
5. F.A. Hayek, *The Road to Serfdom*, pp. 42–43.
6. G.H. Sabine, *History of Political Theory*, p. 607.
7. R.J. Bennett, *The Geography of Public Finance*, p. 17.
8. *Ibid.*
9. C.V. Shields, Introduction, in John Stuart Mill, *Considerations on Representative Government*, p. xxxiii.
10. Schumpeter, *Capitalism, Socialism and Democracy*, p. 273.
11. D. Mechanic, "Growth of Medical Technology and Bureaucracy: Implications for Health Care" in *Technology and the Future of Health Care*, edited by J.B. McKinlay, p. 3.
12. D. Mechanic, *Ibid.*, p. 7.
13. J.L. Wagner, and M. Zubkoff, "Medical Technology and Hospital Costs," in *Technology and the Future of Health Care*, edited by J.B. McKinlay, p. 106.
14. The National Medical Care Insurance Act 1966–1967 established the current medical insurance plan.
15. For an account of the health insurance programmes in Australia from the time of the Second World War see B.S. Hetzel, *Health and Australian Society*, Ch. 8.
16. M. Taylor, *Health Insurance and Canadian Public Policy*, p. 28.
17. *Ibid.*, p. 171.
18. *Ibid.*, p. 183.
19. *Ibid.*, pp. 135–38.
20. *Ibid.*, pp. 158 & 159.
21. *Op. cit.*, p. 269.
22. *Op. cit.*, pp. 271 & 272.
23. S.R. Palmer, and S.D. Short, *Health Care and Public Policy: An Australian Analysis*, p. 69.
24. M. Taylor, p. 418.
25. *Ibid.*

A General Model of Government Intervention

Randy G. Hoffman

The ongoing interactions between government and the governed can be considered as the dynamic aspects of an extremely complex (highly interconnected) system which is in itself conceptually inseparable from the entire national society. Any attempt to predict the broader consequences of an alteration in the behaviour of any group within society must, due to considerations of this complexity, take one of two forms. In one, a particular behavioral change, either transient or sustained, is examined with analytical techniques appropriate to it. The use of this method does not typically involve an understanding of the system that goes beyond what may be learned from such casual observations. Historical evidence from similar phenomena affecting the same group(s) can then be employed to hypothesize the nature of the interactions and dependencies of immediate interest. The weakness of this method for prediction is that the accuracy of predictions will depend upon each new phenomenon being a close replication, in terms of the whole system and the nature of the apprehended changes, to the prior phenomena.

A second method is to study a class of phenomena through the construction of a model that simplifies reality in order that its essential, salient features and cause and effect relationships can be understood. The model will therefore not comprehensively simulate reality; but it should specify logical interrelationships among its components and be complete enough for whatever purpose it is designed.

In this paper, I introduce a model of government intervention to be employed for the purpose of discerning whether a particular application of a governing instrument, regardless of the policy area, is likely to be effective for its stated goals, or at least better or worse than alternative policies for the same purpose. The benefits to be ultimately derived from such a model are the ability to select policy formulations which are of high quality, and to predict the likely performance of intended measures.

Intervention is defined here as the application of any governing instrument: whether moral suasion, resource allocation, or regulation: in short, any way in which a government can give effect to its policy decisions through modifying the behaviour and/or economic and social circumstances of individuals or groups within the private sector. This is a broad working definition of intervention consistent with my aim to model a broad class of phenomena. I shall attempt to show below that the quality or effectiveness of interventions are related to measurements along selected dimensions that may be applied to all interventions. The price of such generality is the lack of an assurance of rigorously accurate determinations of effectiveness in all instances.

THE MODEL

In the literature, two methodologies for studying government intervention commonly emerge. In one, the policy area of intervention is acknowledged, and that area (such as health care or broadcasting) will suggest an appropriate analytical framework, different in many respects from those that might be employed for other interventionist activities. An example is the "General Theory of Regulation" developed over the past two decades by Stigler and Peltzman. Those authors have suggested a transactional analysis specific to regulatory activity in which goods (votes, redistributed wealth, market power etc.) are exchanged between the regulating body and affected groups. The transaction takes place in a way that maintains an equilibrium between

231

the utility values received by the most materially affected parties. The government as well as some private sector groups, who
will then support the government, perceive a profitable transaction; while those suffering disutilities tend to be affected only
marginally, perhaps subliminally, on a per capita basis.[1] This
approach, dealing with the exchange of resources, can be employed to explain the motivating factors behind government's
choice of regulation and society's acceptance of that choice.
More recently, Bryson and Ring[2] have established transaction
dimensions which pertain to various policy mechanisms (governing instruments) and generate qualitative measurements of performance stated in terms of governing principles such as the
degrees of efficiency, justice, and liberty. This analysis, as is
generally the case with transactional approaches, does not adequately address the questions of whether the regulations effectively satisfy their policy goals.

Also, this phenomenological approach addressing motivating
factors is tied to particular policy areas. The analytical framework devised is context specific. In Canada, discussions of
diverse areas of government activity treat them as distinct phenomena, and focus upon the goals to be achieved, the methods
of achievement, and the perceived desirable and undesirable
consequences. Although there are linkages to other concerns, for
example the effect of regional development policy upon national,
aggregate economic performance, the quantitative or literary
models advanced typically do not exhibit the qualities of generality. Their analytical methods are more or less confined to a
select area of policy.[3] In addition, Morah has pointed out that
even in context specific analyses there are many barriers between the measurement of an outcome or result of policy and
the assessment of what formulation and implementation factors
were responsible for the degree of success or failure obtained.
He further states that political considerations are more involved
in the selection and alteration of policies than are considerations of effectiveness based on historical experience.[4]

There has also been significant attention paid to the formulation of a taxonomy of governing instruments with appropriate
categories that could then be used to explain the preferences for
each category according to the situational variables surrounding
each policy decision. Howlett has described American, British,
and Canadian work in these taxonomies, and has observed that

the categories selected reflect national "characteristic processes by which they arrive at policy decisions."[5]

Generally, the categories of governing instruments are depicted as following a continuum from the least coercive (moral suasion), through expenditure solutions, to the most coercive (direct regulatory action). Doern and Wilson, commenting in their 1974 collection of Public Policy essays, and Doern, commenting in his 1978 collection of essays on the Regulatory Process, suggest that lack of effectiveness of exhortation (moral suasion) and the limited supply of expenditure instruments, respectively, tend to motivate government to move along the continuum to direct regulation. Conversely, they observe that this motivation is opposed by the requirement for constitutional clarity (and public acquiescence) that enables direct regulation. Therefore the more "mature" issues, in which well-known and stable public opinions exist, are the likely candidates for this latter treatment.[6]

The concept of a continuum in the selection of governing instruments, and the linkages that Doern and Wilson in Canada and others, internationally, have suggested that exist between points on that continuum and the effectiveness (both in terms of economic efficiency and goal accomplishment) of government's actions, seem to be promising areas for further development. However, it is necessary to develop a comprehensive definition of effectiveness that incorporates qualities related not necessarily to political "spin" or ideological preference, but rather to whether the *tangible* goals of the policy were effectively accomplished. In this way an analytical framework for intervention would exist independently of specific policy areas and ideological preferences. By choosing the measurement dimensions of an intervention appropriately, I shall attempt to show that a generic model can be devised which will have some significant predictive value regarding the consequences of the implementation of the policy. The model which follows does not, however, overlap the territory of the transactional theories of regulation. It does not model the motivational forces that generate intervention. It rather seeks to describe, in terms of dimensional measurements, only the type of intervention. The predictive aspects are then derived from linkages between the particular measurements and useful indicators of quality or effectiveness.

As will soon be apparent, the weakness in this model is its generally qualitative rather than rigorously quantitative nature. It was not my intention, however, to create only a literary model. I shall attempt to show that predictions of effectiveness can be considered as reasonably accurate indications without being overly concerned with precise quantitative determinations. Predictive statements will therefore be analogous to: "tall people are heavier than short people." This is a useful observation that is generally true, although it will sometimes be in error. In this case, the model of people that prompts this statement is one of classification by height. The intervention model below is comprised of classifications that enable conclusions of general truth at least with respect to the relative effectiveness of alternate forms of intervention. But in the study of a specifically intended or completed action, the current role of the model shall be mainly to provide an analytical framework to facilitate a more insightful analysis of the nature of the intervention and its linkage with results or performance.

DIMENSIONS OF MEASUREMENT

The essential nature of the model being proposed is the establishment of three independent dimensions by which an intervention can be measured. They are not the types of intervention suggested by Lowi: distributive, redistributive, regulative, and constituent, or subsequent formulations by others which still follow the traditional political science descriptions of such activities.[7] The critical qualities that the dimensions must possess is that they can be applied to a broad range of actual policies, yield categorical measurements of such policies, and that they can be axiomatically linked to useful and comprehensive quality characteristics. The latter is necessary, as otherwise empirical evidence would have to be gathered to substantiate the linkages, and such evidence must always be situationally specific. The dimensions are, as it turns out, more related to Lowi's political characteristics that are differentiated by degrees of directness or indirectness in the application of legitimate coercion.[8] Below, the dimensions are described, following which I shall attempt to show a relationship between the model as defined by measurements along these dimensions to the effectiveness of an intervention.

Strategic/Reactive

This first dimension probably presents the most severe measurement problem. Although these terms have been widely employed, it is difficult to isolate precise meanings. Such is necessary, however, if the dimension is to be useful; and it is further required that the working definitions chosen should be as unambiguously applicable as possible to actual interventions. Therefore, a purely reactive intervention is defined as one which responds only to the superficial aspects of the issue, without visible concern for underlying or root causes. The word "visible" is important, as otherwise it would be necessary to try to examine the thought processes of members of governmental policy-making bodies not a particularly rewarding line of inquiry. Suppose, for example, a regulatory response to inflation consisted of only a total, permanent ban on price increases. This would be indicative of a complete disregard for the national economic environment and its complex workings, despite what reasoning may have led to this action.

The term reactive is employed because it has been extensively applied by those authors who carry out the analysis of intervention in particular policy areas. Their use of it often denotes a "kneejerk" governmental response to a highly salient and specific issue that gives scant consideration to deeper or broader priorities or consequences. The decision-making process that gives rise to such measures has been termed by Lindblom and others as "incrementalism," or steps in the process of successive limited comparisons.[9] The term "satisficing" is also employed in these instances. It suggests that, when an optimizing policy is not discernible or is impossible, only small policy changes are advisable, which are perceived to offer acceptable results, and which may be thought of as experimentation unlikely to lead to disastrous results. The rationale for reactive interventions, which may or may not be defensible depending upon circumstances, is, however, not of interest here. I simply note it as an "ideal type" which locates one extreme in the continuum that defines this dimension of measurement.

At the other end of the continuum, the probably unattainable ideal type is a purely strategic response that would consider and deal with all the underlying, root issues to any issue. The identifiable, environmental ramifications of any intervention in the short and long terms would be perceived, and a

235

policy would be formulated which would attempt to deal with them, along with satisfaction of the primary goal(s).

The literature generally refers to strategic planning rather than strategic intervention itself. The relationship between them is, however, very close as strategic planning will logically result in the formulation of a strategic intervention. For example, Hartle, writing as a Deputy Secretary of the Treasury Board, defines strategic planning as (1) forecasts of the changes in the indicators of goal achievement that would occur in the absence of changes in the policy instruments; (2) the assignment by ministers of priorities...to problems...on the basis of this information; (3) identification of...policy instrument changes that might be used...; (4) assessment of their relative effectiveness... (5) selection...of the changes in the policy instruments that would most effectively resolve the highest priority problems....[10] This description, which states the necessity of a broad analysis of the impact of alternative interventions is essentially the same process by which I identify strategic intervention as the one that accounts for environmental consequences. The consequences of importance are virtually the same as Hartle's areas of priority.

Real interventions will likely fall along the strategic-reactive continuum according to the analyst's perception of how many of the root causes and potential environmental interactions are being included in a significant way in the formulation of the governmental response. Note that although ex poste analysis will likely, in all cases, expose previously unforeseen areas of both omission and inclusion, I must take care to separate true omissions from attempts at inclusion that simply missed the mark. The accuracy of an attempt to deal with causal factors of an issue must be treated as one measure of the effectiveness of the intervention. It is in fact one of the quality characteristics that shall be dealt with later. Much of the difficulty in measuring the position of an intervention along the strategic-reactive continuum disappears if absolute (and therefore quantitative) determinations are less important than a comparison of the position among two or more alternative interventions designed to fulfil the same policy objectives. Since this relative assessment of effectiveness is often what is precisely at issue when a decision must be made concerning how best to intervene, an ordinal measurement of effectiveness between alternatives is valuable. The model is probably best employed for this purpose.

For example, suppose several firms are discharging industrial waste in a small river. Although there is concern for the quality of the environment, there is also a danger that pollution controls may severely affect the economic life of the community, for which these firms are the principal employers. Government could simply: (1) regulate an immediate reduction in effluent levels; or alternatively, (2) such reductions could be phased in over a certain period of years. Government may also agree (3) to provide grants or tax reductions to defray part of the costs. These monies could be calculated as less than the expected discounted value of future unemployment insurance/welfare payments, and loss of creation of economic surplus that would be required should direct regulation cause plant closures. Suppose the adverse environmental developments of interest are, in order of priority, (1) destruction of the local economy (with a potentially broader multiplier effect), (2) the setting of a precedent in assisting private industry to meet pollution requirements, and (3) the increased expenditure of public funds. It would then appear that the second alternative action, which best deals with side effects one and three is the most strategic in nature. With respect to causal factors, this alternative avoids the outlay of public funds. One identifiable causal factor of pollution could be the private sector's perception that it is government's job to remedy pollution and business' job to operate economically. Note, however, that the second alternative may not necessarily be the highest quality intervention in all respects. For that determination, I must apply the other two dimensions of the model and generate a quality prediction based upon a complete measurement, as I shall show below.

Direct/Indirect

Figure 1 schematically depicts the sequence of effects caused by the intervention "A." For the purpose of a measurement along this dimension, "A" is considered to be either a single component of the exercise of a governing instrument (e.g., a regulation from a group of regulations) or multiple components which are very closely related, both in mode and purpose, and which have the same goal(s). As will become clear below, a single measurement of multiple policy components may include some which are direct and others which are indirect. Similarly, if the intervention is aimed at the accomplishment of multiple goals or

237

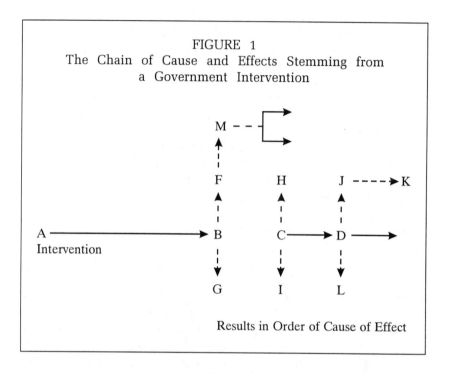

FIGURE 1
The Chain of Cause and Effects Stemming from
a Government Intervention

Results in Order of Cause of Effect

objectives, then the measurement of whether it is direct or indirect may also depend upon which goal is specified. The same policy may be direct in respect of one goal, but indirect in respect of another. This can be contrasted to the measurement along the strategic-reactive continuum where all components of an intervention must be considered simultaneously.

The direct effect of the intervention (component) "A" is "B." (There may also be several direct effects). All other effects which are in turn caused by "B" are indirect. Some of them may be desirable, indirect goals, while others may be side effects that are undesirable. To specify whether an intervention is direct or whether it has various degrees of indirectness, it is only necessary to ascertain whether the action leads to the specific goal being considered without intermediate stages of cause and effect. For example, government subsidies to farmers may have two goals — directly to assist farmers and indirectly to assist food purchasers. The latter result depends upon the price supports being passed to consumers through the distribution system, and is therefore indirect. Below, I will show that the degree of indirectness is also important in making predictions of effectiveness. Other authors have tended to associate direct intervention with the exercise of coercion in the context of regulatory activity. But in this model, it denotes only the closest possible causal link between the application of any governing instrument and the realization of its goal. It is defined in this way because I shall be able to correlate measurements along it with predictions of effectiveness or quality; and because directness is a distinctly separate (independent) aspect of an intervention. In the above example, farmers may be given a choice whether to subscribe to the price support program. (In doing so, they may, for instance, have to adhere to acreage restrictions). There may be other direct formulations which aspire to the same goal that would be coercive; and the intervention may or may not be strategic depending upon how well it deals with underlying factors.

As with the Strategic-Reactive Dimension, it is easier to compare one intervention with alternatives to determine the degree of indirectness. Nevertheless, the chain of cause and effect is usually identifiable, so that determinations with a useful degree of objectivity can be performed; for example, a public infrastructure improvement project to benefit indirectly the local economy. Ordinal determinations of indirectness are logically carried out by counting the various stages of cause and effect until the goal in question is reached. (In Figure 1, it is schematically depicted as the number of links separating it from "B.")

Coercive/Voluntary

There is no continuum for this dimension. The group or individual which the intervention directly affects must either adhere mandatorily to its provisions or its acceptance is voluntary. Many direct regulations are not coercive. For example, government supported health insurance is voluntary in Ontario, although its main goal of subsidizing the cost of health care is certainly direct. It is not coercive even though a person would have no rationale for declining the coverage. Therefore, in the application of this dimension, it should be appreciated that certain "voluntary" measures may be tantamount to coercion.

It should be noted that in the case of indirect interventions which are also coercive, the intervention can only be coercive with respect to its direct effect ("B" as depicted in Figure 1)

239

which is not the intended goal. Therefore, the targeted group of the indirect goal of a coercive intervention may not be the one being coerced. The establishment of an import tariff, for instance, to assist domestic manufacturers to acquire a larger market share is certainly coercive, but only on importers of the foreign, competitive goods. If the goal is defined as encouraging the sales of domestic products, then the consumers who are targeted are not the group being coerced. As was the case when making direct-indirect measurements, it may be necessary to split an intervention into its components in order to measure coerciveness unambiguously.

MEASURES OF EFFECTIVENESS

The linkages that will be demonstrated between the measurement of an intervention along each of the three dimensions and its effectiveness, can at best suggest likely results, or at worst provide a frame of reference for a latter, detailed study that would then add the context-specific component as an overlay. It is important here that the existence of these linkages is supported axiomatically, because such requires no proof or empirical support that might be valid only if given a narrowly defined sphere of activity. That is, the predictions must follow logically from the nature of the dimensions and the measurements that can be made. The dimensions were chosen with this requirement uppermost.

The choice of what quality measures constitute effectiveness of an intervention has been made in what I feel is the most obvious manner, although it may well be that other choices appear equally valid, and could perhaps be considered in addition to those below:

Accuracy

The accuracy of an intervention is simply the degree to which the intended or stated goals are satisfied, when all effects and interaction are substantially complete, or have reached a state of equilibrium. That is, the process of change is virtually completed. If there are goals stated in objective terms, then a quantitative measure of accuracy is simply the ratio of actual to intended accomplishment. When the expected time of goal accomplishment forms part of the statement of a goal basic (as it should), then the ratio measurement should take place at that time. Otherwise, if a reasonable time passes and equilibrium is still not obtained, there must be the exercise of judgement as to when to determine the accuracy.

This definition of accuracy does not include any measure of precision. If the government wished to stimulate the house construction industry, it might offer all taxpayers a continuing shelter allowance tax exemption based on some proportion of their housing expenses. The measure, if sufficiently generous, might be quite accurate as all those who are prospective home purchasers would then perceive mortgage and other housing costs as partially defrayed, and they would have a higher propensity to buy. But the measure would not be precise. Much of the resources thus distributed would accrue to those occupying rental units or home owners with no intention to purchase another unit. Yet, in some cases, the requirement for accuracy might be sufficiently strong that precision considerations are secondary. In other cases, as in the above example, the reverse might be true. Precision must be treated as a separate entity in order that any desired priority between it and accuracy can be reflected in the design and assessment of interventions.

Precision

From the foregoing, precision can be defined as the degree to which the effect of the intervention is limited to only the intended goal(s). The amplitude of all intended effects is compared to those which are unintended (although not necessarily unanticipated), to arrive at this measure. This definition does not presuppose that all unintended results are undesirable although that is clearly the general case (else they likely would be intended). A plethora of scattered results is at best an indication of uncontrolled intervention which will increase environmental turbulence; and at worst, is counterproductive to the intended measures.

Precision is intrinsically a qualitative measure although still an important one. Undesirable environmental consequences can clearly have visible, deleterious social or economic effects, although quantification of them may be impossible.

Efficiency

This is a difficult measurement to assess in the public sector, even qualitatively. It measures the difference or ratio between the resources or utilities created (benefits) and those expended (costs). However, given that such exchanges of value may take place among any groups in any sector of society, economic measures are nearly always insufficient. Values also expressed in terms of social or economic utility units generally pertain. It is perhaps the search for efficiency and the lack of an objective, common unit of value which renders decision making in the public sector a complex activity. In the United States during the early 1970's top level executives were exchanged between business and government to promote a better understanding of the people and their respective task environments in each sector. The following comment was typical of those business executives who spent time working at a policy-making level in the public bureaucracy.

"Most decisions there are very complicated in terms of who they affect what groups in the country for instance and the way those people are affected...there is no right decision...so you settle for the best of a series of alternatives, none of which is close to ideal."[11]

These executives were directly addressing the difficulties in ascertaining an optimal balance of costs and benefits in public sector interventions. Their sensitivity to the problem was due to their prior private sector experience where purely economic measures, such as return on investment, generally suffice, or at least predominate over other criteria for judging decisions.

Nevertheless, merely because efficiency is difficult to ascertain (and attain) is not a reason to omit it from my measures of effectiveness. The implication is rather that the use of the linkages between the model's dimensions and that determinant of quality are rendered less distinct than for the other determinants.

Time Delay

The nature of intervention that stems from a political decision is that sufficient public support (whether broadly based or located within influential pressure groups) must be perceived before action is taken. Governments far prefer to act when they have established a defensible rationale. This fact tends to force a "management by crisis" flavour to the use of governing instruments, which certainly degrades the public sector's ability to act in timely fashion. When the government is ready to act, results are often required "yesterday." Any additional time delay caused by the design of the intervention is generally an adverse quality of some importance.

Time delay is not a difficult factor to measure even quantitatively. It is simply the period of time between the implementation of an intervention and the accomplishment of the desired goals. In order that it not be confused with accuracy, the ultimate level of achievement is not at issue. Of importance is only that the degree of achievement is no longer significantly increasing at the time that defines the end of the measurement period.

Private (Productive) Sector Environmental Effect

The definition of this last suggested determinant of quality has to be carefully, and somewhat narrowly, defined to avoid it becoming too vague to be used. Obviously, certain measures (for example, the establishment of a minimum wage, unemployment insurance, laws governing product safety, pollution standards, and even corporate income tax) could have a measurable, deleterious effect on the private sector's environment which may be evidenced by a reduction in economic performance indicators such as the GNP. These effects are derived from the chosen, intrinsic nature of a specific intervention and are therefore not to be considered here. They result from an exercise of political preference. My concern is in respect of the choice of the mode of the intervention as described by the dimensions of the model. I wish to establish a linkage by which a mode of accomplishing the same results will be perceived to affect the environment of the private sector more or less deleteriously than other modes, given that government wishes to maintain a viable private sector.

A relatively complex example is the effort to reduce inflation. Allowing and encouraging high and highly variable interest rates is one method in which environmental instabilities are established or increased. Industrial expansion plans are in doubt because of the cost of debt capital, and the reception of the stock market to a share offering making the consumer demand for products all the more volatile. Behaviour that will optimize on the part of corporations is less discernible by their managements. Profits will then tend to be adversely affected; unless the nature of the business offers built-in protection, such as for

243

chartered banks. Alternatively, wage and price controls are aimed at the same objective with relatively little short run environmental turbulence. This is not to say that the latter mode is preferable to industry. But it seems to be resisted more for the ideological aspects the removal of management and labour's discretionary power over price and wage decisions, and the long run distortions it will cause, if the regulations remained in place. (And which might then have to be resolved by rationing.)

Whether business favours the objective of government action is not at issue here. It is arguable, in any event, whether the private sector was happier in 1981 with high interest rates, than in the earlier 1970's with wage and price controls. It can be shown that, in Canada, for many key industries such as steel, automobile manufacturing, appliances, transportation, food production etc., performance has been more severely disrupted in the more recent attack on inflation. Some of the blame for that must be attached to the environmental instability inherent to the chosen mode of action to combat inflationary pressures.

The assumption upon which the inclusion of the environmental effect is justified, is that the maintenance of a favourable business environment is desirable. This is easy to demonstrate. Canadian society, even though existing as a mixed economy, is still almost totally reliant upon the private sector for the production of most of its goods and services. While the government may have interventionist objectives, there is nothing to be lost, and much to be gained or maintained by pursuing these aims in a less disruptive fashion, if it can be so done with similar effectiveness. This is not tantamount to a pro-business orientation for government. Adherence to that value also requires that the goals of interventions themselves will reflect it. In the context of the above examples, those goals may be perceived by business interests as very unfavourable. But even in these instances, the infliction of further damage purely through the choice of the means to achieve those goals, can only be judged as a negative contribution to the intervention's quality.[12]

A useful characterization of business environments depicts them as consisting of both formal and informal groups which interact through resource exchanges. Turbulence, which is the unpredictable component of variability inherent in those interactions,[13] is the parameter of environmental degradation which government intervention (among, of course, other causes not at issue here) can engender, apart from any deleterious effects that result solely from the specific goal of the intervention. Turbulence causes change that is less predictable as its intensity increases. Excessive turbulence will tend to degrade the performance optimizing competence of private sector organizations.

LINKAGES BETWEEN THE MODEL AND EFFECTIVENESS

Figure 2 summarizes the linkages that are discussed below. I have attempted to impute a linkage only where there is a logical justification for it that is not derived from specific examples of intervention. Rather, it must be based upon an easily demonstrated, abstractly justified relationship between the dimension and the determinant of quality. Of course, as observed above, the requirement of generality and measurement difficulties leads to exceptions or examples where contradiction is unavoidably perceived. The relationships between the quality determinants and the position of an intervention along the three dimensions of the model are best considered as likely tendencies. This can yield useful information as it establishes an analytical frame of

---

FIGURE 2

Linkages Between Dimensions of the Model and Quality Measures of Effectiveness

Three Dimensions of the Model

Quality Determinants	Strategic/ Reactive	Direct/ Indirect	Coercive/ Voluntary
Accuracy	*/*	*greater*/less	*greater*/less
Precision	*greater*/less	*greater*/less	*/*
Efficiency	*/*	*greater*/less	*greater*/less
Time Delay	*/*	*less*/greater	*less*/greater
Environmental Effect on Private Sector	*less*/more deleterious	*less*/more deleterious	marginally *less*/more

* indicates the lack of a generally supportable linkage

---

reference by which historical, present or future interventions can be considered. It follows that the most reliable predictive use of the model is to compare two or more alternative modes of intervention designed to accomplish the same goal. A search for tighter, more deterministic linkages would, at this stage of the model's development, be fruitless; the result being that no linkage could be established.

With respect, first, to the strategic-reactive dimension, the very nature of the strategic approach, as defined above, almost assures a more precise accomplishment of the government's goal. The highly strategic intervention attempts at the outset to counteract, through its design, the dampening of undesired side effects and unfavourable changes in environmental inter-actions through a close analysis of cause and effect in the context of the issue at hand. For that reason, an unplanned deleterious environmental effect upon the private sector is very likely minimized. Less turbulence (uncontrolled changes) will, by definition, create less environmental disruption. Other qual-ity determinants, however, do not suggest linkages with the strategic-reactive dimension which can be logically supported.

The dimension which suggests the strongest overall linkage with effectiveness is the direct-indirect. The depiction of the causal chain of intervention consequences in Figure 1 is a use-ful illustration in this regard. First with respect to accuracy, a direct intervention (the intended result would be "B" in Figure 1) is clearly likely to better reflect this quality. A measure that directly accomplishes the intended result(s), and which does not rely upon an extended chain of cause and effect (as would be increasingly the case if the intended result was C or D, etc.), is much easier to design accurately. The shorter the chain of events between cause and desired effect, the easier it is to per-ceive the details of the relationship and incorporate them in the design of the appropriate intervention (cause).

The argument to support generally greater precision for di-rect intervention as opposed to indirect, rests upon a similar ra-tionale. Unless the environment is in an extreme state of instability (turbulence) any changes in existing interactions, such as those caused by an intervention, will eventually allow the environmental area affected to settle to a new stable state. The analogy of ripples in a pond dying out as their distance from the original splash increases, is appropriate. Therefore, it is probable that as the effect being considered moves from B to E,

J, K, or M, the amplitude or intensity of the effect lessens. If one of the latter results is a desired indirect goal of the measure, unwanted antecedent effects which are direct, or less indirect, may well be stronger than the desirable one(s).

It can be concluded, therefore, that precision of indirect interventions is generally inferior to the direct or less indirect modes. And if the precision is lower for the reason of an extended chain of cause and effect, the amount of resource expenditure in that instance is likely required to be greater to accomplish a given indirect, desired result. There will be a tendency for the resources expended to be spread out over unwanted effects. Therefore, efficiency of the direct intervention also tends to be superior. This latter linkage can only apply when the direct intervention requires an expenditure of public money; or decreases the utility of some group(s) and increases it for others. Direct actions which do not perceptively involve value exchanges would avoid an efficiency measure, except perhaps in terms of sociopolitical utility, measuring the latter always being a difficult measurement problem.

Finally, there are two reasons to suspect that environmental degradation will usually be more severe in the case of indirect intervention. First, the higher relative amplitude of unwanted (and perhaps unplanned) antecedent and/or side effects may engender the results. Second, the longer the chain of cause and effect, the more difficult it is to design the intervention for the desired intensity of results. This may lead to some situations where "overkill" occurs. The stronger measure will then adversely affect environmental stability throughout the causal chain (which will be more extensive than the illustration of Figure 1). Conversely, the inherent lack of predictability in lengthy causal chains may lead to interventions which underachieve the results and force a revamping of the policy and adjustment of initial measures. In that instance, additional environmental changes are generated. Neither of these problems would be as prevalent when the direct mode is used.

The coercive-voluntary dimension separates measures which are mandatory and therefore more predictable in effect, from those which may be avoided by the exercise of such a preference on the part of the intervenees, and which are therefore less predictable in effect. It is precisely the degree of predetermination that provides the linkages with the quality determinants. The two most obvious linkages concern accuracy and time delay. When it is known that the group(s) primarily affected by the intervention must comply, accuracy will generally be greater than for the converse. Similarly, with coercive measures, the variable time required to decide whether to comply is omitted. Time delay for effects is nearly always less.

The argument for a linkage to the quality determinant of efficiency is almost as straightforward. It rests upon the proposition that in order to attract adherence to a voluntary measure, more resources will tend to be required than if a coercive approach was taken.[14] As an example consider that to raise funds voluntarily, government must offer bonds at competitive interest rates while a mandatory tax suffers no such constraints.

Finally, the environmental effect on the private sector has a weak linkage to this dimension, that may still be useful, if less reliable. First, mandatory measures will certainly change the environment in a more predictable way than measures which may be optionally avoided. The accomplishments (and hence environmental consequences) of voluntary interventions can only be well assessed ex poste. However, coercive measures tend to reduce flexibility of response to environmental change. Flexibility of response assists the strategically superior firm to achieve differential advantages over less apt or less efficient competitors. Reduction of such flexibility is therefore a deleterious environmental change, in that excellence in strategic and tactical planning may yield less tangible results. These two effects can perhaps be perceived as striking a rough balance. To tip that balance, consider that additionally, a more complex formulation is often required of the voluntary intervention. It must attract adherence through shifting existing environmental opportunities and constraints as perceived by firms or individuals in order to alter their voluntary behaviour. And if satisfactory results are not forthcoming, then adjustments must be performed. All in all the linkage in this instance is not very strong; but coercive measures seem to logically cause somewhat less degradation.

CONCLUSION

It is intended that the model presented above and the established linkages will help to provide an analytical frame of reference for the examination of the use and effects of governing instruments. Overall, it has been demonstrated that a strategic, direct, and coercive intervention is a superior mode to accomplish a given goal, assuming that the quality determinants, as defined, are reasonable indicators of such effectiveness. Government has likely perceived this tendency, since, on a case by case basis, the historical trend seems to be toward these types of measures.

As an illustration, consider the formation of the Foreign Investment Review Agency which had to approve or disapprove of significant foreign investments in Canadian Business. Since it could assess the broad impact of the investment on Canadian society before reaching a decision, it should be considered as quite strategic. Certainly, it is both direct (with respect to the goal of limiting foreign ownership) and coercive. The more reactive, indirect and voluntary measures it generally supplanted were such formulations as tax credits for domestic equity investments by Canadians. Whether or not FIRA appealed ideologically to the private sector, the agency, by setting appropriate standards, was able to fine tune its efforts to exclude or include foreign buyers to whatever extent and for whatever reason was desirable. A contrast with the alternative mode shows relative deficiencies with it in respect of all measures of effectiveness.

The dimensions of the model and their individual linkages to the quality determinants can additionally provide insights into the performance of interventions which cannot be categorized as extreme positions with respect to all of the dimensions. For example, it is likely that a direct and coercive intervention that is reactive would have relatively high qualities with respect to accuracy, efficiency, and time delay, but poorer performance with respect to precision and the environmental effect.

This model may be useful in examining the probable outcome of a measure; or, better still, by using it to select an intervention to implement from alternatives. Inherent in the selection of any mode of intervention (as well, of course, in the selection of the goals of the intervention) are political, social, economic, and ideological choices. These cannot appear in the model as they require the application of values that will change from time to time, and from government to government. Therefore, it may be that the practical use of the model is in its consideration as a "template" which can underlay and therefore inform prevailing sociopolitical preferences.

NOTES

1. See George J. Stigler, "The Theory of Economic Regulation," *The Bell Journal of Economics and Management Science*, 1971, 2(1): 3–22; and Sam Peltzman "Toward a More General Theory of Regulation," *The Journal of Law and Economics*, 1976, 14(2).
2. See John M. Bryson and Peter Smith Ring, "A Transaction-Based Approach to Policy Intervention," *Policy Sciences*, 1990, 23.
3. Publications which study the interventionist concerns of government by methods specific to distinct policy areas include; R.W. Phidd and G.B. Doern, *The Politics and Management of Canadian Economic Policy* (MacMillan of Canada, 1978); G.L. Reuber (ed.), *Canada's Political Economy* (McGraw-Hill Ryerson, 1980); G.B. Doern and R.W. Phidd, *Canadian Public Policy: Ideas, Structure, Process* (Toronto: Methuen, 1983).
4. Erasmus U. Morah, "A Comprehensive Approach to Public Policy Evaluation: The Implementation-Outcome Connection," *UBC Planning Papers, Discussion Paper #21*, University of British Columbia School of Community and Regional Planning, July 1990.
5. Michael Howlett, "Policy Instruments, Policy Styles, and Policy Implementation: National Approaches to Theories of Instrument Choice," *Policy Studies Journal*, Spring 1991, 19(2): 1-21.
6. G. Bruce Doern, and V. Seymour Wilson (eds.), *Issues in Canadian Public Policy* (MacMillan of Canada, 1974), p. 339; and G. Bruce Doern (ed.), *The Regulatory Process in Canada* (MacMillan of Canada, 1978), pp. 13–18. See also G.B. Doern and R.W. Phidd, *Canadian Public Policy: Ideas, Structure, Process* (Toronto: Methuen, 1983).
7. Theodore Lowi, "Four Systems of Policy, Politics and Choice," *Public Administration Review*, July-August 1972, pp. 298–310.
8. *Ibid.*
9. See C.E. Lindblom, "The Science of Muddling Through," *Public Administration Review*, 1959, XIX(2): 81; A.O. Hirschman and C.E. Lindblom "Economic Development, Research and Development, Policy Making: Some Converging Views," *Behavioral Science*, April 1962, pp. 211 ff.
10. D.G. Hartle, "A Proposed System of Program and Policy Evaluation," *Canadian Public Administration*, 1973, 16(2): 243–66.
11. Herman L. Weiss, "Why Business and Government Exchange Executives," *Harvard Business Review*, July-August 1974, p. 134.
12. To carry the argument further: if it were deemed favourable to damage the business environment through the choice of a mode of intervention, then that would become one of the *goals*; and this determinant of quality would become inoperative — perhaps being replaced by the contrary statement.
13. This is a simplified depiction of a complex phenomenon which will suffice for the present argument. For a more detailed

description of the nature and causal relationships of turbulence, see Shirley Terreberry, "The Evolution of Organizational Environments," *Administrative Science Quarterly*, March 1968.

14. From the viewpoint of the private sector's environment the government typically creates opportunities for altered behaviour when it intervenes voluntarily, and rigid constraints on behaviour when it intervenes coercively. The nature of the voluntary opportunity is that it must compete with other opportunities for adherence; and it is typically more expensive to create than an involuntary constraint. Other societal costs and benefits associated with the goal (rather than the mode) of the intervention are assumed to generally remain constant.

Beyond Merit:
The Representative Bureaucracy

Fred Ruemper

The purpose of this paper is to examine the current limits of the merit principle in the public service of Canada and to evaluate possible extensions to this system to answer questions of bias in recruiting and employing public servants. The paper will begin with a review of past practices including an assessment of their effect in the public service as well as on the public itself. The final stage will be a presentation of the current situation in one area of the public service, namely the employment of personnel in police forces.

BACKGROUND

The public service has its roots in early agricultural societies which periodically found themselves in need of work that went beyond the personal ability of the leader of the society. Such work might consist of the construction of public edifices or the defense of the society against intruders.

Simpler societies than our own did not require a large public service since many of those activities we now look to government to provide were handled by other institutions in society. Education was provided by the family and/or by the church with the support of the family, welfare was left to the largesse of the well-to-do, health care was mostly provided by the women or a few others but was a private matter, trade and commerce was basically unregulated, crime was a personal wrong for which the victim or family sought redress with the state involved only in occasional adjudication, communication and transportation were quite local concerns which required little help from the state. With such a reduced role for the state, it did not require the support of its own public service agency to manage its employment practices, nor did it require a large tax gathering apparatus.

The state did provide for its own defense when under attack and would occasionally desire the conquest of others. It is in these international relations that the seeds of the modern public service can be found. When state leaders needed a job done they would look amongst those closest at hand. The leadership of the society consisted of a fairly closed group of like minded individuals who shared common ideals about their society and their own role in it. The performance of public duties was seen as something that was done by those in positions of power. The provision of the service was not necessarily remunerative in itself but could be seen as a method of gaining further favour from the leader. Given that such people were the personal representatives of the leader and were often delegated considerable responsibility, it is natural that the leader would choose from amongst an inner circle of close associates. When travel abroad was involved the expense tended to require personal wealth in those chosen.

ARISTOCRACY

This early reliance on what was essentially the aristocracy of the society established a pattern of public service employment which was to continue as the need for a more permanent public service grew. The first phase of public service systems were based on a reliance on the aristocracy of the society and as with the aristocracy itself a major element in those appointments was inheritance or birthright. This passing down of what were essentially public jobs such as a tax collecting or judging was fairly practical. It provided for a great deal of stability in the society. People of all classes knew what to expect in the future and were given no reason to think it was worthwhile to contemplate change. Furthermore the work itself was not really all that essential to the survival of the society so that a weak performance was not that serious a matter. The key elements were the homogeneity of the leadership culture of the society and its continuity.

The aristocratic system was based on a political system which did not make a clear distinction between the legislative or decision making branch of government and the administrative side. Political leaders were public servants in a very broad and practical sense and they counted on the help of their friends to make the government work.

PATRONAGE

The second phase of public service appointments was based on the concept of patronage. This was a natural outgrowth of the aristocratic system since the aristocracy itself had a major basis in patronage. Leaders and their societal elite had an interdependent relationship. No leader could govern on fear alone so there were alliances and arrangements to keep the various power groups in the society happy. Patronage, including public service patronage, provided many opportunities for a leader to endear supporters.

The patronage system accompanied the industrial revolution. Industrialization gave rise to a wealthy bourgeois class which challenged the landed gentry for social and political status. It would be fair to say that the aristocracy saw government as a partner in maintaining the status quo. The industrialists saw government as a partner in an economic revolution. Furthermore the industrialists had learned in their factories and warehouses that their own success was not based on family background but rather on their own ability to organize production, sales and distribution. Similarly they were most successful when they recruited employees on their ability to do the job and dismissed those unable to perform the work. This valuing of performance over tradition was carried over to their expectations of government.

An important aspect of patronage as a basis of public service appointments was that it modified the aristocratic tradition of making an appointment based on who one was. The modification expanded the tradition to include some recognition of what one had previously done or might possibly do in the future. The focus was not on the actual job for which the person was being appointed but rather on the more general benefit to the society or its leadership, however even this represented an important shifting of ground as it broke the tradition of a basically closed public service and raised the possibility of change and growth.

So much has been written about the horrors of patronage in the public service that one is reluctant to find a kindly word or two for the practice. In the historical context it was important as a transitional phase. It also reinforced the reality of the two way relationship between the leadership and the public service. They have never been isolated elements in society, rather they share common needs and goals and the patronage system made this clear. Patronage was the glue that kept the leadership united and made it possible for the leaders to create a loyal and dependent group of followers.

The patronage system continued to be functional so long as the work expectations were of a low level or were general enough in their requirements that they could be performed by any reasonably educated person. The expectations of society on the public service and the leadership continued to be modest with most of their needs being cared for by the family, immediate community, and the church. The apparent advantages of the system more than compensated for any difficulties that might arise.

MERIT

By the time the bourgeoisie had supplanted the landed gentry from the seats of power, the structure of public service had changed such that the offices of the politician and of the public servant had become separate. This came partly as a result of the numerical growth of the role of the public service. The duties to be performed exceeded the capacity of the politicians in office. This separation coincided with the first of what would come to be a long series of inquiries into the public service. In 1853 a report titled "The Organization Of The Permanent Public Service" recommended a selection process for the British civil service which was designed to evaluate the ability of the candidate. This report by Sir Stafford Northcote and Sir Charles Trevelyan marks the formal beginning of the merit system in the British public service and had a major effect on the colonies since they shared the same political system. The Northcote-Trevelyan report suggested a system of examinations designed to identify suitable candidates based on their general literacy. The examinations were not, however, designed to measure their ability to perform specific and narrowly defined job related tasks.

The foundation of the merit system in the concept of general literacy eventually led to the development in Britain and to a lesser degree in Canada of a formal system of civil service examinations. These examinations were designed by graduates of the British middle and upper class schools and placed a heavy reliance on knowledge of the classics for a successful performance. Preparation for taking the exams consisted of attending the expensive, traditional universities. This had the effect of restricting the highest levels of the civil service to the wealthy. Gradually the system was expanded to include the principles of public notice of positions and interviews to determine the most suitable candidates. In the lower levels of the civil service there was not the same reliance on knowledge of the classics but the general principle of valuing formal education continued nonetheless. Merit consisted of the criterion of education which in turn was measured by the examinations.

Four forces have modified the traditional concept of merit. The first was the political demand to give preferential treatment to veterans of military service. The second was the fluctuating demand for employees, especially the huge increases during times of war. The third has been the accelerating rate of job specialization. The fourth has been the political pressure for equity in the civil service job market.

Veterans

Soldiers have always been accorded some kind of reward or benefit from their war-lords at the end of battle or on the occasion of their retirement. Soldiers have long regarded this as a survival benefit and governments have commonly seen fit to accord it. Demobilized soldiers have often stayed in the land of their conquest and frontiers such as the Canadian west were

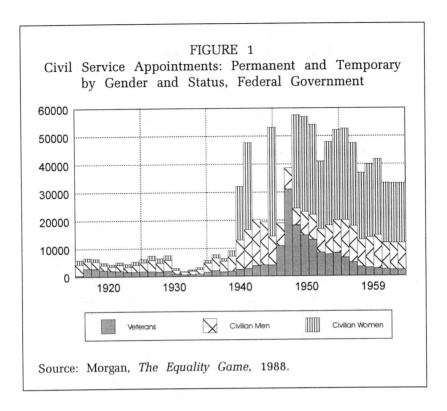

FIGURE 1

Civil Service Appointments: Permanent and Temporary by Gender and Status, Federal Government

Legend: Veterans, Civilian Men, Civilian Women

Source: Morgan, *The Equality Game*, 1988.

settled by soldiers with land grants. From 1920 to 1959 in Canada 25 per cent of all federal civil service appointments were to veterans. There have been times in Canadian history when it was quite difficult to secure a public service job without military experience. A further distortion of the situation results from the fact that almost all veterans are men while women represented over 40 per cent of all permanent and temporary appointments. Figure 1 shows a 40 year analysis of the appointments of veterans, civilian men and civilian women. The preferential treatment of veterans is sometimes described as an affirmative action program. Nicole Morgan in her report "The Equality Game" published by the Advisory Council on the Status of Women says of the Civil Service Employment Act "The Veterans' Preference Clause was the longest and most powerful affirmative action program ever applied in the federal service..." (Morgan 88:6). An alternative conclusion might be that rather than being the fore-runner of the modern affirmative action program it was actually the last breath of a patronage appointment system that was over two hundred years old. In either case it represented a distortion to the merit system of appointment as it then existed. No case was ever made that veterans had acquired special qualities during their military service which made them better candidates for a civil service job. The system of merit was still supposedly based on educational qualifications.

FLUCTUATING DEMAND

The second distortion arose from the fluctuating demand for additional employees particularly during wartime and the post war years. Again Figure 1 provides graphic illustration of these changes. When demand was high the Civil Service Commission found it necessary to reduce or at least change its standards. One important change was to hire more women and to drop the discriminatory practice of requiring women to resign when they got married. Eventually women became a regular part of the federal civil service workforce. The pressures of demand for workers also forced the Civil Service Commission to shorten the time it usually took to fill a position. All of this lead to a reduction in the merit system as it had previously existed and forced changes in the hiring procedures.

Job Specialization

The third change has been the result of increasing job specialization. The original merit system hired people with a general education. This provided them with a broad background and the ability to be flexible and adapt to the varied demands of public service. The emergence in the 20th century of highly skilled jobs rendered this concept unworkable save for a few categories of managerial jobs. A casual reading of the "Help Wanted" section of the daily newspaper will provide plentiful evidence that the civil service these days is engaged in recruiting specialists rather than generalists. Even the generalist manager seems to be on the wane with increasing calls for specialization in public administration.

Employment Equity

The final change has been the political call for employment equity. Employment equity is a term coined by Judge Rosalie Abella in her Royal Commission Report on Equality in Employment. She developed the term to replace the expression "affirmative action" which had received criticism during the public hearings of her commission. She proposed "...that a new term 'employment equity', be adopted to describe programs of positive remedy for discrimination in the Canadian workplace" (Abella, 1984:7).

Employment equity is a political issue that has gained the support of women and a variety of minority groups. The original goal was the elimination of adverse discrimination in the workplace. As Abella notes in her introduction "One hundred years ago, the role for women was almost exclusively domestic; 50 years ago some visible minorities were disenfranchised; 25 years ago, native people lacked a policy voice; and 10 years age, disabled persons were routinely kept dependent. Today, none of these exclusionary assumptions is acceptable" (Abella, 1984:1). She equates the concept of equality to the concept of fairness and goes on to add, "It is not fair that many people in these groups have restricted employment opportunities, limited access to decision-making processes that critically affect them, little public visibility as contributing Canadians, and a circumscribed range of options generally" (Abella, 1984:1).

The elimination of discrimination in employment practices is a noble cause which has received formal support from governments to a growing degree since the end of the second world war. The provinces and the federal government have enacted human rights codes which specifically prohibit employment discrimination against visible minorities, women and other designated groups. The first of these codes (in Saskatchewan) is now nearly 40 years old and despite this long period of effort, and the exemplar of a powerful civil rights movement in the United States, workplace discrimination continues to a sufficient degree that the federal government established the Royal Commission on Equality in Employment in 1983.

This Royal Commission was stimulated by a series of reports to the Minister of Employment and Immigration which showed that despite specific bars to discrimination the reality was that women and minority groups were under-represented in the workforce and thus denied the benefits of employment. The main discovery during this process was that the primary difficulty was not overt or intentional discrimination (the various human rights codes could control most of that behavior) but rather the problem was with systemic discrimination. Abella described this to include:

> "...practices or attitudes that have, whether by design or impact, the effect of limiting an individual's or a group's right to the opportunities generally available because of attributed rather than actual characteristics.... It is not a question of whether this discrimination is motivated by an intentional desire to obstruct someone's potential, or whether it is the accidental by-product of innocently motivated practices or systems. If the barrier is affecting certain groups in a disproportionately negative way, it is a signal that the practices that lead to this adverse impact may be discriminatory" (Abella, 1984:2).

Systemic discrimination is a no fault concept which is defined by the impact instead of the intention of the employment practice.

The commission was given a mandate to "inquire into the most efficient, effective and equitable means of promoting employment opportunities, eliminating systemic discrimination, and assisting all individuals to compete for employment opportunities on an equal basis..." (Privy Council Order 1983–1924). The commission was to examine the employment practices of certain large crown corporations such as Canada Post, the CBC, CMHC, Petro-Canada, the CNR, Air Canada and Atomic Energy of Canada.

The terms of reference for the Abella Commission are clearly directed at the question of equity in the workplace from the perspective of the employee. Abella makes it very clear that her first concern is the issue of fairness for the people who have been denied employment opportunities. It is interesting to note however that a second theme of potentially equal importance to the country as a whole was present from the opening paragraphs of the Privy Council Order. The issue raised was that in economic terms it was important that people "are employed to the full extent of their productive potential" (Privy Council Order 1983–1924). This is a recognition that the benefit of employment equity programs can be viewed to extend beyond the individual who has been disadvantaged and that society may also be a victim of this discrimination. The question of the extent to which society needs the benefit of the contribution of all of its citizens is a central theme of this essay and will merit examination as the other side of the employment equity issue.

Employment Equity Strategy

Abella outlined a strategy for eliminating systemic discrimination and achieving employment equity as follows:

(a) a clear statement of executive support, the appointment of senior management accountable for implementing an employment equity program, the establishment of an implementation structure, the assignment of appropriate resources, and the development of a suitable labour-management consultative process;

(b) the design and implementation of an organizational plan to include:
   i) the identification and removal of discriminatory barriers in a company's hiring, training, promotion, and income policies;
   ii) alternative corrective systems;
   iii) special remedial measures designed to remove the effects of previous discrimination;
   iv) quantifiable goals with an appropriate monitoring and assessment system to ensure that women and minorities are equitably represented and remunerated at all levels within the organization. (Abella, 1984:193)

Instruments of Implementation

The Abella Commission noted the historic failure of voluntary programs designed to encourage compliance based on public pressure and an exposure of results through a mandatory reporting program. Her conclusion was that mandatory compliance programs were the only realistic alternative. The Commission recommended legislation which contained three components:

- a requirement that federally regulated employers take steps to eliminate discriminatory practices;

- a requirement that federally regulated employers collect and file annually data on the participation rates, occupational distribution, and income levels of employees in their workforces, by designated group; and
- an enforcement mechanism. (Abella, 1984:205)

The method of compliance uses the so called "bottom-line" approach which measures successful compliance in terms of the outcome for the employees rather than through an evaluation of the policies and practices to see whether they seem reasonable. Plans must produce results to be considered successful. If the results do not meet expectations of equity then the practices must be examined to identify discriminatory practices. The bottom-line approach assures that the issue of style versus substance will be resolved in favour of substance. The history of human rights legislation has shown that it is difficult and ultimately meaningless to try to establish intent on the part of employers. In the modern era all employers would deny that they discriminate in employment practices even if their workforce was totally homogenous. By avoiding the designation of fault by an employer it is possible to save face and get on with the remedial action which the results dictate.

Workforce Analysis

A key requirement of this approach is data collection. Two types of data are required. The first is performance data by the employer which reports the participation rates for the various designated groups in the organization. Abella recognized that there was more than just the variable of whether a person was hired by an organization and added the further question of the level or type of work for which the employee was hired as well as salary. For this analysis she developed a universal classification of work into twelve categories. This has become known as the Abella Categories:

1. Upper-level managers.
2. Middle managers.
3. Professionals.
4. Technicians and semi-professionals.
5. Supervisors (white collar).
6. Foremen/women (blue collar).

7.   Clerical.
8.   Sales.
9.   Service.
10. Skilled crafts and tradesmen/women.
11. Semi-skilled manual workers.
12. Unskilled manual workers.

(For a complete description of these categories refer to Appendix D of the Abella Commission Report.)

Employers were to report the number of female and male employees in each of these categories for each of the designated groups. Salary data provided salary ranges by category and quartile distributions by sex. These tables provided the performance data for the organization.

Worker Availability

The second set of data required is the benchmark against which performance is to be measured. Initially Abella refers to this as data on the availability of potential candidates from the designated groups. Such data can be acquired from Statistics Canada. The premise at this stage is that it is unreasonable to expect an employer to hire someone who does not exist.

The question of availability is not as straight forward as the question of whether someone could become available for a particular type of work. This is very much related to the likelihood that they would ever be hired. It would be foolish of a woman to undertake the effort and commitment involved in learning the trade of plumbing if she had no expectation of ever being hired as a plumber. On the other side, a business seeking to hire a woman plumber would not find one available. To break this cycle Abella proposes that the definition of availability be broadened to include data on overall demographic rates and employment rates. She further advises that:

> ...governments at all levels would be expected to work toward correcting the legislative, economic, social, physical, educational, and communication barriers that depress the expectations and opportunities for women, native people, minorities, and disabled persons. (Abella 1984:212)

Taken to its logical conclusion, availability becomes demography. This leads to the expectation that the workforce will reflect the community in terms of the designated groups. Any limitation to this ideal would be a considered short term consequence while the appropriate remedies are being worked through the system. For occupations which do not require much entrance skill or require only a general type of education then an early match between the workplace and society would depend only on job turnover rates.

Success in an employment equity program can be measured in terms of the relationship between the composition of the workforce and the availability data. In the ultimate sense the expectation would be that the workforce would mirror the society, but such an analysis does not lend itself to an ongoing evaluation of the performance of a program.

On-Going Evaluation of Performance

A more relevant measure of performance would involve a comparison of worker availability to the proportion of new-hires from the designated group. For example if women represent 15 per cent of a particular workforce but represent 40 per cent of those potentially available for the work we would recognize that the situation is in need of a remedy. The goal would be that 40 per cent of the workforce be women. The key measure of whether the situation will be remedied is the proportion of new employment opportunities which are given to women. If 15 per cent of new openings go to women the net result will be no change. If 10 per cent of the jobs go to women there will be a reduction in the proportion of women employed and this reduction will ultimately be to 10 per cent. If 25 per cent of the jobs go to women there will be improvement to a maximum of 25 per cent. If 40 per cent of the jobs go to women the ultimate improvement will be to 40 per cent however the rate of change will slow as the 40 per cent ceiling is approached. The difference between these two measures can be likened to the difference between speed and acceleration. To achieve a higher speed we must increase our acceleration. In terms of human resources management the preceding analysis refers to a stock and flow model wherein goals and progress toward achieving them can be simultaneously monitored. Figure 2 shows a stock and flow model using the illustrative data from above.

A study by Harvey and Blakey entitled "Strategies for Establishing Affirmative Action Goals and Timetables" was

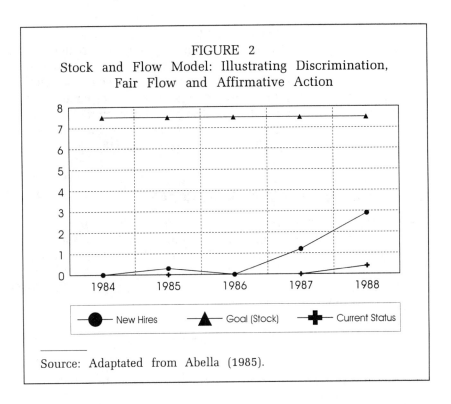

FIGURE 2

Stock and Flow Model: Illustrating Discrimination, Fair Flow and Affirmative Action

Source: Adapted from Abella (1985).

commissioned by Abella as background research for her report (Abella, Equality in Employment — A Royal Commission Report — Research Studies: 1985). It evaluated a variety of strategies and included rules for modifying the rate of change depending on the distance from the goal. A typical hiring decision rule would be that the hiring rate (or flow) be one and one half times the goal. This would specify that 60 per cent of all new hires be women until the goal (or stock) of 40 per cent is achieved. An additional rule might be that no group exceed 50 per cent of the openings, in which case the flow rate would be 50 per cent.

By plotting flow rates against availability data it is possible to determine whether discrimination, fair flow or affirmative action is taking place. Human resources managers are then able to directly evaluate the effects of their hiring policies.

The above discussion has been limited to the basic case of hiring new employees but the same model can be applied to other aspects of employment equity such as promotion, demotion and layoff, salary, training and other employment benefits.

The employment equity model describes both a policy goal of fuller and fairer employment of all groups of society as well as a series of strategies for achieving this goal. A cornerstone of the policy is the requirement of government involvement both to provide a positive example in its own practices but also by passing legislation designed to gain compliance the plan.

THE REPRESENTATIVE BUREAUCRACY

The history of civil service appointments in this century has involved a program of attempting to eliminate the worst consequences of the patronage system which developed during the preceding century. The patronage system had distorted the composition of the public service and hampered its ability to perform the functions expected of it.

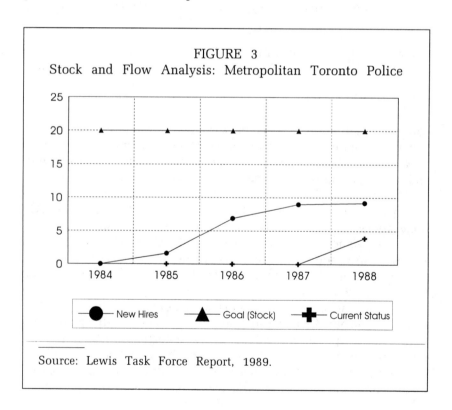

FIGURE 3
Stock and Flow Analysis: Metropolitan Toronto Police

Source: Lewis Task Force Report, 1989.

The Merit System

The merit system was the remedy adopted. It had the laudable consequence of hiring and promoting people based on their personal abilities rather than their connections or social class. In sociological terms the merit system replaced ascribed status with achieved status as selection criteria. The main effect was to eliminate the aristocracy and the friends of politicians. The key measure of merit which emerged was that of education. Formal education provided an ideal indicator of merit, it had high face validity, people generally accepted that education leads to qualification. Furthermore it is quite objective to evaluate and it does provide an indication of the persons ability and motivation.

For those doing the selection, education provided the comfort of a relatively unappealable selection criterion. Any appointment based on education was a safe appointment. If events later proved otherwise, the decision itself could not be faulted. This attribute of the merit system became increasingly important as

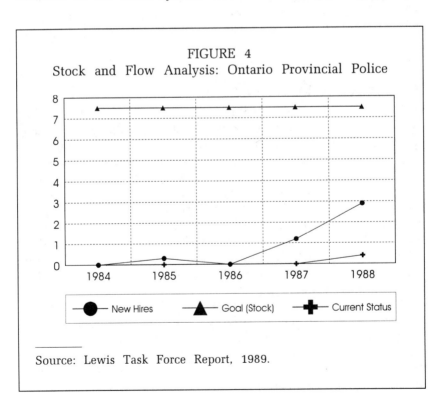

FIGURE 4
Stock and Flow Analysis: Ontario Provincial Police

Source: Lewis Task Force Report, 1989.

the civil service developed systems of checks and balances designed to enhance the basic human rights of employees and to protect them from arbitrary decisions.

Additional support for a merit system based on education came from the growing need to hire people with specialized skills. If a scientist or a technician was required then what could be more natural than to select someone based on their education in that particular field. This kind of recruiting was position based in that people were hired for a specific position in the civil service rather than being hired for a career with their actual posting to come later.

The most serious consequence of basing merit on education has been the creation of a civil service composed largely of those from the middle and upper middle classes. Education is not universally valued, nor is it universally available. The use of education as a selection criterion had the effect of drawing the civil service from a relatively narrow segment of society. Furthermore this situation become worse the higher one looked in the civil service. The use of education in selecting candidates came to mean the exclusion of many people from public employment.

Trend Toward Representativeness

Mid-way through this century a powerful new trend has emerged which has had a profound effect on the merit principle. This has come to be known as the "representative bureaucracy." A representative bureaucracy is one which reflects the society in terms of certain key characteristics such as gender and minority group membership. In the ideal representative bureaucracy the proportion of civil servants who are women or minority group members would exactly equal the proportion in society. The characteristics are those of ascribed rather than achieved status and the proposal that people should be employed in the civil service on the basis of these characteristics has met with serious opposition.

The reasons in support of the concept of the representative bureaucracy can be categorized according to the beneficiary of the change. One set of reasons are focused on the issue of fairness to the individuals who have been discriminated against by the existing merit system, i.e., those who are under-represented in the civil service. Part of this argument rests on the notion that public service jobs are paid for by all tax payers and everyone should have an equal opportunity to benefit from this employment. This category amounts to the employment equity case which was previously described.

The second category has to do with the view that the public is entitled to be served by people from their own background. In Canada this perspective has been strongly advanced by the Francophone segment of our population. Service in English to a person who does not speak English is a denial of service. The denial may have some legitimacy if the language spoken by the person is obscure but it has no legitimacy when it is one of Canada's official languages. Similar arguments are made on behalf of other ascribed characteristics such as gender, race, religion or disability. The perspective is that when one is being provided with a public service then one is entitled to fully sympathetic service provided by a civil servant who is able to understand our needs. Any group which does not receive such service is being discriminated against.

The third category sees the public service itself as the beneficiary. Increasingly the trend has been a transfer of true decision making power away from the politicians to the bureaucracy. We have come to expect so much from government that it is quite beyond the ability of our elected representatives to provide. The result is that the civil service has come to play a much larger role in preparing legislation and giving direction to the political agenda. If the bureaucracy has become more powerful then we need to examine who is making these decisions for us. Do they have the benefit of the best information and resources available? Do they represent a broad section of public interests? Are they even aware of the concerns of the different segments of society? Will their agenda represent the needs of all of society or will it represent the needs of the group from which they are drawn?

A second aspect of this category which sees the public service itself as the beneficiary of a representative bureaucracy has to do with the recruitment limitations resulting from the traditional concept of merit. Using education as the measure of merit has had the effect of creating a practice of hiring white, English speaking, middle class males. But in Canada the labour pool of such candidates is either static or declining, furthermore the private sector actively recruits from the same group. The result is that potentially better candidates from other groups are ignored while there is intense competition for one group. The public service needs all the help it can get to manage the immense expectations of society and cannot afford to overlook any potential resources.

Reconciling Merit and Representation

A merit system based on education has been such an entrenched feature of bureaucratic service that change is difficult. Change to a system based on an ascribed status such as gender, race, etc. is particularly difficult as it seems a backward step toward a system based on patronage. Patronage is no longer an acceptable use of the public service and politicians who attempt to use it for this purpose soon find themselves in difficulty with their parliamentary colleagues or the watchdogs in the public media. Hardly a month goes by without some public scandal surrounding the inappropriate use of public resources by a politician. Patronage in public life today is restricted to only a relatively small number of posts that are either closely allied with members of parliament, such as the prime minister's office staff, or are ceremonial in nature such as a senate seat. The day when the staff of the Post Office or other government agency changes with each election is gone.

We have become an achievement oriented society and we do not long for a return to a system that rewards us for our ancestry. Instead we hope to be recognized for who we are and what we have done. On the surface the merit system would seem to do this but in practice it has not. The model proposed by employment equity is of benefit in assessing the situation. The employment equity model judges employment practices by their effect rather than by their intent. The Royal Commission By Judge Rosalie Abella was established for the express purpose of learning why the existing system had failed and to propose remedies.

REFERENCES

Abella, Judge Rosalie Silberman (Commissioner). 1984. *Equality in Employment: A Royal Commission Report* (Ottawa: Supply and Service Canada).

———. 1985. *Equality in Employment: A Royal Commission Report — Research Studies* (Ottawa: Supply and Services Canada).

Cryderman, Brian K. and Chris N. O'Toole. 1986. *Police, Race and Ethnicity: A Guide For Law Enforcement Officers* (Toronto: Butterworths).

Ericson, Richard V. 1982. *Reproducing Order: A Study Of Police Patrol Work* (Toronto: University of Toronto Press).

Fletcher, Joseph. 1989. *Results of the Survey on Racial Prejudice* (Toronto: University of Toronto, Department of Political Science and The Centre of Criminology).

Hoffman, Randy. 1989. *A General Model of Government Intervention*, this volume (North York: Captus Press).

Lewis, Clare (Chair). 1989. *The Report of the Race Relations and Policing Task Force* (Toronto: Ministry of the Solicitor General).

Morgan, Nicole. 1988. *The Equality Game: Women in the Federal Public Service (1908–1987)* (Ottawa: The Canadian Advisory Council On The Status Of Women).

Auditing for Parliament

Office of the Auditor General
of Canada

FOREWORD

Canadians are telling their elected representatives that they want the best possible value from the use of public funds they send to their federal government in Ottawa. Members of Parliament, in turn, look to the Auditor General to help them find out whether that value is being obtained by the government.

The aim of this booklet is to explain how the Office of the Auditor General helps Parliament perform its role and how the Office fits into our parliamentary system of government.

Parliament, the government and the public service are the guardians of public funds entrusted to them for delivering programs and services to benefit Canadians. An important part of the confidence that people have in our democratic institutions is their belief that public funds are spent wisely and effectively. There must be, and there must be seen to be, value for money spent,

Source of Information: Office of the Auditor General of Canada. Reproduced with the permission of the Minister of Public Works and Government Services Canada, 1997.

compliance with authority and environmental stewardship. In a significant way then, confidence in our national government depends upon clear and timely accountability by the government for its performance.

I firmly believe that the Office of the Auditor General plays an important role in the functioning of our parliamentary system and that in fulfilling its mandate, it can and must influence the attitude of the government and public servants toward effective management of and accounting for public funds.

L. Denis Desautels, FCA
Auditor General of Canada

A GOVERNMENT ACCOUNTABLE TO PARLIAMENT

The people's right to control how public funds are collected and spent is one of the cornerstones of democratic government. In Canada, like other parliamentary democracies, this control is carried out on behalf of the people by their elected representatives, the members of Parliament.

The government of the day must obtain the permission of Parliament before it can collect or spend money. After it spends public funds, the government must also report on its use of the money authorized by Parliament. This obligation of government to answer for its actions is called accountability.

A process has been developed to hold the government to account. The government must report on its performance by submitting to the House of Commons: the annual spending plans or Estimates of all departments and reports on their past year's activities, and the annual financial statements showing all federal spending, borrowing and taxing, known as the Public Accounts of Canada.

These documents provide members of Parliament with a great deal of information for holding the government to account. But one more link in the accountability process is needed: independent assessment of that information. Members of Parliament need this impartial assessment so that they can effectively assess the government's performance and gain assurance that the information provided accurately reflects the results of the activities authorized by Parliament.

The Auditor General of Canada audits government operations and provides the information that helps Parliament to hold the government to account for its stewardship of public funds.

A BRIEF HISTORY

John Lorn McDougall, a former member of Parliament, was appointed the first independent Auditor General of Canada in 1878. The job was previously performed by a government official, the deputy minister of Finance.

The Auditor General of that day had two main functions: to examine and report on past transactions and to approve or reject the issue of government cheques.

The Auditor General's annual Reports to the House of Commons in this era were weighty documents, sometimes as long as 2,400 pages! They listed every single government transaction, from the purchase of bootlaces to contracts for bridge building. These detailed records revealed a focus different from the work of the federal audit Office today. But like today, the Auditor General of the late 19th century was expected to report on whether public money was spent the way Parliament intended.

In 1931, Parliament transferred responsibility for issuing cheques to a newly created government official, the Comptroller of the Treasury. This drew a clear line between the duties of government and the auditor: the government was responsible for collecting and distributing public funds, while the auditor was responsible for examining and reporting on how those funds were handled.

The work of the Office began to move in its current direction in the 1950s, when the Auditor General began to report on "non-productive payments." These were transactions that, while legal, provided no apparent benefits to Canadians. The reports were controversial, however, because government officials felt the Auditor General was commenting on government policy and therefore going beyond his mandate.

New legislation, the 1977 Auditor General Act, clarified and expanded the Auditor General's responsibilities. In addition to looking at the accuracy of financial statements, the Auditor General was given a broader mandate to examine how well the government managed its affairs. The new Act maintained the important principle that the Auditor General does not comment on policy choices but does examine how those policies are implemented.

In June 1994 the Auditor General Act was amended to provide for the production of up to three reports per year in addition to the annual Report.

Further amendments to the Act in December 1995 established the position of Commissioner of the Environment and Sustainable Development within the Office of the Auditor General. These amendments also impose an obligation on government departments to publish annual sustainable development strategies.

VISION AND MISSION OF THE OFFICE OF THE AUDITOR GENERAL OF CANADA

Vision

We are committed to making a difference for the Canadian people by promoting, in all our work for Parliament, answerable, honest and productive government.

Mission

The Office of the Auditor General of Canada conducts independent audits and examinations that provide objective information, advice and assurance to Parliament. We promote accountability and best practices in government operations.

Elaboration of Mission

In achieving our mission, we want to make a difference by promoting:

- a fair and frank accounting of government's stewardship of financial and other resources
- efficiency and productivity in the public service
- cost effectiveness of government activities
- collection of revenues owed to the Crown.

Other effects we want to produce through our work are:

- objective assurance on matters found to be satisfactory and unsatisfactory

275

- compliance with authority
- deterrence of fraud and dishonesty.

ROLE OF THE AUDITOR GENERAL: TO AID ACCOUNTABILITY

The Auditor General aids accountability by conducting independent audits of federal government operations. These audits provide members of Parliament with objective information to help them examine the government's activities and hold it to account.

For the Auditor General to be effective, it is important to be objective. To help achieve this objectivity, Parliament has taken steps to keep the Auditor General independent of the government.

The Auditor General is independent of the government of the day, and is appointed for a 10-year period. The

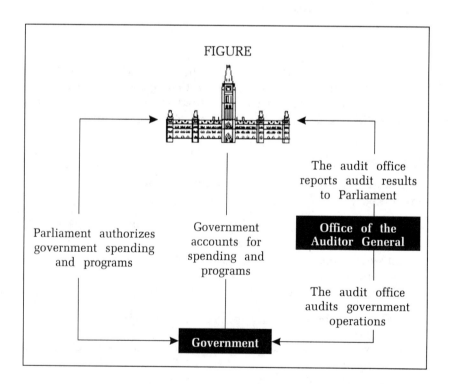

FIGURE

Parliament authorizes government spending and programs

Government accounts for spending and programs

Office of the Auditor General

The audit office reports audit results to Parliament

The audit office audits government operations

Government

Office has the freedom to recruit its own staff and set the terms and conditions of employment for staff. The Auditor General has the right to ask the government for any information required to do the job as outlined in the Auditor General Act. Moreover, the Auditor General submits his reports directly to the House of Commons, through the Speaker.

WHAT ARE THE AUDITOR GENERAL'S RESPONSIBILITIES?

The 1977 Auditor General Act directs the Auditor General to address three main questions:

- *Is the government keeping proper accounts and records and presenting its financial information accurately?*
  This is called "attest" auditing. The auditor attests to, or verifies, the accuracy of financial statements.

- *Did the government collect or spend the authorized amount of money and for the purposes intended by Parliament?*
  This is called "compliance" auditing. The auditor asks if the government has complied with Parliament's wishes.

- *Were programs run economically and efficiently? And does the government have the means to measure their effectiveness?*
  This is called "value-for-money" or performance auditing. The auditor asks whether or not taxpayers got value for their tax dollars.

  "Value for money" is an approach to auditing that examines management practices, controls and reporting systems. In addition to information in attest and compliance reports, legislators also need information on how well the government has implemented its policies and programs. Value-for-money audits, which are sometimes called performance audits, do not question the merits of government policies; rather they help legislators judge how well the policies and programs were implemented.

The attest, compliance and value-for-money audits combine to form an audit framework that, over time, provides a complete view of the organization. The term "comprehensive auditing" is used to describe this audit framework developed by the Office to meet requirements of the Auditor General Act.

Crown corporations are also subject to a form of comprehensive audit, established in 1984 with amendments to the Financial Administration Act. While the Auditor General may not be the auditor of all Crown corporations, the audit provisions for those organizations are the same. They include: annual audit; an audit opinion on the fairness of the presentation of the financial statements and one on compliance with authorities; a provision to raise other matters as the auditor considers appropriate; and a periodic special examination, including an audit opinion on the fulfilment of management responsibilities.

The 1995 amendments to the Auditor General Act gave the Auditor General the responsibility to report to the House of Commons on the extent to which departments have met the objectives set out in their sustainable development strategies and action plans, and on all other questions related to the environment and sustainable development that he considers should be brought to the attention of the House of Commons.

WHAT DOES THE AUDITOR GENERAL AUDIT?

The Office of the Auditor General audits most areas of the Canadian government. This includes a vast range of activities: health, culture, the environment, finance, agriculture, transportation, and scientific research, to name a few. In total, audit coverage includes:

- about 70 federal government departments and agencies ranging from small boards to large, complex organizations whose activities extend across Canada and overseas;
- about 40 Crown corporations, for example, the Canadian Broadcasting Corporation and the Royal Canadian Mint. Under the Financial Administration Act, most Crown corporations must undergo a value-for-money audit (called a special examination) every five years. In addition, their financial statements are audited annually;
- about 10 departmental corporations;
- about 60 other entities and special audits;

- areas of responsibility shared by more than one department, such as immigration;
- issues that affect the entire government, for example, personnel matters or the use of computers;
- the governments of the Yukon and the Northwest Territories and some 15 territorial agencies; and
- some United Nations agencies, such as the United Nations Educational, Scientific and Cultural Organization, and the International Civil Aviation Organization.

With the creation of the position of Commissioner of the Environment and Sustainable Development in December 1995, the Auditor General's responsibilities related to environmental matters increased considerably. The Commissioner, on behalf of the Auditor General, reports annually to the House of Commons on all matters related to the environment and sustainable development that he considers should be brought to its attention. In addition, government departments must publish annual sustainable development strategies and action plans that are audited by the Commissioner.

HOW DOES THE OFFICE DO ITS WORK?

Attest Auditing

Every year, the Government of Canada publishes the Public Accounts of Canada, which contain the government's annual financial reports. Included in the financial statements of the government is an aggregation of the financial results of all departments, agencies, Crown corporations, and several large special funds. The Auditor General's Office performs attest audits of the financial statements of the government and most Crown corporations. Attest audits result in opinions that indicate whether reliance can be placed on the organization's financial statements. In addition, some agencies and Crown corporations publish their own financial statements; the Auditor General examines these statements and expresses an opinion on their fair and consistent presentation.

Auditors plan and perform attest audits using their knowledge of accounting and auditing and of the government organizations being audited. As part of these audits, they gather evidence, on a test basis, to support the amounts and disclosures in the financial statements. Audit procedures might include comparing the results of operations with planned results, checking the reliability of a department's financial control systems and checking samples of transactions and balances. Specialized computer programs are used throughout the audit.

In reporting the results of audits, the Auditor General may call attention to other matters of importance.

Compliance Auditing

The audit team reviews transactions to see if the department or agency conformed to all laws and regulations that govern its operations. This involves checking the spending authority contained in the annual budget and relevant legislation.

Value-for-money Auditing

Because of the large size of some departments, the Office focusses each audit on a selected number of activities. In this way, the major programs and aspects of the department can be examined over a number of years.

A value-for-money audit, which can last from 6 to 18 months, has three stages: planning, examination and reporting. At all stages, the multidisciplinary audit team works closely with an advisory committee of experts who offer advice and review audit results. In the planning stage, the audit team studies the program and its working environment. Team members identify areas to be examined during the audit and establish the audit criteria — standards to which the audited activities can be compared. During the examination phase, the audit team gathers and tests evidence and analyzes findings. This may require field work that can range from checking inventory in government warehouses to examining the management of an agricultural research station. At this point, the department may decide to make changes based on the preliminary findings. In the reporting phase, it is decided what will be included in the Auditor General's Report to the House of Commons.

Comprehensive Auditing

The term "comprehensive auditing" is used when an audit of a department encompasses all of the three preceding components:

attest or financial auditing, compliance auditing and value-for-money auditing.

Special Examinations of Crown Corporations

In addition to value-for-money audits of departments and agencies, the Office also carries out audits (special examinations) on Crown corporations at least once every five years. In the planning stage, a plan is submitted to the audit committee of the Board of Directors, which includes criteria against which the identified key areas will be assessed during the examination. The audit report resulting from the examination is provided directly to the Board, and, in exceptional circumstances, to the responsible minister and Parliament.

REPORTING AUDIT RESULTS

Since 1879, the principal instrument for reporting has been the Auditor General's annual Report to the House of Commons. With the amendment of the Auditor General Act in June 1994, the Auditor General may produce up to three reports per year in addition to the annual Report. In any given year, these reports contain the results of:

- comprehensive audits of federal departments and agencies, and of issues that cross departmental lines;
- government-wide audits (for example, the use of computers);
- follow-up reports, which review the actions taken by departments in response to previous audits; and
- audit observations, which are significant matters that are not included in any of the above-noted audit reports.

Some other audit results are reported through different means:

- Audit opinions on transactions, financial statements, compliance and other matters relating to Crown corporations are submitted to the responsible minister for tabling in Parliament.
- Special examinations of Crown corporations are reported directly to their Board of Directors; in certain cases, they are

also submitted to the responsible minister and to the House of Commons through the annual report of the corporation.

- Opinions on the government's financial statements (attest audits) are included with the publication of the Public Accounts of Canada every autumn.
- Audits requested by the Governor in Council (Cabinet) on matters of interest to the Government of Canada and not covered by the Auditor General Act are reported in different ways, depending on the circumstances of each audit.
- Audits of the governments of the Yukon and Northwest Territories are reported annually to their legislative assemblies.

REPORTING BY THE COMMISSIONER OF THE ENVIRONMENT AND SUSTAINABLE DEVELOPMENT

The 1995 amendments to the Auditor General Act established the position of the Commissioner of the Environment and Sustainable Development within the Office of the Auditor General. These amendments also require departments to prepare sustainable development strategies and action plans by December 1997 and to update them at least every three years. The Commissioner, on behalf of the Auditor General, reports annually to the House of Commons on the extent to which departments have met the objectives and implemented the plans set out in those strategies. He does this in a new annual "green" report required by the amendments. The report also includes the Commissioner's observations on the number, nature and status of environmental petitions sent to the Auditor General and forwarded to the appropriate minister(s), who must respond directly to the writer within specified time frames.

THE PUBLIC ACCOUNTS COMMITTEE AND OTHER PARLIAMENTARY COMMITTEES

Although the Auditor General's Reports attract considerable attention when they are released, their long-term impact is felt when they are examined by the House of Commons Standing Committee on Public Accounts. The Committee reviews whether public money was spent for the approved purposes and with due regard to efficiency, economy and effectiveness.

It bases much of its work on the Auditor General's Reports. Throughout the year, the Committee holds hearings attended by the Auditor General, the audit team, and senior public servants of the audited departments to review audit findings. After the hearings, the Committee may report and make recommendations to the House of Commons. The audited departments are generally expected to report back to the Committee on what they have done in response to these recommendations. In this way, the Public Accounts Committee ensures completion of the accountability loop.

In addition to the Public Accounts Committee, many other parliamentary committees hold hearings on report chapters.

WHO WORKS AT THE OFFICE OF THE AUDITOR GENERAL?

The Office staff has a wide range of experience and skills. In addition to accountants and finance experts, the broad scope of government auditing also requires specialists from many other fields, including engineers, lawyers, economists, computer experts, management specialists and sociologists. The staff is organized into teams that are assigned to the audits of specific departments, agencies or Crown corporations. Most of the audit staff works out of the head office in Ottawa, and regional offices are located in Vancouver, Edmonton, Winnipeg, Montreal and Halifax.

Audit work is supported by staff who research and develop audit policies and methodologies and run extensive training programs.

The Office also offers training for students who are articling for the Chartered Accountant, Certified General Accountant, and Certified Management Accountant programs and for recent graduates with a Master's degree who seek experience in value-for-money auditing.

INTERNATIONAL ACTIVITIES

The Office of the Auditor General audits a number of United Nations agencies and has served as one of the auditors of the

UN itself. The Office has also been one of the most prominent supporters of training programs for auditors from national audit offices of developing nations. Every year, senior government auditors from developing countries come to the Office as part of the International Audit Office Assistance Program and spend nine months in Canada becoming familiar with Canadian techniques in public sector auditing. The program is funded by the Canadian International Development Agency (CIDA) and administered by the CCAF-FCVI Inc.

The INTOSAI Development Initiative (IDI) is another international training activity supported by the Office. INTOSAI, which stands for International Organization of Supreme Audit Institutions, is made up of the heads of national audit offices from around the world. The IDI Secretariat is attached to the Office of the Auditor General of Canada and offers an extensive training and information exchange program to the INTOSAI membership and, in particular, to national audit offices of developing nations.

HOW IS THE AUDITOR GENERAL HELD TO ACCOUNT?

An external auditor appointed by the Treasury Board audits the Office of the Auditor General annually. The auditor's report is submitted to the Treasury Board and tabled in the House of Commons. In addition, the Auditor General's Report chapters are reviewed and discussed in hearings before some 15 parliamentary committees. The Auditor General, like government departments, also submits annual spending estimates to Parliament, and the Public Accounts Committee calls on the Auditor General to explain the spending estimates and management practices of the Office. As well, the Office is subject to scrutiny by the Official Languages Commissioner on language issues, by the Public Service Commission on staffing and classification practices, and by the Privacy Commissioner on the Privacy Act. The Institute of chartered accountants of Ontario certify Office practices as suitable for training and apprenticeship for new chartered accountants.

Organizational and Administrative Renewal at the Immigration and Refugee Board

James C. Simeon ▨ ▨ ▨ ▨ ▨ ▨ ▨ ▨ ▨

INTRODUCTION

Much of the work of government is done in the line departments within the public bureaucracy, which

This chapter was initially presented as a paper at the Institute of Public Administration of Canada Annual Conference, Victoria, British Colombia, August, 1996. The opinions expressed in this paper are solely those of the author and do not represent the views of either the Immigration and Refugee Board (IRB) or any of its employees.

The author would like to thank Nurjehan Mawani, Chairperson of the IRB, Urich Ferdinand, Assistant Deputy Chair (ADC) of the Toronto University Regional Office of the IRB, for their permission to publish this paper. I should also like to thank Rick Stanisby, ADC Professional Development for the IRB, for his comments on earlier drafts of this chapter. I am also grateful for the assistance and advice of a number of other people at the IRB who provided their suggestions and comments on earlier versions of this chapter. Among these who I should like to give special thanks are Michèle Hurteau, Jennifer Benimadhu, Sandra Kline, and Bill Jackson.

are led by ministers of the Crown, Cabinet Ministers. Other organizational entities, such as Crown corporations or public enterprises and Statutory Regulatory Agencies or Administrative Tribunals, which Cabinet Ministers are also responsible for in Parliament, but which they do not lead or direct, also play an important role in government operations.

Recently, a number of tribunals or quasi-Judicial Boards have undertaken major initiatives in organizational and administrative renewal. This is perhaps most evident with the recent changes introduced at the Immigration and Refugee Board (IRB). One of these new initiatives involved the development of the Immigration and Refugee Board's (IRB) Mission Statement:

> The Immigration and Refugee Board is an independent tribunal established by the Parliament of Canada. Our mission, on behalf of Canadians, is to make well-reasoned decisions on immigration and refugee matters, efficiently, fairly, and in accordance with the law.

Another important initiative was an effort at "cultural transformation" through the use of internal focus groups.

This chapter begins with the IRB's structure and operations; it then reviews the factors that led to the impetus for organizational and administrative renewal at the IRB. The article then examines the internal focus group exercise on vision and values and its impact.

The public bureaucracy is often seen as a monolith which is not only resistant to change, but actively opposed to it. Contrary to this simplistic view, the public bureaucracy is comprised, in fact, of diverse organizational entities performing a variety of tasks. Furthermore, the public bureaucracy is frequently incorrectly viewed as a static entity; rather, it should be viewed more properly as a dynamic and continuously changing social organism.

Whether in the public or private sector, organizational change is never a simple or easy process. One of the central issues that must be addressed in efforts at administrative reform is how organizational change can be successfully implemented within the public sector. The IRB's efforts at organizational and administrative renewal are instructive, since they illustrate the methods and techniques utilized in managing change within the public sector.

IRB: STRUCTURE AND OPERATIONS

The Immigration and Refugee Board is Canada's largest independent administrative tribunal. Since its inception in 1988, the IRB has established itself as one of the foremost governmental agencies of its kind in the world. It is recognized within Canada and abroad for its legal innovation in the area of immigration and refugee law as well as its administrative ingenuity and efficiency. This chapter will review the organizational and administrative changes that have been recently introduced at the IRB as part of a program of renewal. It will concentrate primarily on the IRB's use of focus groups to initiate a fundamental cultural change within the organization.

The IRB has three principal functions which are carried out in three distinct divisions. The Convention Refugee Determination Division (CRDD or Refugee Division) hears claims for Convention refugee status made by persons in Canada, in accordance with Canada's obligations under international conventions and Canadian law. The Immigration Appeal Division (IAD or Appeal Division) serves as an independent tribunal for persons who have been denied admission to Canada or ordered removed from Canada, as well as to Canadian citizens and permanent residents whose family members have been refused landing in Canada. The Adjudication Division (AD) conducts immigration inquiries on persons seeking admission at a Canadian port of entry believed to be inadmissible, or on persons in Canada believed to be removable; and it conducts detention reviews for persons who have been detained during the examination, inquiry, or removal process.e.

The board's Chief Executive Officer is the chairperson, Nurjehan Mawani, who reports to Parliament through the Minister of Citizenship and Immigration. The three IRB divisions are independent of each other in their decision making, but are affiliated administratively to make the most efficient use of facilities and services.

During 1995, the CRDD received 26,072 claims. Of the 17,189 claims concluded, 9,614 (56 per cent) of the claimants were found to be Convention refugees while 4,096 (24 per cent) were found not to be Convention refugees. Another 3,479 claims (20 per cent) were withdrawn or abandoned.[1] In 1995, the IAD had 4,489 new appeals filed in the division, an increase of 45 per cent from the previous year. Of these new appeals in 1995,

3,420 were appeals made by sponsors, 1,063 were appeals from removal orders, and 6 were appeals made by the minister.[2] The Adjudication Division concluded 11,594 inquiries and 10,765 detention reviews in 1995.[3]

The IRB's head office is in the National Capital Region. The board is geographically organized into regions, districts, and points of service. The three regions are Montreal, Toronto, and Vancouver. Each of these major urban centres have IRB Regional Offices. The Prairies and Ottawa/Atlantic comprise the board's two districts, with district offices located in Calgary and Ottawa. Cases are processed in other municipalities throughout Canada. The "points of service" are the various locations across the country where the CRDD, IAD, or Adjudication Division hear cases and conduct inquiries.

Members of the CRDD and IAD are appointed by order of the Governor-in-Council. The Appeal Division may consist of not more than 30 full-time members. There is, however, no limit on the number of members for the Refugee Division. One member from the CRDD and one from the IAD are designated as deputy chairpersons. Members are also appointed as assistant deputy chairpersons (ADCs) for the Refugee Division in each of the board's regional offices. Co-ordinating members (CMs) are also appointed in the larger regional offices to provide management support to assistant deputy chairpersons. There is also one ADC responsible for members' professional development for both the Refugee Division and the Appeal Division.

The Adjudication Division is headed by a director general, with a director responsible for each of the three regions. Adjudicators are appointed pursuant to the Public Service Employment Act, unlike the members of the CRDD and IAD, who are appointed by the Governor-in-Council for fixed terms of office not exceeding seven years.

RESTRAINT, RESTRUCTURE, AND RENEWAL

It is a truism that all governments are currently in a retrenchment mode. Demands for public services have not declined, yet the resources available to provide these public services have been dramatically reduced. Accordingly, governmental organizations have been forced to adapt to continuously reduced resource levels. The new strictures of declining resource levels have forced some governmental organizations to "re-engineer" or "re-invent" themselves.

This trend is not, of course, limited to the public sector. As Lynda Hurst, feature writer for the *Toronto Star*, noted:

> Companies in the '90s have de-layered, restructured, re-engineered, downsized, right-sized; all chilling euphemisms for letting people go. Those left after the cut(s) have been introduced to life in the new knowledge economy: to total quality management and "continuous learning," to mission statements and employee empowerment, to circle management and team-team-team-teamwork.[4]

Gary Nyp in a recent article reviews how various companies in Canada are seeking to adjust to the new realities of the marketplace. He states:

> Across North America, organizations and the executives that lead them are looking for similar results in a fiercely competitive global marketplace. There's a new context for business and new principles driving the change, many based on management philosophies like Total Quality Management (TQM).
>
> The first tremors were felt in the mid-1980s, when Japanese automakers were making sizeable dents in North America's auto industry. Executives realized that business as usual would leave the domestic auto industry far behind, and launched a critical analysis of their own business practices.[5]

Hence, one of the most important challenges facing management, in both business and public administration, is managing change within a diminishing resource environment. And, it is within this context that organizational and administrative renewal at the IRB has occurred.

Legislative and Procedural Changes at the IRB

During the past year the IRB has experienced significant legislative and procedural changes. This was started with the announcements made by the Minister of Citizenship and Immigration on March 2, 1995. The minister announced that legislation would be introduced to allow the board to conduct Refugee Division hearings with single-member panels. The minister also announced the creation of an advisory committee on member appointments, with Mr. Gordon Fairweather, the IRB's founding chairperson, as its Chair.

289

Then, on March 3, 1995, the chairperson announced the adoption of a number of enhancements to the Refugee Division's procedures for determining Convention refugees.[6] The chairperson stated that the Refugee Division would operate on the basis of a specialized board of inquiry model. She also announced that there would be a heightened emphasis placed on information gathering:

> Refugee Claims Officers will be assigned to work in geographic teams with Refugee Division Members. In assisting Members, Refugee Claims Officers will be primarily responsible for research, information gathering and analysis related to individual claims. They will also assist in conducting more focused hearings which will result from the early identification of issues.[7]

Other changes that effected the work of the IRB resulted from changes to the Immigration Act, Citizenship Act, and Customs Act that were part of Bill C-44 which was proclaimed on July 10, 1995. For instance, permanent residents convicted of serious crimes are not eligible to have Convention refugee claims referred to the CRDD if the minister is of the opinion that they constitute a danger to the public in Canada. Also, permanent residents cannot appeal removal orders to the IAD if they have been convicted of serious crimes and the minister is of the opinion that they constitute a danger to the public in Canada. Further, after a claim has been referred to the CRDD, a Senior Immigration Officer with Citizenship and Immigration Canada may revoke the referral where (i) the claimant has been convicted of a serious crime, (ii) the claimant has made multiple claims, or (iii) the decision to refer the claim was based on fraud or misrepresentation. Moreover, where a sponsored application for landing is refused, no appeal may be made to the IAD in respect of a person convicted of a serious crime who, in the opinion of the minister, constitutes a danger to the public in Canada. Finally, the implementation of Bill C-44 modified the Immigration Act by expanding the jurisdiction of the Senior Immigration Officer, thereby extending the authority of immigration officials in the Department of Citizenship and Immigration in ways that reduced the number of cases conducted by adjudicators, while increasing the proportion of complex inquiries.

IRB Action Plan for Renewal

In January 1995, the chairperson announced that Joe Stanford of the Canadian Centre for Management Development (CCMD) would be retained to "take the pulse" of the board.[8] In effect, Mr. Stanford's task was to identify issues that had to be resolved to allow the board to function as a fully integrated team. In November 1995, a program of organizational renewal was announced in the board's "Action Plan for Renewal." The "Action Plan for Renewal" outlined a number of initiatives that the board would pursue as part of its program of organizational renewal:

- continuing support for enhancements to the refugee determination process;
- working towards an improved delivery capacity;
- working towards an approach to deal with Members' concerns;
- work force adaptability;
- a code of ethics and conduct incorporating the board's vision and values; and
- a new classification system and a workable redeployment capacity.[9]

One of the early initiatives undertaken by the board, on the advice of Joe Stanford, was to define the board's Mission Statement. In July 1995, the board's full management team, including senior managers from all divisions, branches and regions, met to establish the board's Mission Statement, and to begin the work of setting the board's vision and values.[10] The board's executive team developed the following Mission Statement:

> The Immigration and Refugee Board is an independent tribunal established by the Parliament of Canada. Our mission, on behalf of Canadians, is to make well-reasoned decisions on immigration and refugee matters, efficiently, fairly, and in accordance with the law.[11]

The "Action Plan for Renewal" also outlined a plan for a focus group exercise on vision and values which would seek input from a representative cross-section of the IRB on the organization's key values and vision for the future.[12] The focus group exercise would begin by selecting internal facilitators who would operate in teams and travel across the country to conduct focus groups in the regional and district offices. The internal facilitators would be carefully selected and given special training

291

to conduct focus groups. It was also envisaged that internal facilitators would serve a valuable role in the future as "agents of change" within the organization.

Three major organizational changes have already been initiated and implemented. The IRB is in the process of amalgamating its three Toronto offices, the two CRDD regional offices and the Adjudication Division offices located on Edward Street. The Operations Branch has been given a new mandate and been reorganized. It has been transformed into the Program, Policy and Standards Development Branch. Further, regional directors, responsible for the administrative operations of regional offices, now report directly to the board's Executive Director rather than the Director General of the previous Operations Branch. The IRB is also moving toward improving its client services by providing a "single window service" for such common services as finance, administration, and personnel.

INITIATING CULTURAL TRANSFORMATION THROUGH FOCUS GROUPS

Drawing from the work of Terrence E. Deal and Allan A. Kennedy's groundbreaking book, *Corporate Cultures*, Eileen Shapiro notes, in *Fad Surfing in the Boardroom: Reclaiming the Courage to Manage in the Age of Instant Answers*, that organizations will only change "if they invest in a massive 'cultural transformation' effort or 'change management' program."[13] Given that organizational cultures are malleable, Shapiro argues that organizational cultures can be transformed by changing "'the internal game,' the set of implicit, unwritten rules about how to survive and excel within the organization."[14] Shapiro's prescription is "to uncover the objectives and rules of the internal game and change **them** as a first and fundamental step in transforming the culture."[15] She bases her belief on the following three observations:

1. Every organization has an internal game that sets the rules for how to survive and excel within the organization; if you want to change the culture, part of your plan must include changing the internal game.

2. The rules people use for navigating the internal game seldom look anything like the rules in the policy books; if you want to change the internal game, you first need to uncover the real rules.

292

3. Those who excel at the internal game are not always those who contribute to performance; if you want to fine-tune the game, you need to find ways to assess the true contributions of the participants and reward the worthy.[16]

Shapiro, therefore, counsels that the first step in commencing "cultural transformation" or "change management" within an organization is "to start by identifying the factors that most closely influence actual behaviour: what is permitted and what is rewarded, versus what is prohibited and what is punished, and what is funded and supported versus what is starved and ignored."[17] It is only after one has uncovered the real rules of the internal game, Shapiro argues, that one can then move to alter those rules which stand in the way of the needed changes within the organization.

Focus groups are perhaps one of the most effective ways of uncovering the "rules of the internal game." However, it is important to stress that focus group research is a **qualitative** methodology. According to Ron Zemke and Thomas Kramlinger, "the objective of a focus group is to acquire a set of responses from a group of people familiar with the topic, service, experience, or product being discussed."[18] Thomas Greenbaum notes that focus groups "can be very helpful in providing inputs into a decision-making process and in helping design a research instrument that can provide statistically reliable data. But it is generally not advisable to use focus groups to make decisions."[19] In the private sector, focus groups are often used to test new product ideas. Thomas Greenbaum states that:

> Participants in focus groups can be very helpful in **reacting** to new product ideas that are presented to them during a session, but they almost never are the source of a new product idea themselves.
>
> Nor is the focus group technique itself designed to create new product ideas. Brainstorming and Synectics are much better techniques for developing the strengths of a group to achieve this objective.[20]

However, focus groups can be constructively used as part of a program to assess the effectiveness of an advertising campaign. The role of focus groups in this regard would be to "ascertain consumer attitudes toward the campaign, to help determine how well the campaign communicates the intended message, and to identify parts of the message that are not believable or easily understood."[21] Another way in which focus groups are used is to develop hypotheses to be tested by means of surveys or observational techniques.[22] Perhaps one of the most serious abuses of the focus group technique is to use it ostensibly for research purposes but in reality to capture the attention of a target group to sell products.[23]

Since the focus group technique is a qualitative methodology and focus group participants are not selected at random it cannot provide results that are projectable to a larger universe. Moreover, the sample size of individual focus groups is too small to be representative of the views of those within the larger group or organizational setting from which they are drawn. Consequently, those who have the responsibility for moderating and analyzing the outcome of a focus group session must be careful to ensure that their conclusions accurately reflect the participants' views about the subjects under discussion. Moreover, they should guard against assuming the views of focus group participants necessarily apply to everyone within an organization or the universe from which they are drawn.

Focus Groups at the IRB

Following the release of the "Action Plan for Renewal," the board began to recruit people who could be trained to become internal facilitators and run focus groups on visions and values. The fifteen people who were selected underwent a challenging screening process and three days of training in Ottawa.[24] The training was based on experiential learning which required each of the internal facilitators to prepare focus group research designs based on a set of packaged resource materials.[25]

The fifteen people selected came from the regional and district offices across the country. They consisted of five members, four from the CRDD and one from the IAD, and ten staff, including three senior staff from the board's National Headquarters in Ottawa. Overall, the fifteen facilitators were fairly representative of the IRB with individuals from various divisions and levels within the organization.

After completing the three-day training session the internal facilitators were tasked with putting together a facilitator's guide, which included a checklist for setting up focus groups off-site (yet reasonably close to the various regional offices to allow participants ready access to the sessions), a moderator's script for the focus group exercise, an outline of the themes that facilitators could use for questioning participants, data capture and data analysis forms, and the instructions for completing these forms after each focus group session.[26]

Of the fifteen people selected and trained as internal facilitators, ten where chosen to deliver the actual focus group sessions. The ten internal facilitators were divided into five teams of two. One facilitator acted as a moderator while the other served as a data capturer. The focus group sessions were conducted off-site in order to ensure the participants felt completely open to express candid views on the topics discussed. The internal facilitators also wanted to avoid the situation where participants would be tempted to return to their offices to take telephone calls or do other work during the focus group sessions. It was agreed that the extra expense involved in conducting focus groups off-site was justified, because providing a completely neutral venue would enhance the validity as well as the richness and quality of the data gathered during the sessions.

Each focus group represented, as much as possible, a cross-section of the organization in that region of the country. Employees and their direct supervisors were prohibited from participating in the same focus group session. Focus group participants were also assured that their comments would be treated as confidential and that there would be no attributions made to individual participants.

All focus group facilitator teams followed a similar format for their focus group sessions. Three specific goals were presented to the focus groups at the beginning of each session:

1. to identify the values, attitudes, behaviours, ethical principles, or "rules of the game" that our organization needs to fulfil its mission and foster a harmonious work place;

2. to identify how we can realize these values; and

3. to identify how we can measure our progress in realizing these values.[27]

Each focus group session lasted about three hours and developed its own unique dynamic which reflected the mix of participants involved in the session and the region or district in which the session was held. Participants in the focus groups told their personal stories and related their own work experiences at the board. These stories and experiences helped to illustrate the underlying values practised at the board.

THE FOCUS GROUP FINDINGS AND RECOMMENDATIONS

After completing the twenty-three focus group sessions, one facilitator from each of the five teams met in Ottawa to analyze the data collected from the focus group exercise. At this meeting, the values identified from the focus group sessions were grouped into a number of distinct value clusters. Eventually, they were refined into five value clusters. These included:

- relevant, responsive, and accountable management;
- open, honest, timely communication;
- valuing people;
- working together effectively;
- excellence in delivery.[28]

In essence, these five value clusters provide the central pillars or foundation of the culture that focus group participants identified should be espoused and promoted at the board.

The general perception of the facilitators was one of being overwhelmingly impressed with the tremendous enthusiasm, commitment and concern the focus group participants demonstrated for the board in all regions and districts across the country. Focus group participants took great pride in working for an organization committed to fulfilling Canada's international obligation to provide protection and refuge to those individuals and families in genuine need as well as applying and enforcing the statutory requirements of the Immigration Act with respect to those who seek entry to and landing in Canada. The number and quality of the suggestions made by focus group participants, for improving the board's overall efficiency and effectiveness as an organization, was quite remarkable. Internal facilitators were left with the overall impression that the employees of the board are not only extraordinarily well qualified but highly motivated and dedicated to the work they do for the IRB.

A distillation of the recommendations made by focus group participants resulted in the identification of three key recommendations for addressing the perceived shortcomings of the board. The first is "transforming management," which calls for a change in the management style prevalent at the board. What is advocated is a change in management style which would foster a greater sense of trust at the board and an elimination of territorial behaviour among management and others.[29] To this end, a cadre of senior managers will be assigned to guide the process of organizational and administrative renewal at the IRB. The second recommendation calls for the establishment of a "renewal team" to work under the direction of the Director General, Renewal, to coordinate, facilitate, and monitor the renewal efforts at the board. Accordingly, eleven renewal team members have been selected from the regional and district offices across the country and from the three divisions and from different positions and levels throughout the organization. Appointments to the renewal team are on an assignment basis and are not permanent. Renewal team members are intended to serve as "change agents" for the organization. The third recommendation is for a series of task groups to be set up to deal with a wide ranging set of issues, including:

- setting standards for excellence in delivery;
- simplifying and/or re-engineering work processes;
- helping managers and employees be more mutually accountable.[30]

The recommendations that would be made by the task groups would be reviewed by the cadre of senior managers and, if deemed appropriate, implemented on a contractual basis in the regional offices across the country.

BUILDING MOMENTUM FOR RENEWAL

A "Draft Focus Group Report on Values" was distributed to all employees of the board in order to validate the focus group exercise findings. Consequently, all those employees who did not have an opportunity to participate in the focus group exercise will have a chance to provide their input into the final report. Although the final report has yet to be issued, it may not be too early to provide an assessment of the focus group exercise.

Overall, the focus group exercise must be considered a success from a number of perspectives. First, it provided an opportunity for IRB employees, irrespective of position, to shape

the values and vision of the board in the very midst of its renewal. Second, it provided those who participated in the focus
group sessions the chance to discuss workplace issues and concerns with colleagues in different divisions and at different levels of the organization. Normally, of course, employees within
an organization would not have this type of contact with their
co-workers. Since all participants were treated as equals in the
focus group sessions there was a genuine opportunity for employees to learn about each others' experiences. Many of the
participants told internal facilitators that they learned a great
deal by listening to the comments of their co-workers in the
sessions. This educational aspect of the focus group exercise
should not be underestimated. Third, the focus group exercise
provided a clear indication of the most significant concerns of
the employees within the organization. Fourth, it also provided
many useful and interesting recommendations on how various
issues and problems could be addressed. These were eventually
condensed and captured in the draft report's recommendations
for renewal. Fifth, the focus group exercise provided the employees of the board an opportunity to have their concerns,
ideas and views considered and incorporated in the board's organizational and administrative renewal. Sixth, the focus group
exercise provided the necessary impetus to help ensure the success of the board's program of renewal. It helped to ensure that
all employees had their say on what the board's core values
should be as well as what its vision for the future could be. In
this sense, it helped to empower and unite all the employees in
the organization. Finally, and perhaps most importantly, the focus group exercise achieved its principal objective of identifying
the central values that everyone within the board would like to
see as the cultural foundation of the organization.

NOTES

1. Immigration and Refugee Board, *1995, The Year in Review*, "The
   Work of the Convention Refugee Determination Division."
2. *Ibid.*, "The Work of the Appeal Division."
3. *Ibid.*, "The Work of the Adjudication Division."
4. Lynda Hurst, "Consultants sell art of borrowed wisdom," *The Toronto Star*, February 24, 1996, p. B1.
5. Gary Nyp, "Agents of change, Managing in the turbulent '90s,"
   Laurier Campus, Spring, 1996, p. 9.

6. Immigration and Refugee Board, "Refugee Status Determination Process to be Strengthened," *News Release*, March 3, 1995.

7. *Ibid.* Refugee Claim Officers were formerly known as Refugee Hearing Officers. Their role is to assist panels by ensuring that all relevant information concerning a claim is presented to the panel. Although they play a neutral role in the refugee determination process they receive their direction from members who are assigned to particular claims.

8. Immigration and Refugee Board, *1995, The Year in Review*, "A Message from the Chairperson."

9. Immigration and Refugee Board, "Action Plan for renewal," "Message from the Chair and Executive Director," Nurjehan Mawani, Chairperson, Jean-Guy Fleury, Executive Director.

10. *Ibid.*, p. 2.

11. *Ibid.*, p. 4.

12. *Ibid.*

13. Eileen Shapiro, *Fad Surfing in the Boardroom: Reclaiming the Courage to Manage in the Age of Instant Answers* (Addison Wesley Publishing Company, 1995), p. 51.

14. *Ibid.*, p. 53.

15. *Ibid.*

16. *Ibid.*

17. *Ibid.*, p. 63.

18. Ron Zemke & Thomas Kramlinger, *Figuring Things Out* (Addison-Wesley, 1992), p. 85.

19. Thomas Greenbaum, *The Handbook for Focus Group Research* (Lexington Books, 1993), p. 59.

20. *Ibid.*

21. *Ibid.*, p. 60.

22. Zemke & Kramlinger, *Figuring Things Out*, p. 85.

23. *Ibid.*, p. 61.

24. Internal facilitator candidates had to complete three exercises and a personal telephone interview before being selected. The exercises included an "Internal Consultant Self-Assessment," the Myers-Briggs Type Indicator, and the Bradford Dunlop Team Relations Indicator.

25. Facilitator training was designed by Bradford-Bachinski Limited, Ottawa.

26. Immigration and Refugee Board, *Focus Group Internal Facilitator's Guide*.

27. Immigration and Refugee Board, *Draft — Focus Group Report on Values*, June, 1996, p. 2.

28. Immigration and Refugee Board, *Draft — Focus Group Report on Values*, p. 4.

29. *Ibid.*, p. 20.

30. *Ibid.*, p. 22.

Public Sector Innovation in Canada

Eleanor D. Glor

Most Canadians have looked to their governments to address key problems and issues of the nation, concerns such as working conditions, business environment, transportation and communication infrastructure, social and health problems, and the environment. Especially since the Second World War they have also looked to government to manage the economy and support the disadvantaged. In recent years, however, as the growth rate of government revenues declined, and the dominant ideology changed from liberal to conservative, the role of government has been rethought, with an emphasis on eliminating budget deficits, reducing debt and taxes, and lessening the role of the state. One paradigm within which innovation occurred was replaced by another. Always, the role of the state was bracketed by a dominant paradigm.

Public services have been organized as bureaucracies in order to support governments and implement initiatives, but not typically with a mandate to innovate. For the most

Portions of this paper have been published previously in *Optimum*, 1997, 27(2). Reproduced with the permission of the Minister of Public Works and Government Services Canada, 1997. The opinions expressed in this paper are those of the author.

part, policy was developed by the elected officials and public servants, while the civil service implemented it. Today, public services are being asked to take on novel roles reflecting new values like service to the client as opposed to service to the public, shrinkage rather than growth, and innovation. While the emphasis of innovation was policy from the 1940s through the 1970s, today, the focus is administration, management, and efficiency.

This chapter outlines Canadian governments' relationships to innovation over the last 50 years and explores barriers to it. Growing out of this experience, it also identifies means to support public sector innovation, and suggests a framework for avoiding the impediments, and creating an innovative government.

What Is Innovation?

Many different definitions of innovation are in use — a sampling is outlined in Appendix I. For some, innovation is any activity which is new for the government introducing it. Using this definition, the same activity could be an innovation thousands of times, as long as it was new to the organization adopting it. This definition is treated here as innovation dissemination, not innovation. This chapter focuses instead on the first time the activity is introduced anywhere or at minimum in Canada. Innovators, then, are the group of first adopters in the forefront of change. Innovation is "the conception and implementation of significant new services, ideas or ways of doing things as government policy in order to improve or reform them, and involves taking risks. An innovative government is an innovator or early adopter of many innovations within a short period of time." (Glor, 1997b) This chapter examines innovation in the federal, provincial, and municipal public sector in Canada today.

Innovation for What?

Rather than taking a leadership role in "busting paradigms" and considering a full range of possible options, governments have tended to follow trends in society and adopt measures around which a clear consensus has already developed. Only in the face of undeniable social movements[1] has government been

301

prepared to move out of the dominant paradigm which said that the role of government was to serve the most powerful interests in society. Most of the nationalizations in Canada, for example, were conducted by Conservative governments, in order to help out an industry rather than to change power relationships. Some innovations have had revolutionary impacts, however. The conversion from steam to electricity as the main source of power and the introduction of the computer, for example, have both had huge impacts on the world of work — what we do, how we do it, who does it and how many do it (Rifkin, 1995). This is not to say, however, that innovations must produce revolutionary results to be innovations. It is to recognize, rather, that innovation is imbedded in a political context and can have impacts on power. Most innovations in government have, in fact, produced incremental changes, however. More fundamental changes were not approved, probably not even conceived. Government was sometimes proactive, often it introduced incremental innovations, but it did not, for the most part, change the basics of how we function in society and the positions of the powerful and of the disadvantaged.

Innovation has not typically been a goal in itself. It has been a response to a situation which has for some reason become unsatisfactory — because of an intolerable situation or because a better approach has been discovered. Innovation is also a tool that offers a process for addressing those unsatisfactory situations. The difficulties involved in changing involuntarily, or even voluntarily, are many. Most important, however, is a clear vision of the goal, the values and the kind of society which the innovator wishes to create and which the innovation serves. Changes are always imbedded in a set of values, and these should be understood, and explicitly described and agreed upon, in innovation. Innovative Japanese companies take this approach as well (Nonaka and Takeuchi, 1995). Only by making values the basis of innovations is there any chance they will accomplish the goals set and contribute to improving society, as they should. What that improvement should be can be difficult to describe, but one version of it is Christian Bay's: we should seek to create a "healthy polity" (Bay, 1968 a, b). A healthy polity could be defined as one which reduces suffering and increases well-being for the population of a country (Doughty, 1997).

INNOVATION IN GOVERNMENTS

Because of a general lack of focus on it, public sector innovation has not been well documented. Just a few studies have examined public sector innovation in the last 30 years, and these have each looked at different areas (Table 1). Following a flurry of interest in the 1970s, interest in public sector innovation has grown again during the 1990s. Today's interest is not based exclusively in academia but also in governments and public servants' professional associations.

For governments, the most important issue is how to innovate when they want to do so. Elected and appointed officials have not generally recognized the need to be innovators, and so are not as well organized as some private corporations, to innovate. Because of this lack of emphasis on innovation, and because government has many other competing objectives, numerous barriers stand in the way of innovation in government. These impediments vary somewhat by level of government.

The following analysis of innovation in government is done separately for policy and administrative innovation because the patterns of their development have been somewhat different. The leaders in policy and administrative innovation are typically different, for example — elected officials for the first, appointed ones for the second. Although the distinction is not always easy to make, in this paper policy refers to what is done by government — policies and programs which it delivers. Administration is concerned with how it is done — the management, processes, and infrastructure (human resources, information systems, administration, assets management, and finance) that support policy. This analysis also suggests that the governments which were innovators (first implementers) may have been different for policy and management innovations.

POLICY INNOVATION

The literature on policy innovation has reviewed a limited number of innovations. Mohr (1969) studied 93 innovations, Gray (1973) 12 and Walker (1969) 88 (Table 2). In Canada, Dale Poel (1976) studied 25 policy innovations introduced by Canadian provinces from the 1940s to the 1970s and Glor (1997b)

TABLE 1
Comparison of Canadian Administrative and Policy Innovations by Government

Scope Government	IPAC Finalists & Medal Winners 1990–97 Admin. National	Gow Admin. National	Glor Admin. Sask & National	Poel Policy National	Glor Policy Sask & National	Total Innovations
Canada	11	6	4	N/A	7	26
Ontario	12	4	2	5	3	27
Quebec	4	0	0	2	0	5
BC	12	3	1	4	1	20
Alberta	4	2	1	2	2	9
Manitoba	0	0	0	3	2	7
Sask	2	0	13	10	109	131
N.S.	0	1	0	4	0	5
N.B.	1	1	0	1	0	3
Nfld	0	0	0	0	0	0
PEI	0	0	0	0	2	2
Total	46	17	21	33	126	235

Source: Institute of Public Administration (1990–97), *Public Sector Management.*
NOTE: Statistical tests are not performed because the same intensity of examination and knowledge of governments was not available for all studies. As a consequence, no firm conclusions can be drawn about which governments were innovative, except that Saskatchewan was innovative.

TABLE 2

Comparison of Policy Innovation Studies

Author	Subject Area	Period	Number of Cases	Concentration of Innovations Discovered [Mean no. of innovations per year]	How Innovations Were Identified	Region Covered
Mohr	Public Health	1945–1964	93	4.7	Survey of participant observers	Illinois, Michigan, New York, Ohio, Ontario
Gray	education, welfare, civil rights	1784–1969 (185 yrs)	12	0.1	Word of Mouth	USA states
Walker	comprehensive	1870–1966 (96 yrs)	88	0.9	Word of Mouth	USA states
Poel	comprehensive	1940s–1970s (30 yrs)	25	0.8	Word of Mouth	Canada provinces
Glor	comprehensive	1971–82 (11 yrs)	126	11.4	Participant Observers	Sask, federal and provincial gov'ts

Sources: Mohr, 1969; Gray, 1973; Walker, 1969; Poel, 1976; and Glor, 1997.

identified 126 innovations which were introduced first primarily in Saskatchewan, [from 1971–82] but were also initiated in the rest of Canada (Table 1).

Federal Policy Innovation

The federal government should be Canada's primary public sector policy innovator. It becomes aware of public sector innovations abroad in the course of its normal business much more than other governments and political parties, which often must identify the need, assign additional resources and create specific mechanisms such as task forces in order to identify these initiatives. Because of its size, the federal government has also had more resources with which to innovate: it has a budget equal in value to that of all the provinces combined. While some federal officials argue its budget is largely "outside its control," this is true for provincial and municipal governments as well, which likewise earmark large portions of their budgets for third parties. Moreover, the federal government did research and funded others to do much more research than other governments. To some extent this was the equivalent of research and development (R&D) for private sector innovators. The federal government thus had high potential to become an innovator because of its size, its large research and development budget and its many contacts outside the country.

The federal government has indeed been the first government in Canada to introduce a number of new policies, such as creating a single department to serve the north; creating an open, honest environmental public consultation process, with financial assistance made available to interest groups; establishing a comprehensive environmental assessment of a development project (MacKenzie Valley Pipeline); introducing a human rights code; creating a strategy for reducing drug prices (bulk buying); establishing a science council; and providing short-term developmental funding for health and social preventive, community-based projects. While this is not a complete list, it is a rather short 40-year list, especially for the largest government in Canada, compared to 126 policy innovations over 11 years in the Saskatchewan government (Table 1). The federal government was not the most active policy innovator among Canadian governments, as it should have been. Why was this?

Barriers to Federal Policy Innovation

Several factors stood in the way of policy innovation by the federal government. For the most part, the federal government *did not interpret its role as a policy and program innovator*. Because of the separatist threat and growing provincial and regional sentiment, the federal government perceived its role as *a consensus builder and preserver of national unity*. The need for consensus, moreover, constrained the number of innovations which were introduced. Many national innovations, like unemployment insurance (UI) and Canada Pension Plan (CPP), required not just consensus but unanimity, something very difficult to achieve in the Canadian federation. Instead of innovating itself, the Government of Canada *facilitated adoption of innovations by "laggards,"* jurisdictions which lacked either the will or the resources to adopt demonstrated improvements. The requirement for consensus or unanimity was a useful tool in convincing laggards to adopt innovations.

The federal government's focus on maintaining national unity permitted less attention to other matters. As part of its unity strategy, moreover, the federal government until recently required that most programs be universal and identical across the country. Important objectives may have been achieved, but this *did not allow local solutions and innovations to bloom*.

Shared jurisdiction. Under the Constitution, the provinces are responsible for health, social services, welfare, education, natural resources and the environment — all important and expensive program areas. For the most part the federal government could only legislate in these areas when it was able to secure the agreement of the provinces to do so. This it was able to achieve in introducing UI, which required an amendment to the Constitution in 1940, and the CPP, hospital insurance and medical insurance during the 1960s. Alone, the provinces lacked the resources to fund these programs in keeping with post-WWII expectations. Thus the provinces had a financial motive to cooperate with initiatives promoted by the federal government which included shared-cost funding. *Provinces also needed national programs* to achieve the universal coverage and the magnitude necessary to permit programs to function well. Crop failures due to drought or hail damage, for example, tended to be regional or local rather than national, so a crop insurance program was viable on a national basis, but could become highly indebted on a provincial basis.

The *federal role* in innovation also hinged on *its capacity to fund programs*. One reason the federal government could fund programs was because its tax rate was double that of the provinces. During the late 1970s, however, in order to meet provincial demands for more power and to manage its growing fiscal problems, the federal government began to devolve some of this tax room to the provinces.[2] This allowed them to fund, manage, and control health and social programs themselves. The federal government has been less likely to introduce health and social innovations since that time. Beginning in the 1970s, both the federal and provincial governments (except Alberta and Saskatchewan during the 1970s and early 1980s) ran deficits, and hence were not in a position to fund many new programs.

Since then, the federal government has had trouble initiating new programs which ultimately required provincial financing on an ongoing basis. In the health and social services field, the federal government created research and development programs during the early 1970s, which provided short-term (three years) funding for new programs. The programs funded services and projects in predetermined categories and in keeping with the progressive thinking of the time, but it did not fund provincial programs nor innovations, specifically. As a result, nongovernment agencies were funded to create programs aimed at priority target groups (e.g. adolescents, disabled, seniors). Services were often delivered by small, isolated, not-for-profit agencies created specifically for that purpose. Once federal funding ran out, the agencies sought funding from provincial and municipal governments, with declining success over time. This approach became less and less acceptable to the other governments. While these federal development programs served to initiate new services and sometimes novel approaches, for the most part they facilitated the dissemination of programs throughout the country. Their focus was not on innovation as such and they put pressure on the provinces to shift their funding from potential new provincial government programs to not-for-profit sector programs.[3] The potential for learning implicit in these programs was also not realized because they were not typically evaluated in a way which allowed governments to conclude whether the approaches were more successful or more cost-effective than previous ones.

Finally, even when it came to areas of its own jurisdiction, the federal government had the *largest, most rule-laden bureaucracy* in the country. During the 1980s it also had a *government which did not trust its public servants* nor treat them as its partners in serving Canadians. These factors too reduced the innovativeness of the federal government.

Provincial Policy Innovation

Canadian provinces and their governments are very different one from another, and their policy innovativeness also vary. A comparative study of provincial innovation by Dale Poel (1976), found two innovation streams in the provinces, grouped along ideological lines. On the interest-group liberal (rights-oriented) dimension, Ontario was the most innovative province; on the socialist (equality-oriented) dimension, Saskatchewan was the most innovative province. Overall, Saskatchewan was found to be considerably more innovative than Ontario.

Barriers to Provincial Policy Innovation

Although the American innovation literature suggests large state governments should be the most innovative (Walker, 1969), the large Canadian provinces were not the greatest policy innovators up to 1974 (Poel, 1976), or since (Glor, 1997).

Political leadership was an important determinant of innovation. Ontario had one (Progressive Conservative) government for 42 years, while Quebec had a Parti Québécois government for half of the last 25 years, focused on separation and the federal/provincial context. Saskatchewan, Manitoba, and BC each had NDP governments for at least a portion of the period. Not surprisingly, with their emphasis on change, NDP governments seem to have been more innovative than Conservative ones, although there also were substantial differences among NDP governments in terms of their innovativeness.

Another political factor was the role of a *change of government* and its impact on government policy. In Ontario, one party was in power from 1943 to 1985, so it was a mature government, and the public service correspondingly did not change much either. The Government of Canada changed briefly in 1979, then had a substantive change in 1984 and changed again in 1993. Both Ontario and Canada retained *much the same public servants* at the senior level, although the Government of

Canada engaged many young new public servants at the junior professional levels during the early 1970s. Quebec had a major change of government in 1976, subsequently engaging many new public servants, who reflected PQ perspectives. Bringing in young, new political representatives as well as new public servants seemed to enhance change and introduction of innovations.

In addition, *governments varied in their capacity to create and fund innovations.* As they enhanced their own policy, program, and financial capacity, Quebec, Alberta, Saskatchewan, and a growing number of other *provinces with parties in power different from that federally* were unwilling to take their lead from the federal government, and developed new solutions to their problems. Have-not Saskatchewan's financial situation improved markedly during the early 1970s, thus enhancing its capacity to innovate. Over time, the provinces learned to look more to the federal government to fund programs only, and less to develop them.

As a consequence, while the federal government played a key role funding demonstration projects and disseminating new programs, these were often not federal government innovations. They had, rather, been *introduced in the provinces first* (e.g. business service centres in New Brunswick) or the initiative had been taken by the provincial government to involve the federal government as funder (e.g. crop insurance and cost-sharing of day care costs through the Canada Assistance Plan by Saskatchewan). Sometimes, the federal government approached provinces to demonstrate innovations (e.g. Mincom, the first guaranteed annual income plan in Canada, in Manitoba). The provinces demonstrated the innovations and the federal government helped to disseminate them. I have been told that the federal Department of Finance deliberately chose this role for the federal government, starting in the early 1970s[4] — it was to adopt policies neither early nor late, but in the middle.

Municipal Policy Innovation

Municipal policy innovations have taken a somewhat different turn from those of the federal and provincial governments. Canada is a country with three large municipalities (Toronto, Montreal, and Vancouver), a few medium-sized municipalities (Calgary, Edmonton, Winnipeg, Ottawa, Hamilton, followed by

Halifax and Quebec), and a large number of small and tiny municipalities. Because they are legally controlled by the provinces, municipalities have a limited jurisdiction, which varies by province, but can include local infrastructure, schools, public housing, welfare, public health services, transportation, and leisure time activities, most of which are cost-shared with the province.

The large municipalities are the primary receptors of population in Canada, through internal migration and immigration. Growth, as a consequence, the absorption of new immigrants and dealing with issue-specific pressure groups have been major concerns.[5] Contentious policy differences have therefore tended to centre around control of growth and provision of services, and have not often centred on political party positions. Most municipalities, in fact, do not have political parties.

Growth innovations have focused on developing mass transit systems, limiting growth through zoning and transportation facilities, and developing new housing and services for low-income people, often with federal loan guarantees or funding. Due to municipal and provincial urging, during the 1970s the federal government developed several new programs to support and build housing for the disadvantaged, including social housing, cooperative housing, and self-built housing.

Barriers to Municipal Innovation

Where municipalities could not secure funding from other levels of government, as was often the case, their limited and regressive tax base could provide only a partial back-up. Local governments, moreover, were often influenced by local businessmen and developers, who tended not to support expansion of human services. Lack of funding and will have often stood in the way of local innovation.

Summary: What Has Discouraged Policy Innovation?

The previous discussion suggests a number of factors that have discouraged and inhibited policy innovation in Canadian governments. Federal leadership focused on maintaining national unity. Its approach to unity required universal and identical programs across the country, thus hampering local initiative and innovation to some extent in the more progressive provinces. It did sometimes fund pilots of innovations in the provinces, however. The federal government also was limited by its shared jurisdiction and the necessity to secure provincial consensus or unanimous agreement to change major programs. It used its tax base to fund joint programs, although the federal government transferred some of that capacity to the provinces during the 1970s. The combination of universality, shared jurisdiction, and a willingness to raise taxes favoured dissemination rather than the creation of innovations. The federal government was also, at times, hampered by the largest, most burdened bureaucracy in the country.

Municipalities, provinces, and the federal government shared many factors which discouraged innovation: political disinterest, lack of change of government, little turn-over in public servants, unsupportive relationships (between elected and appointed officials and within the public service), lack of focus on and (especially in the case of small governments) limited capacity to fund innovation. As provinces and large municipalities grew interested in and developed their own policy, program and financial capacity, however, some of them became more innovative.

ADMINISTRATIVE INNOVATION

A few studies have been done of public service administrative innovations. Yin et. al. (1977) identified 140 American information innovations while Gow (1994) examined 17 Canadian management innovations, Borins (1994) reviewed 291 innovations from the Institute of Public Administration of Canada Award for Innovative Management and I found 21 in a Saskatchewan study (including one overlap with Gow) (Table 3).

International Origins of
Current Administrative Innovation Focus

The current focus of government innovation in most Western countries originated with the confluence of continuous fiscal deficits and a change in the predominant ideology beginning with the election of Margaret Thatcher in Great Britain in 1979. This was followed by the election of Ronald Reagan in the U.S.A. in 1980, the Labour Party in New Zealand in 1984 and the Progressive Conservatives in Canada in 1984. Many of the

TABLE 3
Comparison of Administrative* Innovation Studies

Author	Subject Area	Period	Number of Cases	Concentration of Innovations (mean number per year)	How Innovations Were Identified	Region Covered	Type of Analysis
Yin	technological innovation	1965 –75	140 (97 unpublished, 43 published)	12.7	literature	USA: state & local gov'ts	statistical
IPAC	service to the public, empowerment, partnership management, better with less, re-shaping government, making diversity work, mastering change, connecting citizens & government	1990 –97	740	92.5	Participant-observers (Nominees)	Canada: fed., prov. & local gov'ts	statistical
Gow	comprehensive	1960s –1990s	17	0.6	Word-of-mouth (experts)	Canada: fed. & prov. gov'ts	statistical
Glor	comprehensive	1971 –82	20	1.8	Participant-observers	Sask. & some Canada	descriptive

* Recognized innovators = medal winners plus finalists
Note: Administrative includes management, finance, human resource, systems, assets management and process in-novations.

current directions of government were innovations developed and introduced during the early and mid-1980s in Great Britain. These included a re-evaluation of the role of government, leading to major reductions in government services, including health care; hiving off the majority of government agencies into semi-autonomous executive agencies; privatization of Crown corporation and government functions; increased user fees; and introduction of new accountability regimes through management contracts for ministers, deputies, and agency heads. Introducing them for the first time anywhere, Britain spun off about 70% of its government into executive agencies, increased government accountability by introducing health goals and created a Citizen's Charter, a service commitment to citizens as clients.

Canada and other OECD countries adopted many of these British innovations (PUMA, 1990). Canada calls its executive agencies special operating agencies, service agencies, or alternate service delivery and its Citizen's Charter a Declaration of Quality Service. It has not yet adopted health goals, largely because of the difficulties in creating accountability with thirteen federal and provincial governments responsible for health care, and municipal governments and non-government organizations delivering much of the service. Administrative strategies for dealing with restraint used by Canadian federal, provincial, and municipal governments (Table 5) have usually been developed first elsewhere. Canadian governments have been adopters of administrative innovations but more rarely innovators.

The Current Face of Administrative Innovation in Canada

In the face of a major reduction in resources to bring government expenditures into line with revenues which have not been adequate to match expenditures for 25 years, governments face a dilemma trying to maintain services to individuals, groups, and the public today. Revenues have flattened because of corporate downsizing, declining resource industries, a slowed economy, increased unemployment, reductions in corporate income taxes and introduction of new tax-based programs. Increases in individual taxes have not been able to make up the difference, resistance to further tax increases has developed in the face of declining real personal income over the past 10 years, and now some governments are reducing income taxes while increasing

TABLE 4

Government of Medal Winners, Finalists and Entries for IPAC Award for Innovative Management, 1990–97

Government	First	Second	Third	Total Medals Won	Finalists	Recognized Innovators	Entries, 1990–97
Canada	3	1	2	3	8	11	224
B.C.			1	4	8	12	52
Alberta		2	1	3	1	4	39
Saskatchewan		1		1	1	2	19
Manitoba							27
Ontario	2	2	2	6	6	12	167
Quebec	1	1	1	3	1	4	33
New Brunswick			1	1		1	9
Nova Scotia							22
PEI							4
Newfoundland							12
NWT							1
Municipal	2	1		3	5	8	131
Total	8	8	8	24	30	54	740

Sources: *Public Sector Management*, 1990–1997.

Note: The themes of the competitions were: service to the public, empowerment, partnership management, better with less, reshaping government, making diversity work, mastering change and breakthroughs: connecting citizens and government.

fees for government services. Economic stimulation through increased spending is no longer a preferred tool of government, both because of its cost and political opposition. The focus of governments then, is on increasing efficiency and reducing expenditures, without increasing taxes. Sometimes, it is also on reducing the magnitude and power of government.

Following 15 years of constraint and nearly 10 years of restraint, in 1992–3, the federal government's expenditures still exceeded its revenues by 33% overall (Martin, 1994). While reducing this debt, it needed to continue to meet at least some of the expectations of the people, businesses, and other groups of the country. The message being received by governments from Canadians was and continues to be: "We want you to continue to do what you do, but we want it to cost less."[6] The changes governments have introduced to accomplish this task have been in the management and administrative domain, not for the most part in policy areas.

In the U.S.A., the Fiscal Austerity and Urban Innovation Project, a study of local officials in 1000 U.S. municipalities with populations over 25,000 and in 38 other countries, identified the range of approaches to restraint used by municipalities. Table 5 ranks the strategies used by 517 American cities, in order of frequency of use. Whether the federal government is using them is also noted in the table, demonstrating that these same strategies are being used in Canada. Privatization is notably missing from this list, perhaps because it had not yet been demonstrated to be an effective cost-saving mechanism (Gow, 1996; Greenwood and Wilson, 1994; Cigler, 1990; Greene, 1994).

The main strategy employed so far has not been to redesign policies and programs, that is to innovate. Instead, it has been to reduce — to cut subsidies and grants to third parties and budgets to government departments, to introduce and increase user fees, to privatize and to create partnerships to maintain functions which third parties consider important enough to finance, at least in part. This government competition for third party, often charitable funds has, in turn, contributed to a crisis in the non-profit sector.

Governments have reduced the magnitude of their contribution, cutting programs once considered crucial to Canada's national well-being, such as education, health, welfare, and equalization programs. Several have realigned their services, the most striking being Alberta, Ontario with its *Common Sense*

TABLE 5

Cost Reduction Strategies Used by American Municipalities and Government of Canada

Fiscal Austerity Strategy	FAUI 1983–84 % Cities Using No.=517	NLC 1992 % Cities Using No.=620	Brooks 1992 Rank in Use by Ohio Cities 1=most frequent No.=22	1997 Canadian Federal Govt Using? Y=yes N=no
Increase user fees	85	54	4	Y
Improve productivity by management techniques	75	34*	1	Y
New local revenue sources	73	—	3	Y
Attrition reduction of workforce	71	—	7	Y
Reduce spending on supplies, etc.	68	—	11	Y
Draw down budget surplus	64	—	13	Y
Improve productivity by labor saving techniques	63	34*	2	Y
Increase taxes	61	24	14	Y
Hiring freeze	59		15	Y
Reduce capital expenditures	58	44	9	Y
Across-the-board budget cuts	56		10	Y
New intergovernmental revenue	54		5	V. small
Reduce overtime	53		8	Y
Reduce administrative expenses	52			Y
Keep expenditure increases below inflation	51		6	Y
Eliminate programs	48			Y

* = item not directly comparable

continued....

TABLE 5 (Continued)

Fiscal Austerity Strategy	FAUI 1983–84 % Cities Using No.=517	NLC 1992 % Cities Using No.=620	Brooks 1992 Rank in Use by Ohio Cities 1=most frequent No.=22	1996 Canadian Federal Govt Using? Y=yes N=no
Contract services out to private business	46	31*	17	Y
Joint purchasing agreements	46	23*	11	Y
Layoffs	46	40	21	Y
Sell assets	41		22	Y
Reduce locally funded services	40	14	—	Y
Cut least efficient departments	39		16	?
Defer maintenance	37	—	—	Y
Reduce intergovernmental funded services	37			Y
Increase long-term borrowing	36	—	18	Y
Shift responsibilities to other gov'ts	32	3	—	Y
Salary freeze	31	—	—	Y
Contract services out to other gov'ts	29	31	—	Y
Early retirements	26	—	—	Y
Reduce pay levels	23	—	—	N
Controls on new construction to limit population	19	—	—	N

Source: T.N. Clark, "Chapter 8: Strategies That Work: A Menu of Strategies," Table 8.1, p. 215 in T.N. Clark (ed.), *Urban Innovation* (Thousand Oaks, Cal.: Sage Publications, Inc., 1994).

* = item not directly comparable

Revolution and the federal government with *Program Review 1,2 and 3*. Post Program Review 2, Jocelyne Bourgon, Clerk of the Privy Council outlined five core roles of the Government of Canada in her 1996 progress report to the Prime Minister, *Getting Government Right* (Privy Council Office, 1996, p. iv):

- *to strengthen the economy and the economic union* to ensure a prosperous country for Canadians and their children;
- *to enhance social solidarity* by preserving and modernizing the social union so that the caring and sharing society is truly Canada-wide in scope;
- *to pool national resources* to achieve common goals efficiently and effectively;
- *to protect and promote Canadian values and identity* while celebrating Canada's diversity; and
- *to defend Canada's sovereignty* and to speak for Canadians collectively on the world stage.

Such a short list of core roles speaks, however, to the refocusing and reduction being conceived and executed by politicians and public servants. In her remarks to the Annual Symposium of the Association of Professional Executives of the Public Service of Canada (APEX) in 1996, she emphasized that this is never a static list; for example, in the 1996 Speech from the Throne, the government signalled a realignment in labour market, environment, and freshwater habitat roles.

One small shift in the federal government relative to innovation has been the changed role of the Treasury Board Secretariat (TBS). While this is not yet general, the TBS has moved toward a more supportive instead of directive role vis-à-vis line departments. In its quality initiative, for example, departments were not directed to implement quality programs, but encouraged and supported to do so. Building on a national quality network created earlier, gathering together departmental and central agency officials to prepare more than a dozen action guides, emphasizing successes rather than failures, TBS worked with those interested in developing quality programs. Other federal innovations have included moves to industry self-regulation through quality programs and risk-based auditing (fish inspection), shared services among federal departments (Halifax, Place de la Chaudière in Ottawa) and single window entry to federal government services to industry (Canada Business Service Centres) and federal and provincial employment, welfare, and student aid programs (Canada and Alberta). The Department of Fisheries and Oceans has retired ships, double-crewed on some ships and transferred ships among regions, leading to a 10% increase in sea days, an increase in efficiency of 24%, and a reduction in annual operating costs of $1 million (IPAC, 1993). Improved service through greater use of computers and the Internet have been emphasized in Industry Canada, Natural Resources Canada, and Health Canada. A paper burden reduction initiative has led to the redesign of the Record of Employment, cutting the number of forms from six to two, and reducing employer's costs by $100 million a year (IPAC, 1996).

Provinces adopted some of these innovations (e.g. alternate service delivery), and also introduced new approaches. New Brunswick, for example, revamped its conventional training model for literacy programs to introduce a community-based, partnership-focused, and community-driven system. The costs are shared one-third by 400 private sector partners, 45% by the province (no increase in funding) and the rest from other sources. Five hundred jobs lasting up to 40 weeks have been created, 400 volunteers have been involved, programs have been set up in 111 communities, 500 programs are being delivered in 10,000 learning opportunities, dropout rates are down from 50% to 7% and 77% of tests are successfully completed. The delivery cost is $1.39 per student hour, one-fifth the historic cost, while the new program enabled a thirteen-fold increase in training opportunities. (IPAC, 1995)

The Province of British Columbia introduced the first on-line personal property registration system in North America in 1990 (IPAC, 1993). Ontario transferred its Office of the Registrar General to the north, engaged 60% of its work force from target groups, increased productivity 55% and brought per unit salary costs back down to pre-relocation levels through increased use of technology (IPAC, 1994). The Alberta Workers' Compensation Board, facing major increases in costs, shifted from using multi-disciplinary teams focused on body part-specific injuries (e.g. back, lower extremity) to treatment teams organized by occupational categories and allocated by trend data. They used real and simulated work activities at the onset of, and throughout treatment to create "work hardening" (IPAC, 1993).

Ontario privatized its land information systems in 1991, to create Teranet Land Information Services Inc., a partnership among Ontario, Canada and a consortium of private sector companies (IPAC, 1997a). In partnership with the private sector, Ontario piloted in 1993, then fully introduced in 1996, fifty-eight 24-hour *ServiceOntario* Self-Service Kiosks in shopping malls. These provide motor vehicle stickers, vehicle record searches, address changes for both the Ministries of Health and Transportation, payments for court and parking fees, and other services. The kiosks feature product (e.g. licence plate) and receipt dispensing with credit card payment (IPAC, 1997b). Ontario also introduced a paper burden reduction exercise for the business community, creating a single-window, client-oriented transaction process through its Clearing the Path project (IPAC, 1996).

Municipal governments have faced similar problems to those of the federal and provincial governments, *viz.* greater demands for service at a time of both lower revenue growth rates and reduced transfers from provincial and federal governments. Because municipalities are not legally allowed to run operating deficits, they have been forced to come to grips with scarce resources very quickly. Most municipal and provincial governments have balanced their budgets, but they have not yet felt the full impact of transfer reductions.

The approaches used by municipalities in Canada to deal with restraint have been varied. The city of Charlottetown, for example, resolved a long-standing dispute between the city and its police force over implementation of 12 hour shift schedules. Through facilitation by an expert with unique problem solving skills, they developed a solution which met the needs of the police officers for an improved lifestyle and at the same time avoided a projected 9.5% increase in the operational budget of the Police Department. The solution reduced the cost of overtime by 50% and the overall Police Department budget by 4% (IPAC, 1993). The city of Toronto introduced the Bridges Program to facilitate the movement of women employees into nontraditional occupations, those where the workforce was less than 30% women. It combined classroom sessions, shop training and a three-week work placement (IPAC, 1991). Montreal improved access to services by opening 14 Accès Montreal offices in communities across the city, in order to save citizens repeated journeys, act as a clearing house for information on services and activities, and allow people to consult documents and make requests of municipal departments (IPAC, 1990). Saint-Augustin-de-Desmaures, a suburb of Quebec City, was the first city worldwide to obtain its high level of certification under the ISO 9001 quality standards (IPAC, 1996). The city of Vancouver created integrated service teams which resolved community issues like "problem houses" characterized by brawls, fires, and hassling of children. Teams drew their members from city departments, schools, and health services. Problems were effectively dealt with, communities becoming safer and more pleasant, yet costs were absorbed by existing services (IPAC, 1997).

The most comprehensive picture of administrative innovation in Canada is that provided by the IPAC Award for Innovative Management. IPAC received 740 nominations for its award over eight years, identifying 30 finalists and 24 medallists (Table 4), in eight management categories. Among recognized innovators (governments reaching the finals and winning medals), the most innovative governments were Ontario, B.C., and Canada. Among those which won medals, that is, "significant innovators," the most innovative government was Ontario, followed by B.C., and then Quebec, Alberta, Canada, and (mostly large) municipalities with the same number. Among these, however, Alberta and Canada never won a gold medal. These governments have been recognized by their peers as management innovators during the early and mid 1990s, in the eight areas examined (Table 4 lists themes).

Administrative innovation is clearly occurring in federal, provincial, and municipal governments. The innovations are typically adoptions of the innovations of other governments or purpose-made solutions to specific problems; none of the Canadian innovations seems to have been recognized internationally as an important new way of doing the business of government. Overall, the excellent reputation of Canada's administration continues to grow, however, as represented by comments made by officials of the International Monetary Fund (IMF) and World Bank, and requests for advisors, orientation, and training from other countries.

Barriers to Administrative Innovation

The list of IPAC innovators also reveals some things about the less innovative governments. Large governments are prominent in the list of medallists — Ontario notably, followed by Quebec and Canada, although smaller governments have also been significant innovators, mostly B.C., Alberta, and large municipalities. These are, however, the next largest governments. Therefore, despite a small province's predominance as a policy innovator in Canada, small governments are the least likely to win the IPAC innovative management award.

Again, as with policy innovations, two of the governments identified as introducing the most administrative innovations, Ontario and B.C., were provinces with NDP governments (of a total of three NDP governments at the time). The Quebec Parti Québeçois government was, until 1996, a social democratic government as well. Likewise, the radically Conservative successor to the NDP government in Ontario and the neo-conservative government of Alberta are being recognized as innovators. Although this evidence is neither comprehensive nor conclusive, what evidence exists points to radical governments being more innovative than Conservative or Liberal ones. Having a Liberal or Conservative government, therefore, could be a barrier to innovation.

While Ontario and B.C. won six and four medals respectively (the largest numbers won), Canada, which is twice the size of all provincial governments combined, only won medals three times — two thirds and a second place. At the same time, the federal government was a beehive of change, federal public servants participated actively in the IPAC Innovation Award, submitting entries to the competition more frequently than any other government, and were often finalists (Table 4). Why could this be? IPAC officials suggest that the federal innovations submitted have generally not been as innovative as other medalists' submissions. The federal government has tended, for example, to introduce new technology into existing processes, rather than to redesign both its technology and its processes. It has introduced a great deal of change and innovated somewhat, but has not perhaps been as creative as the most innovative governments. Thus, as with policy innovation, the federal government is an innovator, but not the most innovative government. The federal government perceived itself to be an active innovator, however, as revealed by the numbers of nominations it submitted.

The barriers to innovation discussed above and outlined in policy and administrative research are summarized in Appendix II. Key areas in which barriers became apparent were lack of will, an unsupportive culture, lack of resources, poor implementation, poor communication, and lack of jurisdiction.

WHAT SUPPORTS INNOVATION?

While the kinds of innovations created and adopted by Canadian governments have been identified, and the barriers to innovation in Canadian governments explored, strategies which could encourage innovation have not yet been examined.

Saskatchewan stood out as a strong *policy innovator* during the 1940s, 1950s, and 1970s. Suffering very difficult economic times leading up to these periods of innovation, it elected new CCF/NDP governments, known for their reform focus and making deliberate efforts to create new solutions to long-standing problems. A mentality promoting change developed in their populations, and was reflected in their election of an innovative political party, and the recruitment of creative public servants.

Five factors have been identified as essential to the capacity of the Blakeney government to produce and implement innovative policies: developing public acceptance, readiness, commitment, excellent management, and a focus on results (Glor, 1997b). Public acceptance implied both general acceptance of change in the population and acceptance of individual initiatives. Readiness was created by the political party and by the public service through generating good ideas, political and public service commitment, and allocating adequate resources to innovations. Management recruited good people, strengthened existing staff and created a culture of excellence, based on a professional perspective and active participation in professional organizations. As well, management provided superior leadership, created a supportive environment and effectively implemented and evaluated programs. Finally, the government formed and maintained a focus on results.

What can encourage *administrative innovation*? Basing his conclusions on the IPAC management award results, Borins suggested that pressure from outside factors had been the major motivator, including political mandate or pressure; consumer, employee or other stakeholder dissatisfaction; new leadership; an organization unable to meet demands for its services; a changing environment: inertia which had become dysfunctional; financial or resource constraints; failure to understand or reach markets; crises or visible failures; new technology creating new opportunities; and failure to coordinate policies and practices (Borins, 1994).

TABLE 6

Processes for Overcoming Barriers to Innovation in the Public Sector

Stage 1 Readiness	Stage 2 Negotiate Approval	Stage 3 Implement Innovation	Stage 4 Evaluate	Stage 5 Learn
Create a climate/culture favourable for innovation	Reduce risks	Develop change strategies	Develop evaluation mechanisms	Identify, collect and focus on feedback.
Closely align personal and organizational interests	Test Solutions: Establish full-scale pilots and demonstration projects	Plan for introduction of innovation	Benchmark	Consult with public and interest groups
Use organizational conflict to stimulate creativity	Develop business plans	Implement Strategies	Create favourable results	Understand media perspectives
Introduce procedures for encouraging non-routine thinking	Develop strategic plans	Introduce innovations	Incorporate innovations into daily activities of organization	Poll
Stimulate different skills, views, perspectives	Overcome obstacles	Develop excellent management and administration	Create political benefits	Understand election results
Recognize the problem	Find adequate resources	**Develop Human Resource Strategy**		Recognize innovation

continued....

TABLE 6 (Continued)

Stage 1 Readiness	Stage 2 Negotiate Approval	Stage 3 Implement Innovation	Stage 4 Evaluate	Stage 5 Learn
Define the problem	Build momentum	Identify, attract, recruit and retain excellent, innovative people	Recognize, analyze, & identify the learning available from failures.	Introduce more innovations into political platforms.
Develop a solution which involves:	Communicate the solution (develop communication strategies)	Create concrete rewards for innovators	Deal with the negative consequences of the innovations	Create organizational rewards: expand/revise successful innovations
• A process for creating and scanning for ideas, examples & models		Reduce disincentives for innovation.	Realize the benefits from the positive consequences of the innovation	Create personal rewards
• Using tools e.g. identifying best practices		Create balance where disincentives fewer and less powerful than incentives		Promote innovators
Consult		Develop behavioural patterns to institutionalize the new policies		Create Innovation Fund

continued....

TABLE 6 (Continued)

Stage 1 Readiness	Stage 2 Negotiate Approval	Stage 3 Implement Innovation	Stage 4 Evaluate	Stage 5 Learn
Develop innovators		Focus on results		Make information on successes available
Build capacity to identify, attract, recruit & retain excellent, creative, people		Monitor progress		Reward success
Develop procedures for evaluating and choosing among proposals				Recognize and acknowledge failure
Reduce risk				Contract out/cancel projects/programs which cannot be rescued.
Develop and implement small-scale pilots and demonstration projects				Tolerate failures: treat them as a necessary step on the road to success
Build momentum				
Develop champions and leaders				

A FRAMEWORK FOR OVERCOMING BARRIERS TO INNOVATION

Understanding the barriers to innovation permits perception of the processes needed to support it. Table 6 outlines a process for removing and avoiding the impediments outlined above. The innovation process has two major phases — the conceptualization and testing of an innovation, then its approval and implementation. Conceptualization is the coupling of new with existing ideas to create an innovation, while approval and implementation involve promotion and change management that will foster a climate permitting current and future innovation. There are five stages in the innovation process:

- *Readiness* involves creating a climate favourable to innovation that permits individuals to be creative alone or in groups. It is reinforced by ensuring that personal and organizational interests are aligned, by using organizational conflict to stimulate creativity, and by encouraging non-routine thinking. Introducing variety through the composition of the group stimulates expression of different perspectives. An environment of trust encourages openness. This stage needs creators. Creativity can be enhanced or reduced, depending on the approach taken to defining the problem(s) and developing solution(s). An emphasis on "paradigm busting" helps. Risk can be reduced and momentum built by developing and implementing small-scale models.

- *Negotiating approval* is tricky for an innovator and often approval requires a champion and direct contact with the minister of the department. Innovation means risk-taking, so methods to reduce risk are appropriate if they do not hinder the innovation. Strategic and business planning help. Full-scale pilot and demonstration projects demonstrate the potential for success and point out the problems. Though they risk loss of an opportunity, pilots and demonstrations contribute to building momentum, as does active communication about the innovation.

- *Effective implementation* requires change managers who develop planned change strategies; consider explicitly how the innovation will be introduced; and develop implementation, human resource and communication strategies. This stage must develop the behavioural patterns that will institutionalize the new policies and focus on results. There will be many small failures along the way, so tolerance for failure and tenacity to hold out for eventual success are key.

- *A focus on results* provides a means for testing the innovation. It requires not only success on formal evaluations but also the creation of favourable results for both the government and the public service.

- *Learning from the innovation, feedback, and mistakes* goes a long way toward building a climate favourable to innovation, and may point to the next innovation. Punishing failure, on the other hand, is certain to kill interest in innovation. The creation and use of feedback is therefore necessary for future innovation and will occur whether formalized or not. Collecting and focusing on feedback enhances trust and ownership of employees, the public, interest groups, the media and politicians. Treating failure as a false step rather than a conclusive catastrophe contributes to this approach. By creating the right signals as the results of an innovation become known, and by clearly recognizing and celebrating both success and failure, future innovation is made possible.

While this process is not a prescription, and innovations will not always follow it, innovation created to solve problems will often contain this pattern. The process is described in Figure 1.

APPROACHES TO IMPLEMENTATION OF INNOVATION

Innovations are usually purpose-driven. They are not typically introduced because governments recognize the need to be innovative, but rather as solutions to problems, such as scarcity of resources.

Processes such as that outlined above to enhance and support innovation and creativity are rationalist approaches. They define problems and develop solutions to the problems as defined, following a linear process and creating an effective solution. There are, however, other ways to approach innovation.

The redundant approach, rather than following a straight line to a solution, examines more and broader options by seeking detailed input from more staff groups. More than one group

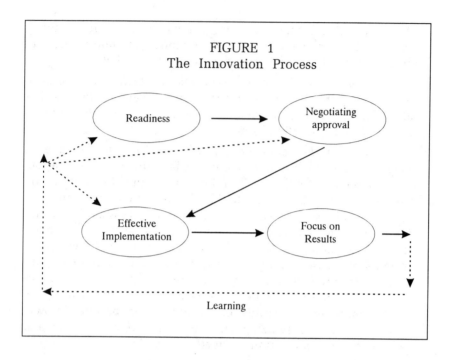

FIGURE 1
The Innovation Process

is made responsible for developing the innovation, producing competition among them. This model is followed in many Japanese companies (Nonaka, 1990). The redundant approach may be difficult to adopt in Western governments, however, because of the focus over the last 10 years on reengineering and business process streamlining. A major element of these cost-reduction strategies has been the elimination of slack, but slack is essential to a redundant approach. By definition, more resources are assigned to the task than is absolutely necessary to solve the problem, in order to come up not with a solution, but with the best solution possible.

Because the Japanese have suffered neither government deficits nor intensive competitive pressure on their companies until very recently, they have not faced the kind of cutbacks encountered by Western governments. Moreover, the Japanese have focused far more on quality approaches than reengineering, the favoured strategy in the West. Thus stakeholders' interests have been constantly considered and made part of the development process, producing innovations and quality improvements which pleased customers and expanded markets.

PARTNERS IN INNOVATION

While an understanding of the innovation process is important, people make it possible. Innovation is a partnership among the public, elected governments and public servants, with each playing separate roles. As with any other endeavour, the key to success is collaboration of those who want to innovate. Stress and economic scarcity, as discussed earlier, have often prompted the public's openness to innovation and some political parties have been more interested in innovation than others. But who are the public servants most interested in innovation?

They are the newly recruited, newly assigned, young or greatly challenged public servants (those standing on a "burning platform") — those most likely to be willing to change and to try new approaches. These same people, once they have a stake in the current situation, can also become resistant to change. Typically, those who achieve senior positions in a bureaucracy are part of the existing culture and function effectively within it. Their willingness to take risks or let go of power is very limited. When the desire to create fundamental change is combined with status, power, and political support in one person, it increases the likelihood of success. Often, however, innovation in government is driven from the top, by new political and public service leaders and consequently has minimal support in the organization. The best of ideas then suffer from limited and unenthusiastic application. An innovative public service requires horizontal processes that will involve, glean ideas from, and develop the support of all levels and departments. The skills required for this approach are increasing in government today.

The elements, processes, and personal skills described above are not usually present in the public service, but are created periodically when the need and urgency of dealing with an issue overcome the focus on other issues and the desire for constancy. Budget cuts, like surpluses, create the opportunity for innovation, but only a government and a public service organized to deal with the issues and wanting to innovate will respond in a positive manner. Governments and the public service must create the infrastructure, support, and skill sets to sustain ongoing innovation.

Sources of Information on Innovation

Some of these elements, processes, and skill building can and should be in place at all times. Scanning for ideas and identification of best practices, for example, can always be done and should be institutionalized. The current efforts by public servants of Canadian governments, their associations (such as IPAC) and their governmental and private sector partners, to create international associations of public servants (such as the Commonwealth Association for Public Administration and Management (CAPM) and the International Institute of Administrative Sciences (IIAS)), best practice data bases and better access to them through the Internet are facilitating knowledge-sharing about innovation. Some of the more interesting ones at the current time include the worldwide websites and the best practice data bases outlined in Appendix III.

Will greater access to information about what other governments are doing encourage worldwide homogenization of approaches or encourage greater innovation? Probably both. By learning about better ways to work, people will want to build better policy, processes, and administration in their own countries. On the other hand, they may also become more willing to consider change on a broader basis as well, and want to learn how to manage it. This could be read to imply that better informed people are more open to change. While this is probably partly true, it is also true that people will not pay attention to this new information unless it has relevance in their own situations. The factors that will give information relevance and help people attend to it are similarity of political allegiances (e.g. left-wing, liberal, neo-conservative), interests (e.g. business, environmental groups), beliefs (e.g. religion), government, language, culture, and problems (e.g. unemployment, budget cuts). Information by itself will not lead to innovation, but incentives and perceived opportunities combined with information might.

THE FUTURE OF INNOVATION IN THE PUBLIC SECTOR

Although there are many losses to the public and to public servants inherent in the changes occurring in government today, one of the gains is the move away from the disadvantages of bureaucratic government. Executive agencies, for example, are reputedly innovative in Britain and New Zealand, and have the potential to be so in Canada, if they can successfully step outside the failure-safe culture of bureaucracy in government today. With the possibility of greater inventiveness comes the potential for finding better solutions to the problems we face.

CONCLUSION

Government innovations since the 1980s initially emphasized doing more for less (efficiency), and more recently, doing less for less (reductions in spending and programs). Prior to the 1980s, the priority for innovations was policy, finding new and better ways to address key issues, but since then the emphasis has been on streamlining and integration of government processes and administration, more efficient and shared delivery of existing services, and reduction of the size and role of government. The invention of new approaches is a means for elected and appointed public servants to improve the quality and effectiveness of programs and assume some control rather than being buffeted by changes, reduced resources and difficult new problems.

In Canada, as in the United States, declining resources and increased tax pressure may also have produced a change in the values reflected in government. The priority has shifted from equity, redistribution of income and sharing of wealth to self-sufficiency, capitalism and individualist values. As this shift has occurred, government interest has shifted from policy innovations to administrative and process innovations which improve efficiency and reduce resource use. Ultimately all governments have also cut programs in order to balance budgets.

This chapter has taken an open approach to innovation, favouring consideration and application of more than one paradigm. This pragmatic approach to dealing with admittedly difficult problems has better potential for objectively and effectively addressing issues and for allowing government and Canadian society to assert some control over current events. Inherent in this approach is perhaps a sharing of power and building of partnerships rather than the alternating dominance of political and electoral majorities.

In the current context governments and public services must change quickly, innovate more, and innovate more fundamentally. While governments currently provide verbal support for

333

innovation, especially during downsizing and when initiating efficiency enhancement programs, the barriers are typically not overcome. The elements, processes, and skills which are needed, and the values and culture which will support and encourage innovation, are not often put in place. The magnitude of change required today demands not just a willingness to change but that public services organize for innovation that will improve the well-being of both the public and elected and appointed officials. Like the private sector, the public sector should be putting in place the research, demonstration, and cultural change necessary to make innovation not just possible but planned, part of the organization, and legitimate.

Appendix I
Definitions of Innovation

New

Inventing something new
Generating new ideas only
Improving something that already exists
Following the market leader
Attracting innovative people

Dissemination

Performing an existing task in a new way
Spreading new ideas
Adopting something that has been successfully tried
  elsewhere
Seeing something from a different perspective
Introducing changes

Source: Table IV, Lee Zhuang, "Bridging the gap between technology and business strategy: a pilot study on the innovation process." *Management Decision*, 1995, 33(8): 13–21.

APPENDIX II
Barriers to Innovation

1. Lack of Will

- Reluctance to change
- Lack of public support
- Lack of will on the part of elected and/or appointed officials
- Acceptance of failure

2. Unsupportive Culture

- Individual or institutional (structural) resistance to change e.g. lack of structure to encourage cross-fertilization among disciplines, professions, functions, topic areas, departments
- Controlling, limiting accountability frameworks
- A culture in which innovation is unwelcome:
  - if not invented in my branch, I'm not interested
  - Blinkers about what government can/should do, how it should/can do them.
- Ideologically driven
- Financentrism
- Reforms which discourage innovation e.g. re-engineering (eliminating slack)
- Lack of "new blood," derived from changes of government and/or recruiting/transferring new public servants.

3. Lack of Resources

- People, money, techniques, technology
- Ideas
- Structures to develop ideas
- Leadership: leadership which is unwilling/uninterested/ conservative/narrow/rigid/defensive

4. Poor Implementation

- Haste in planning or implementation
- Poor implementation

5. Poor Communication

- Poor reward system: Few rewards, many risks and/or penalties
  - lack of protection for innovators
- Insufficient communication about the innovation with public, media, politicians
- Lack of searching for feedback.

6. Lack of Jurisdiction

- imposed uniformity

Appendix III
Information on Innovation

Worldwide Websites specifically dedicated to innovation

Innovations Worldwide Web Resources (Harvard University list of
public sector innovation sites):
http://www.ksb.harvard.edu/~innovat/resource.htm
The Innovation Journal:
http://infoweb.magi.com/~igvn/journale.shtml
Canada: Innovation and Quality Exchange (see below)
Australia: http;//www.psmpcgov.au/innovation/innovation.htm

Innovation Awards

John F. Kennedy School at Harvard University Ford Foundation
Innovations in American Government Award:
http://ksgwww.harvard.edu/innovat/
The Peter F. Drucker Foundation for Nonprofit Management:
Peter F. Drucker Award for Nonprofit Innovation:
http://www.pfdf.org/index.html
National Information Infrastructure Awards (NII) (American):
http://www.gii-awards.com/index.html

Cases

Kennedy School Case Program:
http://ksgwww.harvard.edu/~innovat/case.htm
Case Studies on Service Delivery Models, Draft, April 4, 1996.
Paper prepared for the Government of Canada Deputy Minister Task Force on Service Delivery
Institute of Public Administration of Canada (IPAC)
http://www.ipaciapc.ca

Performance Measurement

National Performance Review (U.S. Vice President Gore's review):
http://www.npr.gov/
Innovation and Quality Exchange (best practices and performance
measurement, Government of Canada Treasury Board Home
Page): http://www.tbs-sct.gc.ca/tb/iqe/iqemnpgen.html

Other

Canadian Public Sector Quality Network: http://fox.nstn.ca/~riqn/
Database on public-private partnerships:
http://www.ppp.beyondgov.ca/

APPENDIX III (Continued)

Department of National Defense Best Practices Exchange — copy
available from Carrie Munro of CMRS
Tel 613-996-5503, fax 996-9587.
http://www.dnd.ca/vcds/mccrt/d2000e_2.htm#14
Treasury Board Secretariat, *Human Resource Strategies in Times of
Change: An Inventory of Initiatives*, Ottawa: Government of
Canada, May 1995: 400+ best practices.
Health Canada, *Best Practices in Human Resources*.
Ottawa: Government of Canada, March 1996.
Discovery, Invention and Innovation (definitions):
http://www.clearlake.ibm.com/Alliance/database/jfkdb.htm

Public Administration Institutes:

Institute of Public Administration of Canada (IPAC)
http://www.ipaciapc.ca
Commonwealth Association for Public Management:
http://www.comnet.mt/capam/
Local Government Institute, University of Victoria:
http://www.hsd.uvic.ca/PADM/research/lgi/lgi.htm
Linkages to public administration in other countries:
http://www.fin.gc.ca/access/linkse.html

NOTES

1. such as those for public education, women's vote and the progressive movement or in times of clear crisis such as World War I, which lead to the "temporary" income tax; the Great Depression, which saw the introduction of public works; and World War II, which produced unemployment insurance
2. There are some who argue that the transfer occurred on paper only, that the federal government did not reduce its tax take and open room to the provinces to increase theirs.
3. Alternate service delivery is not, perhaps, as new as we sometimes suggest.
4. By Barbara Darling, an official of the Department of Finance at the time.
5. Clark (1994) argues that municipalities perform three kinds of functions, developmental where the municipality seeks to enhance the property value of the locality, redistributive where services nominally aid the disadvantaged and allocational where they provide basic municipal services like policing.
6. Frank Graves, president of EKOS Research Associates Ltd., speaking at the 1997 APEX Symposium, outlined this consistent finding in their polls.

REFERENCES

Bay, C. 1968a. "The Cheerful Science of Dismal Politics," in Theodore Roszak (ed.), *The Dissenting Academy*. New York: Random House.

———. 1968b. "Needs, Wants, and Political Legitimacy," *Canadian Journal of Political Science*, 1(3).

Borins, S. 1994. *Public Sector Innovation: Its Contribution to Canadian Competitiveness*. Kingston: School of Policy Studies, Queens University.

Cigler, B. A. 1990. "County Contracting: Reconciling the Accountability and Information Paradoxes," *Public Administration Quarterly*, 14(3)(fall): 285–301.

Clark, T.N. 1994. *Urban Innovation: Creative Strategies for Turbulent Times*. Thousand Oaks, California: Sage Publications.

Doughty, H.A. 1997. "Toward a Definition of Political Health and Pathology," *Innovation Journal* on Internet at http://infoweb.magi.com/~igvn/journale.shtml

Gery, Gloria. 1991. *Electronic performance support systems: how and why to remake the workplace through the strategic application of technology*. Boston: Weingarten Publications.

Glor, E.D. 1997a. "Encouraging Public Sector Innovation," *Optimum, The Journal of Public Sector Management*, 27(2).

——— (ed.) 1997b. *Policy Innovation in the Saskatchewan Public Sector, 1971–82*. Toronto: Captus Press.

Gow, J.I. 1994. *Learning from Others: Administrative Innovations Among Canadian Governments*. Toronto and Ottawa: The Institute of Public Administration of Canada and the Canadian Centre for Management Development, Government of Canada.

———. 1997. "Managing All Those Contracts: Beyond Current Capacity." in M. Charih, ed., *Public Administration in Canada: Present and Future* (in press). Toronto: Institute of Public Administration of Canada, 1075 Bay St., Suite 401, M5S 2B1.

Gray, V. 1973. "Innovations in the States: A Diffusion Study," *American Political Science Review*, LXVII (Dec): 1174–85.

Greene, J.D. 1994. "Does Privatization Make a Difference? The Impact of Private Contracting On Municipal Efficiency," *International Journal of Public Administration*, 17(7): 1299–325.

Greenwood, J. and D. Wilson. 1994. "Towards the Contract State: CCT in Local Government," *Parliamentary Affairs*, 47(3): 405–19.

Institute of Public Administration of Canada (IPAC). 1990. *Public Sector Management*, 1(1).

———. 1991. *Public Sector Management*, 2(2).

———. 1993–1996. *Public Sector Management*, 4(1), 5(1), 6(2), 7(1).

———. 1997a. *Alternative Service Delivery: Sharing Governance in Canada/ La prestation de rechange des services: pour une gouvernance partagée au Canada*. Toronto: IPAC.

———. 1997b. "Breakthroughs: Connecting Citizens and Government, 1997 Winners of the IPAC Award for Innovative Management." Communique dated May 5.

Martin, Paul. 1994. *The Budget Speech*. Ottawa: Government of Canada, February 22.

Mohr, L.B. 1969. "Determinants of Innovation in Organizations," *The American Political Review*, 63: 111–26.

Nonaka, I. 1990. "Redundant, Overlapping Organization: A Japanese Approach to Managing the Innovation Process," *California Management Review*, 32(3).

Nonaka, I. and H. Takeuchi. 1995. *The Knowledge-Creating Company: How Japanese Companies Create the Dynamic of Innovation*. New York: Oxford University Press.

Poel, D. 1976. "The Diffusion of Legislation among the Canadian Provinces: A Statistical Analysis," *Canadian Journal of Political Science*, IX(4): 605–26.

Privy Council Office. 1996. *Getting Government Right: A Progress Report*. March 7. Ottawa: Minister of Supply and Services, Canada.

PUMA. 1990. *Public Management Developments. Survey 1990*. Paris: Organization for Economic Cooperation and Development.

Rifkin, J. 1995. *The End of Work*. New York: G.P. Putnam's Sons.

Thompson, V. 1976. *Bureaucracy and Innovation*. University, Alabama: University of Alabama Press.

Walker, Jack L. 1969. "The Diffusion of Innovations Among the American States," *American Political Science Review*, LXIII(Sept): 880–99.

Weber, M. 1958. *From Max Weber: Essays in Sociology*, translated, edited and with an introduction by H.H. Gerth and C. Wright Mills. New York: Oxford University Press.

Yin, R., K. Heald, & M. Vogel. 1977. *Tinkering with the System: Technological Innovations in State and Local Services*. Toronto: Lexington Books.

Zhuang, L. 1995. "Bridging the gap between technology and business strategy: a pilot study on the innovation process." *Management Decision*, 33(8).

Appendices

APPENDIX 1

The Constitutional Time Line of Canada

Diane Jurkowski and Janice E. Nicholson

1759 — The Battle of the Plains of Abraham

British sieges of French fortresses in Louisbourg in 1745 and 1758 and the War of the Austrian Succession in 1744 had brought armed conflict to the North American colonies. The Battle of the Plains of Abraham, which lasted only twenty minutes, sealed the fate of Nouvelle France. The French commander, General Montcalm was mortally wounded during the battle. The British counterpart, General Wolfe was killed instantly in battle. One year later, 1760, British reinforcements marched to Montreal and defeated the remaining French forces.

1775 — Quebec Act

To deal with the mounting problems of unrest in Quebec, the British Parliament enacted the Quebec Act, in which England restored the old boundaries of Quebec, extending it to the Mississippi River and including what now Ontario and the American states of Ohio, Indiana, Illinois, and Wisconsin. (This latter territory would change drastically with the American

Revolution.) However, the constitutional significance of the Quebec Act was the declaration of religious and cultural recognition; the free exercise of the Catholic religion was guaranteed and the French civil law was recognized as law. Only the language question was unsettled. (French settlers outnumbered the English by 30 to one and all English proclamations were published in both French and English. This set a precedent that would be difficult to change.)

1791 — Constitution Act

The aftermath of the American Revolution brought an exodus of United Empire Loyalists to the maritime colonies, the western regions of Quebec and the surrounding regions of northern Lakes Ontario and Erie of Upper Canada by 1784. They had experienced an atmosphere of political freedom of self-government in the United States. Their intention of immigrating to the British North American colonies was to retain the political association with England. In order to deal with their political agitation, the British Parliament enacted the Constitution Act, in which representative institutions were established. Although the Governor was appointed by the Crown, he was to be advised by a council whom he would appoint. The council members comprised a small, elite groups of inhabitants representing wealth, education, government, church, and society. In Lower Canada, they were known as the Chateau Clique, while in Upper Canada, as the Family Compact. In their official capacity, they were known to frequently use their offices to advance their own interests in advising the Governor.

1837 — Rebellions of Upper and Lower Canadas

Reform movements to gain control of the executive powers of the governors and their councils were led by Joseph Papineau in Lower Canada and William Lyon McKenzie in Upper Canada. Their assertion included that the Governor appoints to his Council those who had the confidence of a popularly-elected assembly.

1839 — Durham's Report

Lord Durham was dispatched from London to restore order in the British North American colonies. His mandate was to inquire into the case of the rebellions and to suggest measures to solve the dilemma. His report is regarded as a constitutional document as it formed the blue print for self-government of British colonies. Lord Durham's Report made four principal recommendations of significance to representative, responsible government. First, to resolve the struggle between French- and English-speaking inhabitants, it was recommended that Upper and Lower Canadas be reunited. This would result in the absorption and assimilation of the French-speaking people of Lower Canada by the combined forces of the British Crown and the English-speaking people of Upper and Lower Canadas. Furthermore, two recommendations were intended to grant responsible government to the colonial governments. These would not require any radical legislative innovations, but were simply consistent applications of British common law. All Crown revenues were to be placed at the disposal of the colonial governments. Second, all financial issues would originate in the Legislative Assembly and would receive consent from the Crown before being introduced in the assembly. Finally, the report recommended the independence of the judiciary. Members of the court were given a salary and tenure in office based on the British common law system.

1840 — Union Act

The Union Act implemented Lord Durham's recommendations. Upper and Lower Canadas were again united. Members of the council were to be appointed for life by the Crown; however, this was changed in 1856 by making council members submit to an election every eight years. An elected Legislative Assembly of 85 members was also established. English was made the official language of record. However, with the restriction of French, this was made unworkable; so, eight years later, it was amended when both English and French languages were given equal status.

1864

A meeting of delegates from Nova Scotia, New Brunswick and Prince Edward Island was held in Charlottetown to discuss a union of the Maritime provinces. Sir John A. Macdonald and others from the provinces of Canada attended to propose a federal union of the British North American colonies.

1865 — Colonial Laws of Validity Act

A law passed by the British Parliament that stated that any law of a British colony that differed with a British law specifically aimed at that colony, was nulled and void to the extent of the difference. This was important because it set aside the older rule that colonial laws that were inconsistent with English common law could be set aside.

1866

Delegates from the provinces of Canada, New Brunswick, and Nova Scotia met in London to draft the British North America Act.

1867 — British North America Act

The British Parliament enacted the Constitution for Canada. Often referred to as the B.N.A. Act, it created the new Dominion of Canada by uniting the colonies of British North America — Upper Canada (Ontario), Lower Canada (Quebec), New Brunswick, and Nova Scotia. It marked no comparable break with the past, principally because the colonists desired to maintain many of the colonial relationships and legislate authority with England. It allocated legislative powers to the federal Parliament and the provincial Legislative Assemblies, thereby establishing federalism. As a British statute, the B.N.A. Act could only be amended by the British Parliament, except in very limited areas in which the Canadian Parliament was given authority. The provincial legislatures were authorized to amend their own provincial constitutions, except in regards to the office of the lieutenant-governor.

1870

The Province of Manitoba is created by the Parliament of Canada.

1871

British Columbia joins Canada by United Kingdom Order in Council.

1873

Prince Edward Island enters the federation by United Kingdom Order in Council.

1875

The Supreme Court of Canada is established. However, the Judicial Committee of the Privy Council of the Parliament of Westminster remains the highest court of appeal.

1875 — The Northwest Territory Act

The Canadian Parliament makes provision for a separate administration of the Northwest Territories. The Territories are administered from Ottawa until 1967, when Yellowknife is designated as territorial capital.

1878

Substantial modifications are made in the instructions issued to the Governor General, which have the effect of reducing some of his prerogative powers.

1898

The Yukon is created as a separate territory with Dawson City as its capital.

1905

The Canadian Parliament establishes the provinces of Saskatchewan and Alberta.

1909

The Canadian Parliament creates the Department of External Affairs to protect and advance Canadian interests abroad.

1917

All Dominion prime ministers accept an invitation to join with the British War Cabinet in an Imperial War Cabinet.

1919

Canadian representatives take part in the Paris Peace Conference and sign the Treaty of Versailles, which brings an end to the First World War. Canada also becomes a member of the newly-created League of Nations and International Labour Organization.

1926 — Balfour Report

Adopted at an Imperial Conference, the Balfour Report defined the Dominions as "autonomous communities" that are "equal in status" and in no way subordinate to Great Britain.

As well, at the Imperial Conference, Prime Minister Mackenzie King issued a formal statement clarifying that the Governor General should cease to represent the British government and become the representative of the Sovereign.

1937 — Statute of Westminster

The British Parliament repealed the Colonial Laws Validity Act (1865) whereby autonomy of the Dominions was given full legal recognition. Because no agreement had been reached on an amending formula, Canada requested that the B.N.A. Act be excepted from the terms of the statute and that Britain retain the authority to amend the B.N.A. Act.

1939

Canada declares war on Germany one week after Britain has done so.

1945

Canada is one of the founding members of the United Nations.

1947 — The Canadian Citizenship Act

The first such act in the Commonwealth is introduced. For the first time, Canadian is defined as "Canadian citizens" rather than primarily as British subjects born or naturalized in Canada.

1949

Canada is one of the founding members of the North Atlantic Treaty Organization.

The British North America Act, 1949

Newfoundland joins Canada through enactment by the British Parliament of the British North America Act, 1949.

The Supreme Court becomes the final court of appeal in Canada, ending the role of the Judicial Committee of the Privy Council of the Parliament of Westminster in the interpretation of Canadian constitutional issues.

The Canadian Parliament becomes empowered to amend the Constitution of Canada with respect to "housekeeping matters" at the federal level. The basic areas of the Constitution still remain within the sole control of the British Parliament.

1965

Canada adopts it own flag.

1980

The Canadian Parliament adopts *O Canada* as the national anthem.

The Minister of Justice introduces a resolution in Parliament for a Joint Address to Her Majesty the Queen, requesting that the United Kingdom Parliament enact provisions for the patriation of the Canadian Constitution, the coming into effect of an amending formula and entrenchment of a Charter of Rights and the entrenchment of the principle of equalization.

In 1976, the province of Quebec had elected the Parti Québécois with a mandate to hold a referendum on the separation of Quebec. Thus, in the spring of 1980, Quebec held its first referendum on sovereignty-association. The referendum question was defeated by a margin of 40 to 60 percent.

1981

The legality of the justice minister's resolution to unilaterally patriate the Constitution is challenged before the Supreme Court of Canada by Manitoba and several other provinces. The Supreme Court rules on September 28, 1981, that while the Canadian Parliament can legally act alone, there is a "convention" requiring substantial consent of the provinces. After further discussions in early November, the Prime Minister and nine provincial premiers signed an accord on November 5 that broke the impasse. In early December, the House of Commons and Senate approved the revised resolution which formed the basis of Joint Addresses to be sent to London for action.

1982 — Constitution Act

The Constitution Act, containing *inter alia* the Canadian Charter of Rights and Freedoms and a wholly Canadian procedure for further constitutional amendments, is enacted by the British Parliament. On April 17, in a ceremony on the lawn of Parliament Hill, the Queen signed the Constitution Act.

The Constitution Act of 1982 is an act of the British Parliament which enacted a new Canadian Constitution, ending the British Parliament's function by transferring to the Canadian Parliament the power over future constitutional amendments and the British Parliament undertook never again to legislate in respect of Canada.

The government of Quebec did not sign the Constitution Act. However, it is nonetheless a part of the Constitution because when the Constitution Act came before the House of Commons for final approval, Quebec members of Parliament voted almost unanimously in its favour (only three opposed it). To-date, the government of Quebec has not signed the Constitution Act of 1982.

1987 — Meech Lake Accord

The goal of the Meech Lake Accord was to obtain Quebec's endorsement of the Constitution Act of 1982. It was intended as another constitutional amendment. It recognized all five of Quebec's demands, including distinct society, increased powers for Quebec over immigration, a role for Quebec in the appointment of Supreme Court judges, the right of Quebec to a veto over all future constitutional changes, the right of the provincial government to nominate senators and annual convene constitutional conferences of the Prime Minister and provincial premiers. The Meech Lake Accord was readily ratified by Parliament and initially, eight of the ten provinces. However, it died in the Manitoba Legislature because a native member of the provincial Legislative Assembly, Elijah Harper, Jr. refused to give the unanimous approval necessary under Manitoba law for dispensing with public hearings before having the vote on the accord.

With that, the premier of Newfoundland concluded that there was no purpose in having the Newfoundland provincial Legislature vote on the accord since its rejection in Manitoba had ended the possibility of the accord achieving the necessary unanimity.

1992 — Charlottetown Accord

Another round of constitutional conferences was held. When the Meech Lake Accord failed two years before, both federal and provincial governments were criticized for much of the deal-making that went on behind closed doors. This same criticism was levied after the enactment of the Constitution Act of 1982. At question were the legitimacy and practice of the federal-provincial bargaining process and federal unilateralism of renewing a constitution. Not only was there a series of federal-provincial meeting of the First Ministers, but committees of Parliament and the provincial Legislatures as well as Citizen Forums endeavoured to deal with the arduous issues of constitutional amendments. Furthermore, a national referendum would be held to achieve a consensus on constitutional amendments.

An accord was reached by the First Ministers in August in Charlottetown. The Charlottetown Accord included: a Canadian clause; social and economic union; recognition of Quebec as a distinct society; the inherent right to self-government for the First People; reform of Senate; and a great degree of federal and provincial power-sharing.

The Charlottetown Accord was defeated in a national referendum held on October 26, 1992. In order to gain the consensus that the federal and provincial governments sought to achieve in a referendum, it required endorsement from all the provinces. But, in fact, a number of provinces, such as Quebec, British Columbia, and Alberta rejected the accord, while in other provinces, the margin was narrow for either acceptance or rejection.

1995

A second referendum was held in the Province of Quebec. The Parti Québécois was once again elected in 1994 with a mandate committed to Quebec sovereignty. On October 30, 1995, Quebecers were asked once again to decide on the sovereignty of

Quebec. This time, the margin had narrowed to 51 to 49 percent against sovereignty.

1996

The federal justice minister petitioned the Supreme Court to clarify the rules of separation. In 1997, the federal Crown attorneys requested the Supreme Court to appoint legal representation on Quebec's behalf since Quebec has refused to participate in court proceedings.

Bill C-110

A federal statute was enacted on February 3, 1996 granting veto power to Quebec, Ontario, and British Columbia. In addition, any two Prairie provinces with fifty percent of the regional population and any two Atlantic provinces having fifty percent of the regional population, can veto any constitutional amendment. The new formula for gaining the federal government's approval is an addition to the existing constitutional amending formula, which requires seven provinces with fifty percent of the population to approve most constitutional amendments.

APPENDIX 2
Government Organizational Chart

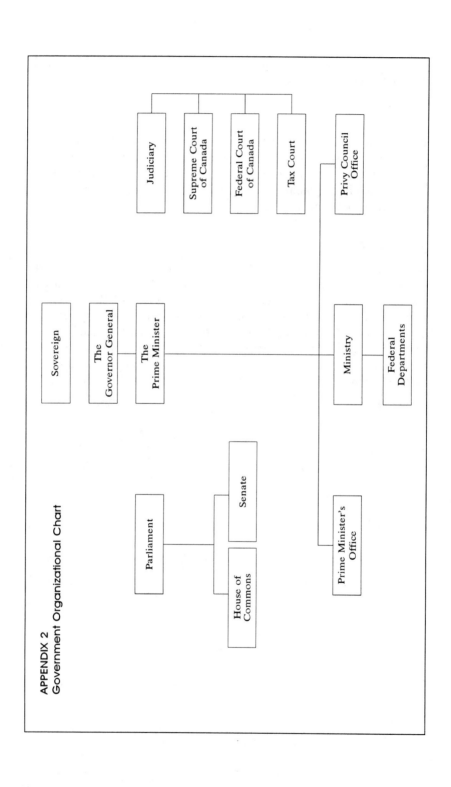

APPENDIX 3

Introduction to Committees of the House of Commons

HISTORICAL BACKGROUND

Since the time of Confederation, the House of Commons has created specialized committees to study matters of national importance. At first, the Standing Orders did not include a list of "permanent" committees, nor did they outline committee powers or the procedures to be observed during committee meetings. House standing committees were created by way of a motion which was usually concurred in at the beginning of each session.

Until 1906, the number of standing committees remained virtually unchanged at nine. In addition, special and joint committees, whose number and mandate varied from one year to the next, were established during the course of each session.[1] Due to the size of standing committees (some had over 100 members) and the rule that a majority was needed to constitute a quorum, a large number of members had to be present in order for meetings to be held and decisions taken.[2] As a result, over the years, the size of standing committees declined (today, the Standing Orders provide that standing committees have a minimum of 7 members and a maximum of 15 members). The number of standing and joint committees, however, has grown

---

Extracted from Parliamentary Internet at http://www.parl.gc.ca. Reprinted by permission of the House of Commons, Ottawa, Canada.

from 11 in 1867 to 22 in the 35th Parliament, not including legislative and special committees.

In 1906, the House listed the "standing" committees in the Standing Orders. These committees were active only when the House gave them an Order of Reference to study a bill or a specific matter. It was only after 1968 that the level of committee activity increased when standing committees acquired responsibility for the study of Estimates.

In the mid-1980s, two special committees (Lefebvre Committee, 1982–83, and the McGrath Committee, 1984–85) were instructed to review the House Standing Orders and this led to a substantial reform of the committee system. Legislative committees came into existence at this time. Standing committees were given the power to examine and report to the House, without first receiving an Order of Reference from the House, on any matter relating to the mandate, operation, and administration of the government department falling within a committee's area of responsibility. Prior to this, the mandates of standing committees were set out in Orders of Reference which the House was required to adopt before the committees could begin their work. Standing committees were also given the task of reviewing Order in Council appointments and departmental annual reports which were automatically referred to them. The creation of a Liaison Committee, the authority to retain the services of expert and support staff, the power to request a government response to a report, the approval of committee budgets by the Board of Internal Economy, and the preparation of annual lists of committee members and substitute members were other changes which came about as a result of the overhaul of the committee system in 1984–85.

In April 1991, further amendments to the Standing Orders affected committees. Reforms included changes in the membership of committees, the possibility of organizing joint meetings of Standing Committees, the right of a Parliamentary Secretary to be a member of a committee, the reorganization of the Panel of Chairmen for legislative committees into four panels, each one corresponding to an envelope, and the broadcasting of committee proceedings. In January 1994, further changes were made to the structure of committees, including the restructuring and renaming of committees, the creation of two new standing joint committees as well as the addition of "associate members" to the membership of committees.

The House of Commons delegates most of the detailed study of proposed legislation and the scrutiny of government policy and programmes to its committees. In delegating these responsibilities, the House of Commons establishes specific terms of reference for their work through Standing Orders or, from time to time, by Special Orders of the House.

TYPES OF COMMITTEES

The various types or categories of committees can be succinctly defined as follows:

- **Committee of the Whole (House).**
  All of the Members of the House sitting as a committee. Presided over by a chairman rather than by the Speaker, it studies appropriation bills and any other matters referred to it by the House.

- **Joint Committee.**
  A committee made up of a proportionate number of members of both the House of Commons and the Senate. It may be either a standing or a special committee.

- **Legislative Committee.**
  A committee created under the Standing Orders on an ad hoc basis to study a bill in detail after second reading. The committee may only report the bill, with or without amendments.

- **Special Committee.**
  A group of Members, or of Members and Senators, appointed to study a particular matter. Once it has made its final report, the committee ceases to exist.

- **Standing Committee.**
  A permanent committee established in the Standing Orders of the House. It may study matters referred to it by standing or special order or, within its area of responsibility, undertake studies on its own initiative.

- **Subcommittee.**
  A committee of a committee, to which the latter may delegate its powers, except the power to report to the House. Not all committees are granted the power to establish subcommittees.

PROCEDURE AND RULES OF ORDER

Committees are regarded as creatures of the House and their proceedings are governed for the most part by the same rules which govern the House proceedings, namely the Standing Orders, precedent and practice. The Standing Orders enumerate a few notable House rules which need not apply (e.g., the election of a Speaker, seconding of motions, limiting the number of times of speaking and the length of speeches). It must be stressed that these rules should not be interpreted as prohibiting committees from seconding motions or limiting the number of times a Member can speak. They are actually permissive in nature, freeing committees from adhering to the rules but leaving each committee to formulate its own rules and restrictions as long as it does not exceed the basic powers delegated to it by the House.

There are some significant differences between the rules of the House and those of committees. For example, while a Speaker's decision cannot be commented upon, the decision of a chairman may be appealed to the committee through a nondebatable motion and can be overturned by a majority of committee members. Furthermore, committees have no authority to decide a question of privilege. A question of privilege is a matter for the House to decide; a committee can decide only whether an alleged breach of privilege should be reported to the House. In general, the same rules and practices apply to committees when considering motions and amendments. However, in committee, motions can be moved without notice and without a seconder; the previous question is not in order; a quorum must be present for a motion to be received and voted upon; and only an official member of a committee is entitled to move a motion.

MEMBERSHIP

The list of members for standing and legislative committees is drawn up by the Standing Committee on Procedure and House Affairs, roughly reflecting the party standings in the House, and concurred in by the House. The list of members for special committees may be contained in the motion establishing that committee. Standing committees have between seven and fifteen members; special and legislative committees may not have more than 15 members. Any Member of Parliament who is part of a committee is entitled to take part in committee debates, question witnesses, move motions, vote, and be part of any quorum.

CHAIR OF THE COMMITTEE

The Chairs of standing and special committees are elected by the members of the committee. It is traditional for joint committees to elect Co-Chairs, one of whom is a Senator and the other a Member of the House of Commons. Legislative committee Chairs are neutral and impartial presiding officers appointed by the Speaker from the Panel of Chairmen; they do not participate in the debate on the bill before them, nor are they responsible for the progress of business on that bill. If a Chair of a legislative committee should become vacant, the Speaker will appoint another member of the Panel of Chairmen to be the Chair.

The Chair serves as the presiding officer of the committee and spokesperson through whom all matters are channelled. Under the Standing Orders of the House, the Chair has the power to maintain order and decorum and to decide all questions of order and procedure. This is the main duty of the Chair. Decisions of the Chair, when rendered, are not debatable but may be appealed to the committee.

The Chair's duties and responsibilities include the following: to preside at meetings and to ensure, in the event of his or her anticipated absence, the presence of the Vice-Chair or an Acting Chair; to chair the Subcommittee on Agenda and Procedure (steering committee); to call meetings on his or her own authority, as authorized by the committee or in the case of standing committees, as requested by four members pursuant to Standing Order 106(3); to recognize Members and to decide their order of speaking in accordance with established procedure; to determine the order in which the committee will examine amendments to a clause in a bill or to a Vote in the Estimates; to prepare budgets; to approve expenditures in accordance with the budget; to sign all committee reports and present them to the House; and to sign contracts on behalf of the committee.

WITNESSES

Standing Orders 113(5), 122, and 108(1)(a) grant legislative and standing committees of the House of Commons the power "to send for persons..." A similar phrase is usually found in the orders of reference creating special committees.

Most witnesses appear before a committee after being invited to do so, such an invitation being issued on the committee's behalf through the clerk of the committee. Should a witness refuse an invitation, the committee may then decide by motion to summon the witness to appear. Committees only rarely use their power to summon people. Since time constraints may make it impossible for committees to hear testimony from every individual and group requesting to be heard, steering committees usually consider lists of potential witnesses and make recommendations to the full committee. The committee decides to whom invitations will be issued.

There are no grounds on which a witness, other than a public servant, can refuse to answer a question. While witnesses are at the mercy of the committee and its collective wisdom, it is important to note that they are only compelled to answer questions that a committee agrees to put to them.

REPORTS TO THE HOUSE

A standing, special or legislative committee makes its views known to the House and brings forward recommendations on matters it has studied by tabling a report in the House. This report must be signed by the committee Chair, or in his absence, a Vice-Chair or another committee member.

There are several types of reports which a committee may present to the House:

- Reports may deal with routine matters affecting the operations of a committee; for example, a committee may ask the House for permission to travel or to defer the deadline set for presentation of its final report. Reports may also bring to the House's attention irregularities in committee rules of procedure or incidents which occurred during a meeting; for example, the fact that a Minister refused to supply documents;
- A legislative committee, which has finished its examination of a bill, reports the bill to the House with or without amendments;
- When a committee has completed its study of the Estimates, it tables a report in the House. This type of report usually

consists of only a brief statement since substantive recommendations are not allowed. The committee may only agree to, negative or reduce Estimates; and

- Normally, a committee tables a report following the completion of an inquiry into matters related to the mandate, management and operation of one or more designated departments, Order in Council appointments and delegated legislation. In this type of report, which may, in some cases, be quite detailed, the committee communicates its findings and makes specific recommendations to the Government.

In the case of standing and special committees, the report must reflect the opinion of the majority of committee members. A separate minority report, therefore, cannot be tabled. However, since May 1991, Standing Order 108(1)(a) has authorized the addition, in an appendix to the report, of dissenting or supplementary opinions or recommendations. For example, pursuant to Standing Order 35(2), when a report includes such an appendix, a committee member who is a Member of the Official Opposition, and who represents those who supported the opinion or opinions expressed in the appended material, may also rise to give a succinct explanation thereof. No other Member may comment on the report at that time.

Under Standing Order 109, a standing or special committee may request that the Government table a comprehensive response to its report within 150 days of the presentation of the report.

LIST OF COMMITTEES

- **Aboriginal Affairs and Northern Development**
  Aboriginal Affairs / Agenda and Procedure
- **Agriculture and Agri-Food**
  Agriculture and Agri-Food / Agenda and Procedure
- Canadian Heritage
- Citizenship and Immigration
- **Environment and Sustainable Development**
  Environment and Sustainable Development /
  Agenda and Procedure
- **Finance**
  Finance / Agenda and Procedure

- **Fisheries and Oceans**
  Fisheries and Oceans / Agenda and Procedure
- **Foreign Affairs and International Trade**
  Foreign Affairs and International Trade /
  Agenda and Procedure
- Health
- **Human Resources Development and Status of Persons with Disabilities**
  Human Resources Development and Status of Persons with Disabilities / Steering Committee on Agenda and Procedure
- **Industry**
  Industry / Agenda and Procedure
- Justice and Human Rights
- Library of Parliament
- National Defence and Veterans Affairs
- National Defence and Veterans Affairs / Agenda and Procedure
- Natural Resources and Government Operations
- Official Languages
- **Procedure and House Affairs**
  Private Members' Business
  Procedure and House Affairs / Agenda and Procedure
- Public Accounts
- Scrutiny of Regulations
- The Quebec School System
- Transport

APPENDIX 4

Canadian Ministry Index

- Agriculture and Agri-Food
- Canadian Heritage
- Citizenship and Immigration
- Environment
- Finance
- Fisheries and Oceans
- Foreign Affairs
- Health
- Human Resources Development
- Indian Affairs and Northern Development
- Industry
- Justice
- National Defence
- National Revenue
- Natural Resources
- Prime Minister
- Public Works and Government Services
- Solicitor General
- Transport
- Treasury Board
- Veterans Affairs

APPENDIX 5

Canada's Court System

Ubi Jus, Ibi Remedium

"Where there is a right, there is a remedy"

When there is a dispute between individuals, or between an individual and the state, either side may go to court to have his or her rights upheld and the dispute settled under the law.

However, "going to court" presupposes many things. First of all, there must be a dependable system of laws. In Canada, our system of private law (governing disputes between individuals) and public law (concerning matters that affect society as a whole) is founded on two ancient and very different forms of justice: English common law and French civil law. Over the centuries, these two systems have been found to be both flexible and durable.

As well, there must be courts to go to: places that are set aside for the hearing of cases; lawyers to plead the facts and law; and judges to weigh the evidence, determine the outcome, and, if necessary, pronounce the sentence.

The courts also require officials to manage their operations. Court administration includes a large number of activities, ranging from issuing summonses and controlling dangerous criminals

Department of Justice Canada. Reprinted with permission of the Minister of Public Works and Government Services Canada, 1997.

in court to scheduling cases, nominating jurors and keeping records. Courts generate a large amount of data. They require the services of many different and well-trained individuals.

SUPREME COURT OF CANADA

The highest court in the land is the Supreme Court of Canada. It is the general court of appeal from all other Canadian courts, civil, criminal and constitutional. It is thus an important institution of Canadian unity. At the top of all federal, provincial and territorial court structures, it melds them into a single national system.

COMMON LAW AND CIVIL LAW

Common law, which developed in Britain after the Norman invasion, is based on precedents. Each decision of a judge is a precedent that may be used to guide other judges in making subsequent decisions. Thus, the common law is constantly evolving. Traditionally, it had not been written down anywhere as a body of law, but there are now compilations of the common law.

In Quebec, the legal system is known as "civil law," or law that is written down in a code. The Civil Code of Quebec is derived from France's Code Napoléon, which is based in turn upon Roman law as established by the Emperor Justinian. Many of the rules set out in Quebec's Civil Code are stated as broad, general principles so that they can be applied to a wide range of disputes. Unlike common law courts, courts in a civil law system look first to the code, then to previous decisions, for guidance.

In Canada, outside of Quebec, the specific statutes enacted by the federal, provincial or territorial governments take the place of the common law with respect to the particular subject matter of the statutes. In Quebec, legislation may also be enacted to deal with specific matters not covered by the Civil Code.

Crimes are defined and penalties are prescribed in the Criminal Code of Canada, which applies to the whole country.

The Supreme Court is composed of a Chief Justice and eight "puisne" (or "ranked after") judges who are appointed by the federal Cabinet. By law, three of the judges must come from

Quebec. By tradition, three come from Ontario, two from Western Canada and one from the Atlantic provinces. The Court sits in Ottawa for three sessions a year — winter, spring and fall. Recently, the Court began using tele-conferencing technology to permit presentations from other parts of the country.

Generally, cases may be appealed to the Supreme Court only with "leave" of the Court. Leave is granted if the case involves a matter of public importance, or if it raises an important question of law, or of mixed law and fact. Leave is not required in certain cases, such as criminal cases when an acquittal has been set aside by a provincial court of appeal or when one of the appeal court judges dissents on a question of law.

The Court also has a special jurisdiction whereby it considers questions of law or fact concerning the Constitution, and provides an opinion to the federal or provincial Cabinet. Canada is the only country in the common law world where the highest court has this "reference" jurisdiction.

FEDERAL COURT OF CANADA

The Federal Court of Canada is organized into appeal and trial divisions and, while it is based in Ottawa, the judges of both divisions may sit across the country. The court reviews the disputed decisions of federal boards, commissions and tribunals. The Federal Court's jurisdiction also includes interprovincial and federal-provincial disputes, intellectual property proceedings, admiralty matters, citizenship appeals, and appeals under certain federal statutes. The Federal Court shares jurisdiction with the provincial superior courts with respect to claims by and against the Crown.

Judges of the Federal Court may also act as Umpires under the Unemployment Insurance Act, and as Assessors under certain acts affecting Canadian agriculture.

TAX COURT OF CANADA

The Tax Court of Canada was created in 1983 to replace the Tax Review Board. Headquartered in Ottawa, the court sits in major cities across the country. Its jurisdiction relates to tax and revenue matters.

COURTS MARTIAL

Courts martial are established under the federal National Defence Act to try members of the armed forces for breaches of the military Code of Service Discipline. A court martial is presided over by a judge advocate, who is a legally trained officer of the armed forces. A court martial might be composed of three or five officers of the armed forces, who have the authority to determine the guilt or innocence of the accused and, in the event of a guilty verdict, to determine the sentence.

PROVINCIAL COURTS

The provinces joining Confederation in 1867 all had their own systems of courts. Except for Quebec, which always had two basic levels, the provinces maintained three distinct levels of trial courts, based upon the British model. At the top were the "superior" courts, so called because they could deal with cases from across the province and had unlimited monetary and substantive jurisdiction; they heard the most serious criminal cases and the largest civil suits. Next were the county or district courts, which were restricted by both the subject matter and monetary value of the litigation and by its geographic location. Finally, there were the "inferior" courts — courts presided over by magistrates or justices of the peace, which dealt with small civil claims and minor criminal offences.

As a result of court reforms over the past 20 years, all of the county and district courts have been amalgamated into the superior trial courts.

The superior courts of the provinces include both trial and appeal levels of court. The trial levels, in turn, may include some or all of the following divisions: small claims; family; and general. The names of the superior courts and their divisions vary considerably from province to province.

The vast majority of criminal trials are not litigated in the superior trial courts. They take place in the "inferior" or Provincial Courts, as the former magistrates' courts are now commonly called. The Provincial Courts may also include family and small claims divisions, as well as a youth or young offenders division. Actual court structure varies from province to province, as do the number and type of divisions within each court. As well, all preliminary inquiries, which are held to determine whether there is sufficient evidence to warrant a full trial in the more serious criminal cases, take place before the Provincial Court judges or justices of the peace.

ADMINISTRATION OF THE COURTS

Normally, each court employs a person who is responsible for managing the administrative work, including the appointment of staff and the management of finances. This person is sometimes known as the "Registrar" but may carry other titles such as "Clerk" in the case of some provincial courts or "Administrator of the Court" in the case of the Federal Court of Canada. These officials may also perform other functions such as informing the legal profession of courtroom procedures; signing orders and judgments; issuing summonses; certifying copies of court proceedings; receiving and recording documents filed in court; and collecting court costs.

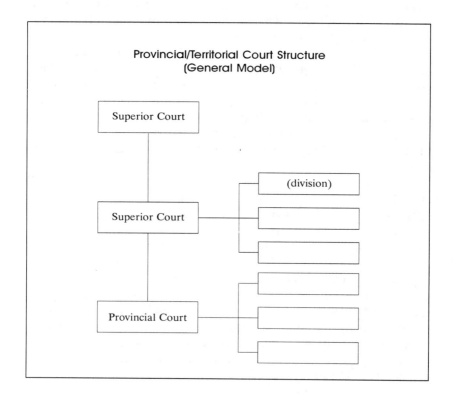

Sheriffs, sometimes assisted by bailiffs, are usually responsible for jury management (that is, they summon, pay, seclude and guard jurors). In some provinces they escort accused and convicted persons, provide security for prisoners, witnesses and the courtroom, and arrest persons for contempt on an order of the judge. Sheriffs and bailiffs are sometimes responsible for serving legal documents, seizing goods, and collecting levies.

Other officials include "masters" or "prothonotaries," who schedule cases, issue summonses, render default judgments, approve the sale of assets in certain circumstances, and keep accounts. Sometimes masters and prothonotaries have additional powers to act as a judge in chambers when the judge is absent or unable to act or when a delay might result in the loss of a right or cause harm to a party. Other judicial officers include family law commissioners, masters in bankruptcy, and the like.

OTHER COURTS

There are many relatively minor legal matters that are not required to be heard in open court, but may be dispensed with by a judge "in chambers." These matters include interlocutory applications to determine a preliminary point at issue and appeals to vary or set aside the orders of masters and registrars.

In fact, there are a number of judicial officers who operate as judges in certain circumstances. They include hearing officers, magistrates, adjudicators, and justices of the peace. These officials perform many pre-trial, informal and formal court proceedings. They may assess penalties under summary conviction on Criminal Code offences, set bail, release prisoners on bail, take informations and issue search warrants. In Ontario, family law commissioners were created to deal with a backlog of divorce petitions. They now operate as judges in many family law matters, conducting hearings referred to them by the Ontario Court (General Division).

In the North, and more recently in the provinces, judges are taking part in aboriginal "circle courts." These courts are unlike the traditional courtroom. In the circle court, the judge, police, social workers, band officials, victims and convicted person sit in a circle to consider an appropriate sentence. The sentence may include some form of restitution, community service and a program of counselling and treatment.

APPENDIX 6

Curia Regis, Privy Council, Cabinet

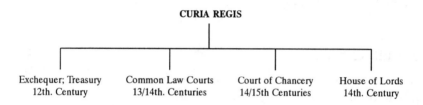

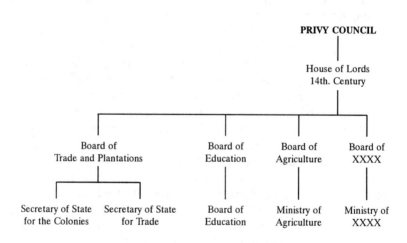

APPENDIX 7

Budget 1997

SUMMARY STATEMENT OF TRANSACTIONS
Fiscal outlook with budget measures[1]

	94–95	95–96	96–97	97–98	98–99
	(billions of dollars)				
Budgetary revenues	123.3	130.3	135.5	137.8	144.0
Program spending	118.7	112.0	109.0	105.8	103.5
Operating balance	4.6	18.3	26.5	32.0	40.5
Public debt charges	42.0	46.9	45.5	46.0	46.5
Underlying deficit	−37.5	−28.6	−19.0	−14.0	−6.0
Contingency Reserve				3.0	3.0
Deficit	−37.5	−28.6	−19.0	−17.0	−9.0
Net public debt	545,7	574.3	593.3	610.3	619.3
Non-budgetary transactions	11.6	11.4	13.0	11.0	10.0
Financial requirements/source	−25.8	−17.2	−6.0	−6.0	1.0
Per cent of GDP					
Budgetary revenues	16.5	16.8	17.0	16.5	16.6
Program spending	15.9	14.4	13.7	12.7	11.9
Operating balance	0.6	2.4	3.3	3.8	4.7
Public debt charges	5.6	6.0	5.7	5.5	5.3
Deficit	−5.0	−3.7	−2.4	−2.0	−1.0
Financial requirements	−3.5	−2.2	−0.8	−0.7	0.1
Net public debt	73.0	74.0	74.4	73.1	71.2

[1] A positive number indicates a source of funds, a negative number indicates a financial requirement.

From *Building the Future for Canadians, Budget 1997, Budget in Brief* by The Honourable Paul Martin, February 18, 1997, Tables 1, 2 and 3. Source of Information: Department of Finance Canada. Reproduced with the permission of the Minister of Public Works and Government Services Canada, 1997.

INVESTING IN A STRONGER SOCIETY

	1997–98	1998–99	1999–2000
	(millions of dollars)		
Sustaining and Improving Canada's Health Care System			
Health Transition Fund/Canada Health Information System	50	75	75
Community Action Program for Children and Canada Prenatal Nutrition Program	33	33	33
Subtotal	83	108	108
Towards a National Child Benefit System			
Canada Child Tax Benefit	50[1]	470[1]	600
Helping Canadians with Disabilities			
Broadening the medical expense tax credit/removing limit on attendant care deduction	5	30	30
Refundable medical expense supplement for earners	5	30	40
Opportunities Fund	30	30	30
Subtotal	40	90	100
Support for Charitable Giving			
Reduced inclusion rate on capital gains	20	90	90
Net income limit/CCA recapture changes	5	5	5
Increased resources for Revenue Canada	5	5	5
Subtotal	30	100	100
Total	203	768	908

[1] Assumes a July 1, 1998 start-up. If implemented earlier, total would be larger by up to $150 million.

FEDERAL REVENUE IMPACT OF
NEW TAX MEASURES

	1997–98	1998–99	1999–2000
	(millions of dollars)		

Personal income tax measures

Enhance tax assistance to education and training

Increase education credit	−5	−45	−80
Make ancillary fees eligible for the tuition credit	−5	−30	−30
Allow a carry-forward of unused tuition and education credits	—	−10	−25
Increase RESP annual limit to $4,000 and allow transfers to RRSPs or to contributor	−10	−25	−40

Helping small businesses

Quarterly remittance of withholdings	−180	−5	−5
Enhancing effectiveness of LSVCCs	—	—	—

Improving the retirement income system

PAR: restoring lost RRSP room	—	—	—
Averaging of CPP/QPP lump sum payments	small	small	small

Towards a National Child Benefit System

Enrichment and restructuring of the Child Tax Benefit	−50	−470	−600

Measures to assist Canadians with disabilities

Broadening the medical expenses tax credit; removing limit on attendant care deduction	−5	−30	−30
Refundable medical expense supplement for earners	−5	−30	−40

Continued....

FEDERAL REVENUE IMPACT OF
NEW TAX MEASURES (Continued)

	1997–98	1998–99	1999–2000
	(millions of dollars)		
Measures to enhance tax assistance to charitable giving			
Reduce the inclusion rate on capital gains arising from the donation of publicly listed securities from 75% to 37.5%	−20	−90	−90
75% net income limit for all donations; include 25% of CCA recapture in the net income limit	—	−5	−5
New method of valuation for easements of ecologically sensitive lands	—	—	—
Increased resources for Revenue Canada	−5	−5	−5
Subtotal	−285	−745	−950
Business taxation measures			
Review of transfer pricing rules	prevents revenue losses		
Restricting investment tax credit claims	prevents revenue losses		
Extension of temporary tax on large deposit-taking institutions	25	45	—
Environmental initiatives	—	−25	−25
Sales and excise tax measures			
Clarify measurement of fuel volumes	—	—	—
Total	−260	−725	−975

APPENDIX 8

1997–1998 Estimates

BUDGETARY MAIN ESTIMATES
BY TYPE OF PAYMENT

1997–98	($ millions)
Program spending in the Estimates	
Transfer Payments	
Major transfers to other levels of government:	
Fiscal Equalization	8,292
Canada Health and Social Transfers	12,500
Territorial governments	1,120
Alternative payments for standing programs	(2,131)
Other	22
Subtotal: major transfers to other levels of government	*19,803*
Major transfers to persons:	
Elderly Benefits	
— Old Age Security	17,140
— Guaranteed Income Supplement	4,778
— Spouses Allowance	390
Subtotal: elderly benefits	22,308
Employment Insurance	13,460
Subtotal: major transfers to persons	*35,768*
Other transfer payments and subsidies	15,899
Total transfer payments[1]	71,470
Payments to Crown corporations	3,909
National Defence	9,916
Non-Defence operating and capital	17,899
Program spending in the Estimates	*103,194*
Public debt charges	*46,000*
Total budgetary Main Estimates	149,194

[1] Excludes National Defence transfer payments.

From *1997–1998 Estimates, Part I: The Government Expenditure Plan and Highlights by Ministry*, Tables 1.2 and 1.3. Source of Information: Treasury Board of Canada Secretariat. Reproduced with the permission of the Minister of Public Works and Government Services Canada, 1997.

PLANNED BUDGETARY SPENDING
BY MINISTRY FOR 1997–98 ($ millions)

Ministry	Statutory	Voted	Total Main Estimates (ME)	Planned Spending Not in ME	Total Planned Budgetary Spending
Agriculture and Agri-Food	636	869	1,505	255	1,760
Canadian Heritage	68	2,457	2,524	24	2,549
Citizenship and Immigration	36	616	652	11	663
Environment	41	476	517	2	520
Finance	64,495	1,543	66,038	—	66,038
Fisheries and Oceans	77	1,000	1,077	19	1,096
Foreign Affairs and International Trade	354	2,870	3,224	56	3,280
Governor General	1	9	10	—	10
Health	49	1,726	1,776	117	1,892
Human Resources Development	23,170	1,736	24,906	70	24,976
Indian Affairs and Northern Development	183	4,125	4,308	84	4,392
Industry	316	2,921	3,237	693	3,930
Justice	249	487	736	135	871
National Defence	724	9,193	9,917	—	9,917
National Revenue	310	1,959	2,269	52	2,321
Natural Resources	57	639	697	(1)	696

continued....

PLANNED BUDGETARY SPENDING
BY MINISTRY FOR 1997–98 ($ millions) (Continued...)

Ministry	Statutory	Voted	Total Main Estimates (ME)	Planned Spending Not in ME	Total Planned Budgetary Spending
Parliament	85	187	272	—	272
Privy Council	40	110	150	—	150
Public Works and Government Services	54	3,533	3,586	59	3,645
Solicitor General	323	2,212	2,535	86	2,620
Transport	767	987	1,754	38	1,792
Treasury Board	208	1,273	1,481	2	1,483
Veterans Affairs	24	1,897	1,922	7	1,928
Consolidated Specified Purpose Account — Employment Insurance	14,102	—	14,102	52	14,154
Other adjustments not allocated by Ministry[1]	—	—	—	845	845
Total budgetary spending	106,368	42,826	149,194	2,606	151,800[2]

[1] Includes provision for the lapse, planned spending not yet specifically allocated by ministry and contingency provisions to cover a number of anticipated pressures.

[2] As set out in the Expenditure Plan contained in the February 1997 Budget.

Note: Numbers may not add up to totals due to rounding.